Miss Kobayashi's DRAGON MAID

11

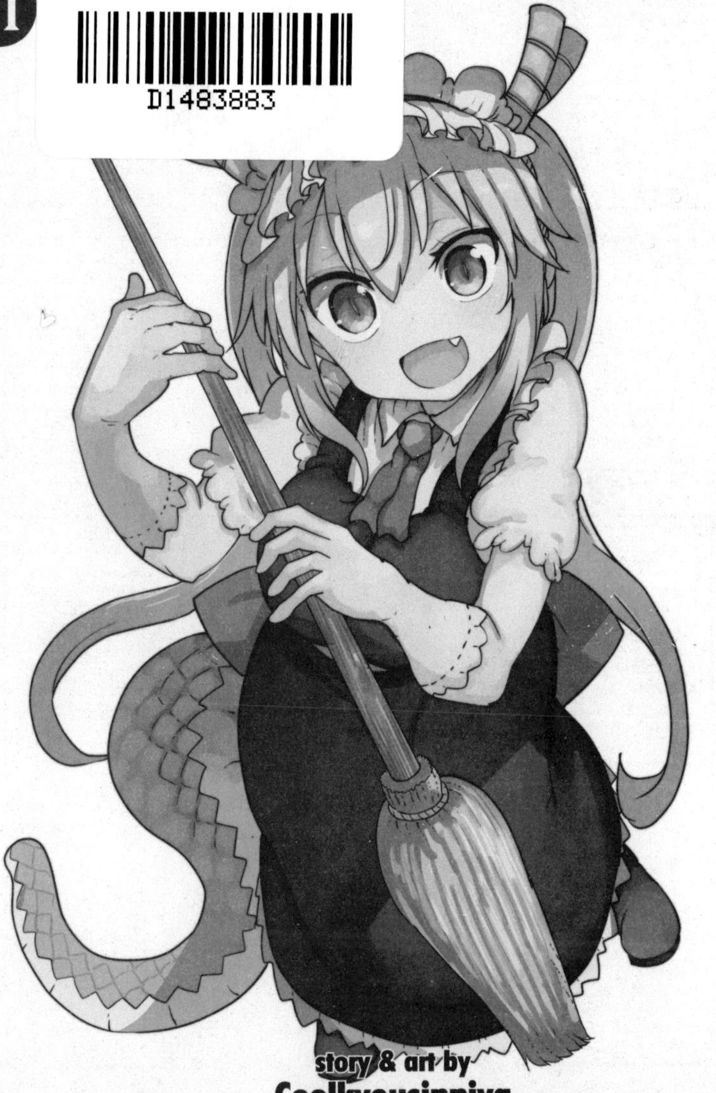

story & art by
Coolkyousinnjya

Miss Kobayashi's Dragon Maid

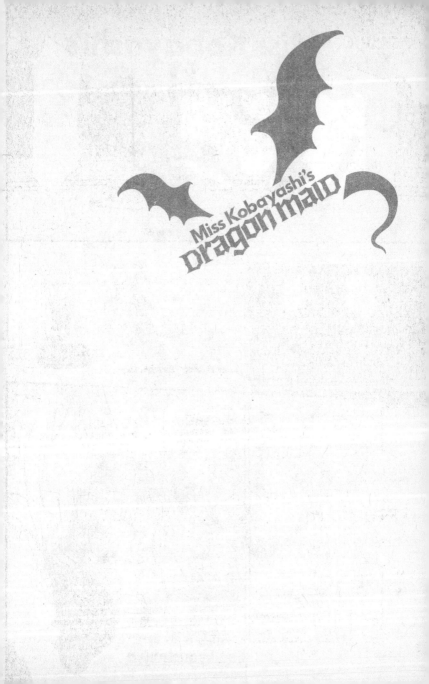

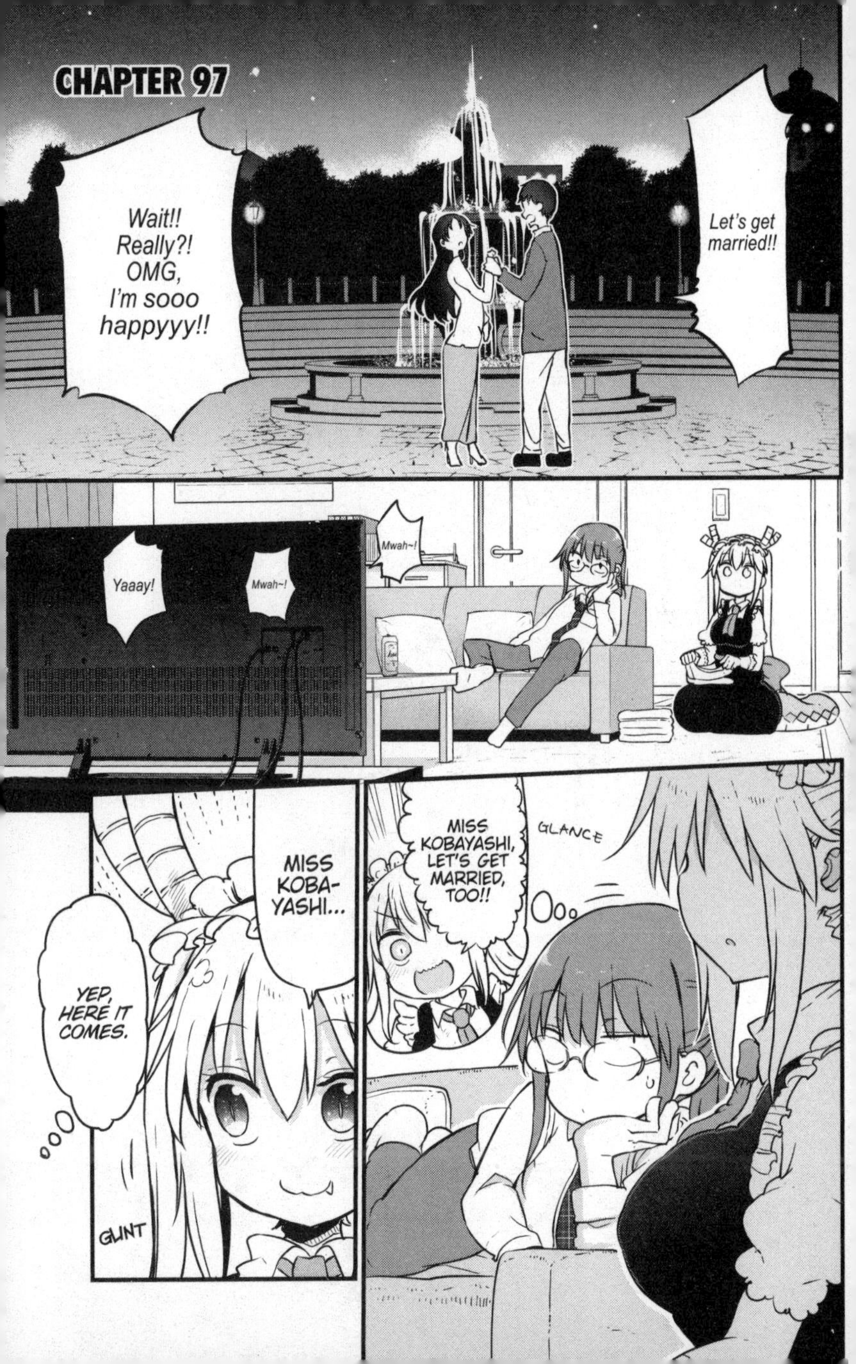
CHAPTER 97
Let's get married!!
Wait!! Really?! OMG, I'm sooo happyyy!!
Mwah~!
Mwah~!
Yaaay!
MISS KOBAYASHI, LET'S GET MARRIED, TOO!!
GLANCE
Ooo
MISS KOBA-YASHI...
YEP, HERE IT COMES.
ooo
GLINT

CHAPTER 97:
KOBAYASHI AND MARRIAGE

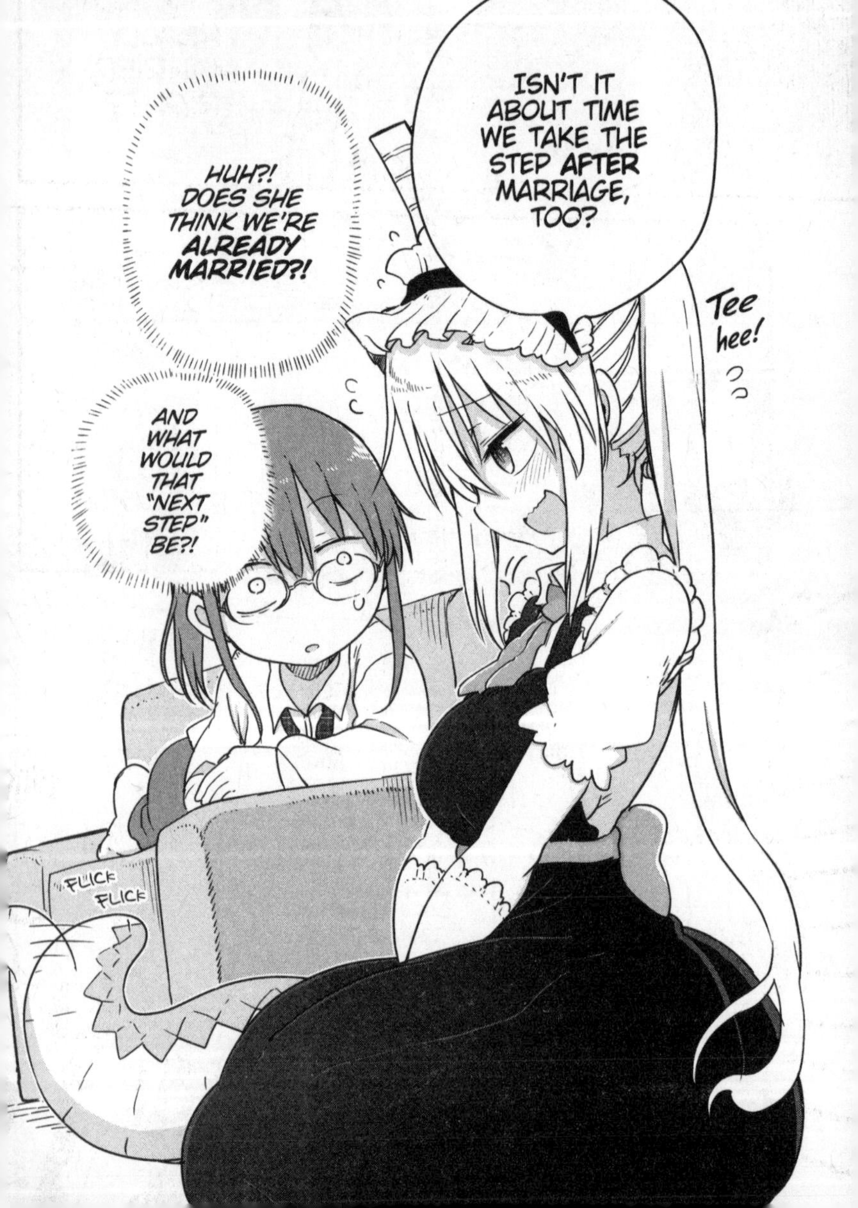
ISN'T IT ABOUT TIME WE TAKE THE STEP AFTER MARRIAGE, TOO?
Tee hee!
HUH?! DOES SHE THINK WE'RE ALREADY MARRIED?!
AND WHAT WOULD THAT "NEXT STEP" BE?!
FLICK FLICK

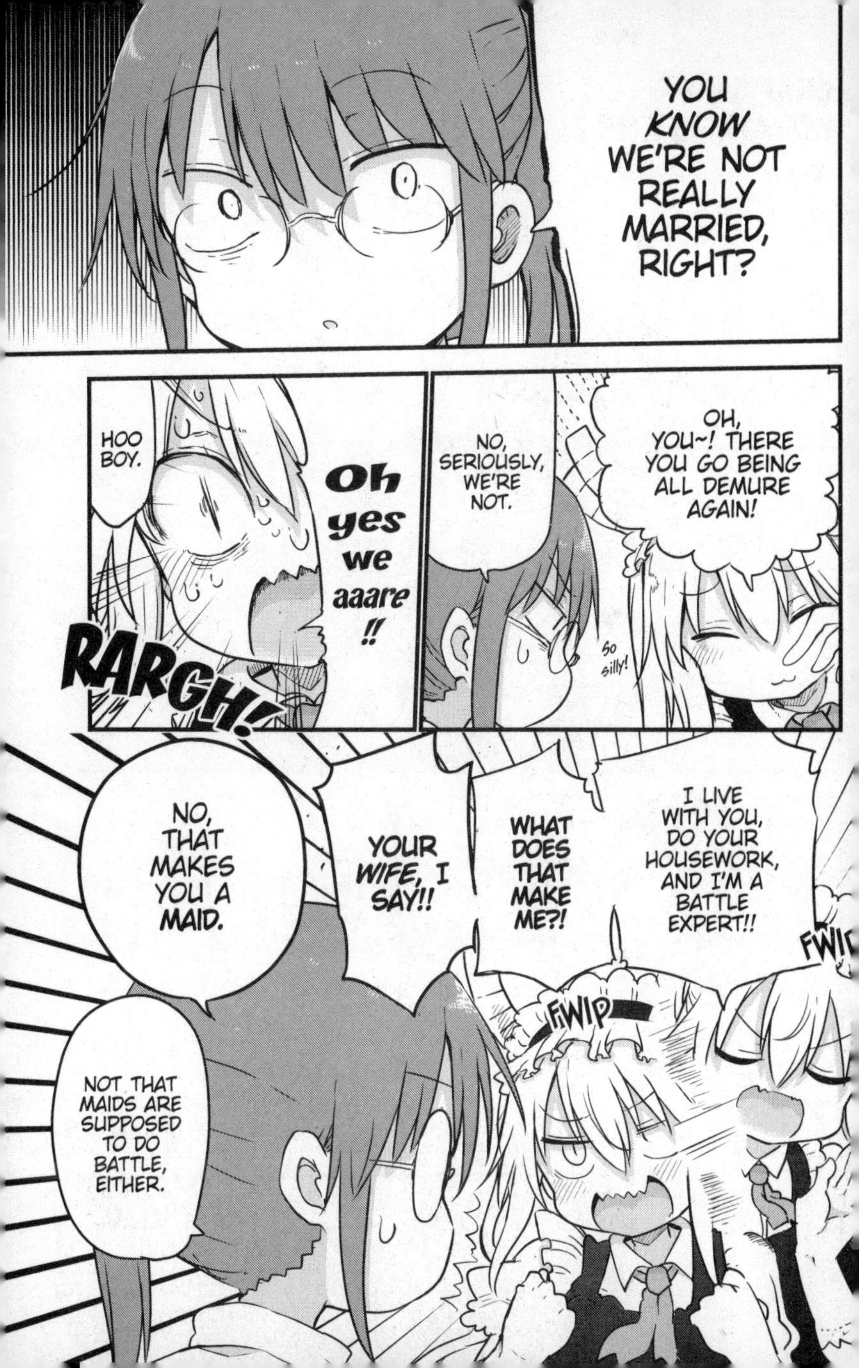

YOU KNOW WE'RE NOT REALLY MARRIED, RIGHT?
OH, YOU~! THERE YOU GO BEING ALL DEMURE AGAIN!
NO, SERIOUSLY, WE'RE NOT.
So silly!
Oh yes we aaare!!
HOO BOY.
RARGH!
I LIVE WITH YOU, DO YOUR HOUSEWORK, AND I'M A BATTLE EXPERT!!
WHAT DOES THAT MAKE ME?!
YOUR WIFE, I SAY!!
FWIP
NO, THAT MAKES YOU A MAID.
NOT THAT MAIDS ARE SUPPOSED TO DO BATTLE, EITHER.

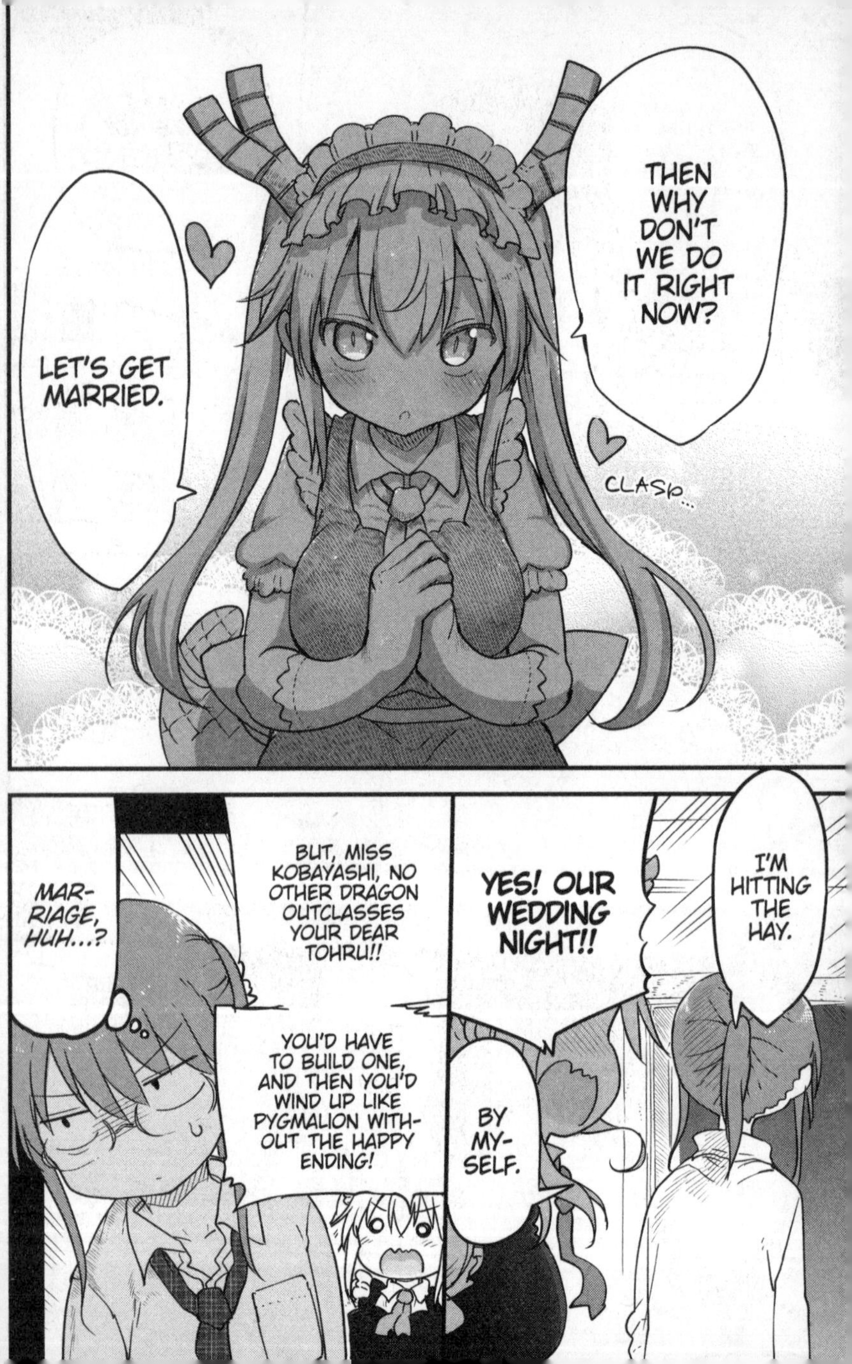
THEN WHY DON'T WE DO IT RIGHT NOW?
CLASP...
LET'S GET MARRIED.
I'M HITTING THE HAY.
YES! OUR WEDDING NIGHT!!
BY MY-SELF.
BUT, MISS KOBAYASHI, NO OTHER DRAGON OUTCLASSES YOUR DEAR TOHRU!!
YOU'D HAVE TO BUILD ONE, AND THEN YOU'D WIND UP LIKE PYGMALION WITH-OUT THE HAPPY ENDING!
MAR-RIAGE, HUH...?

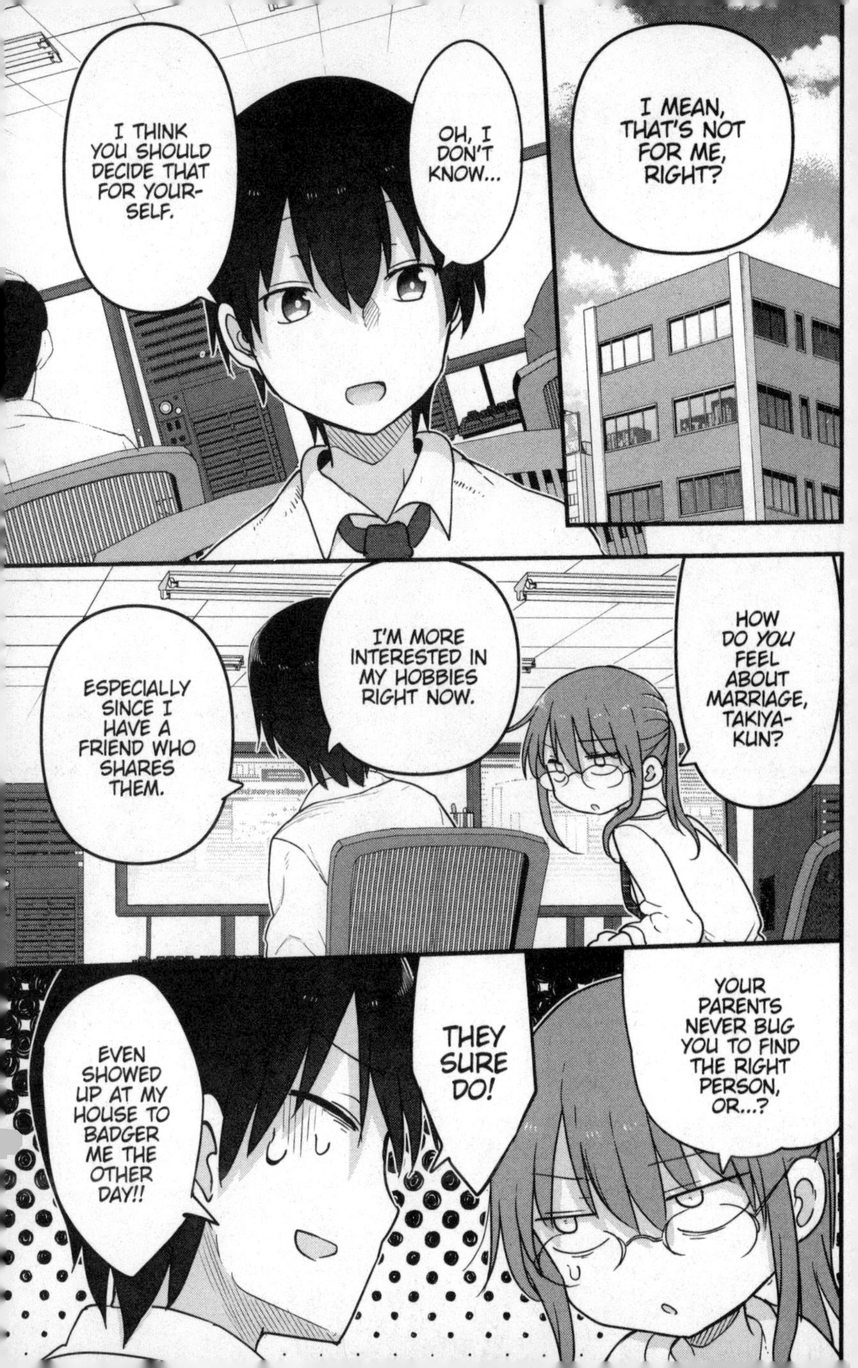
I MEAN, THAT'S NOT FOR ME, RIGHT?
OH, I DON'T KNOW...
I THINK YOU SHOULD DECIDE THAT FOR YOUR-SELF.
HOW DO *YOU* FEEL ABOUT MARRIAGE, TAKIYA-KUN?
I'M MORE INTERESTED IN MY HOBBIES RIGHT NOW.
ESPECIALLY SINCE I HAVE A FRIEND WHO SHARES THEM.
YOUR PARENTS NEVER BUG YOU TO FIND THE RIGHT PERSON, OR...?
THEY SURE DO!
EVEN SHOWED UP AT MY HOUSE TO BADGER ME THE OTHER DAY!!

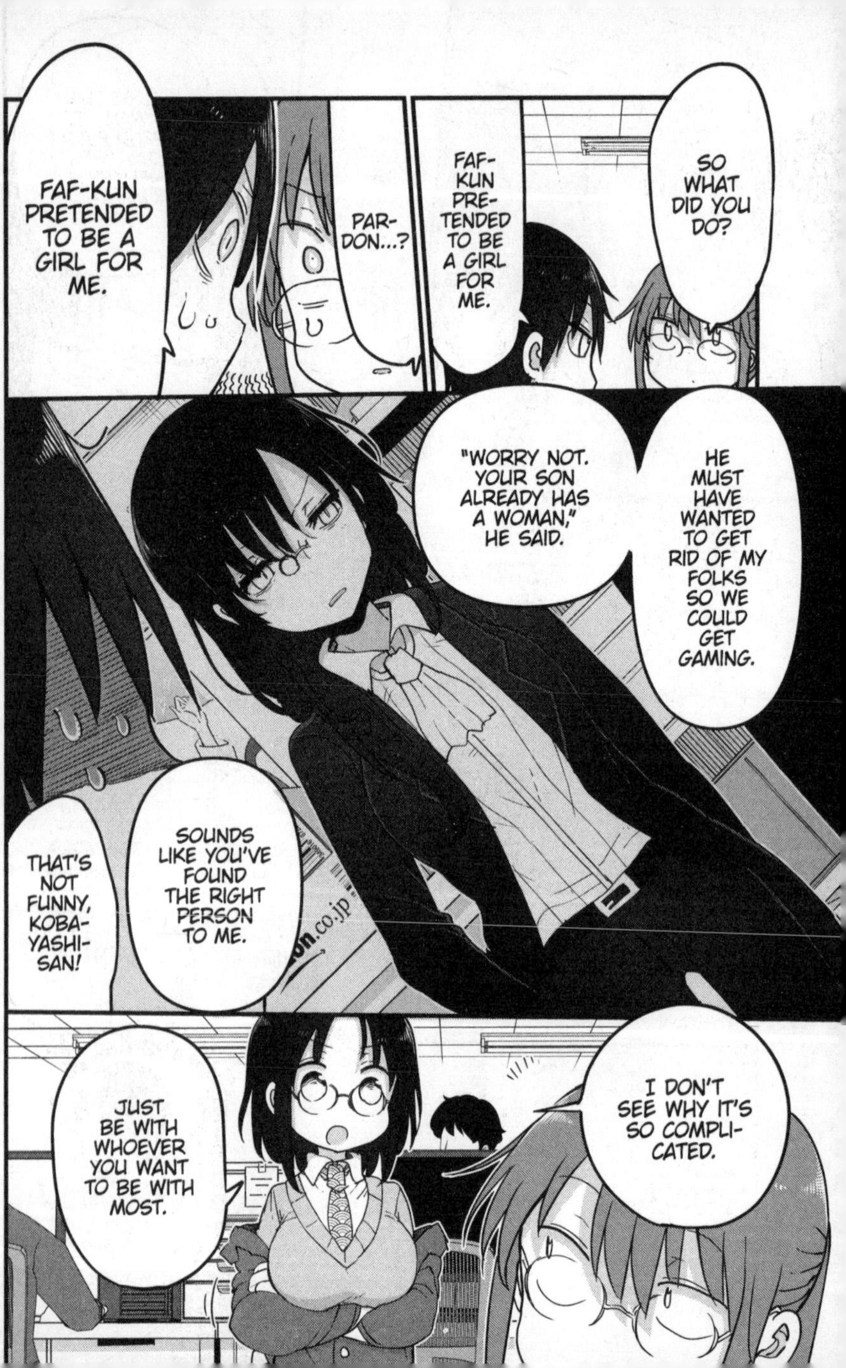
SO WHAT DID YOU DO?
FAF-KUN PRETENDED TO BE A GIRL FOR ME.
PARDON...?
FAF-KUN PRETENDED TO BE A GIRL FOR ME.
HE MUST HAVE WANTED TO GET RID OF MY FOLKS SO WE COULD GET GAMING.
"WORRY NOT. YOUR SON ALREADY HAS A WOMAN," HE SAID.
SOUNDS LIKE YOU'VE FOUND THE RIGHT PERSON TO ME.
THAT'S NOT FUNNY, KOBAYASHI-SAN!
I DON'T SEE WHY IT'S SO COMPLICATED.
JUST BE WITH WHOEVER YOU WANT TO BE WITH MOST.

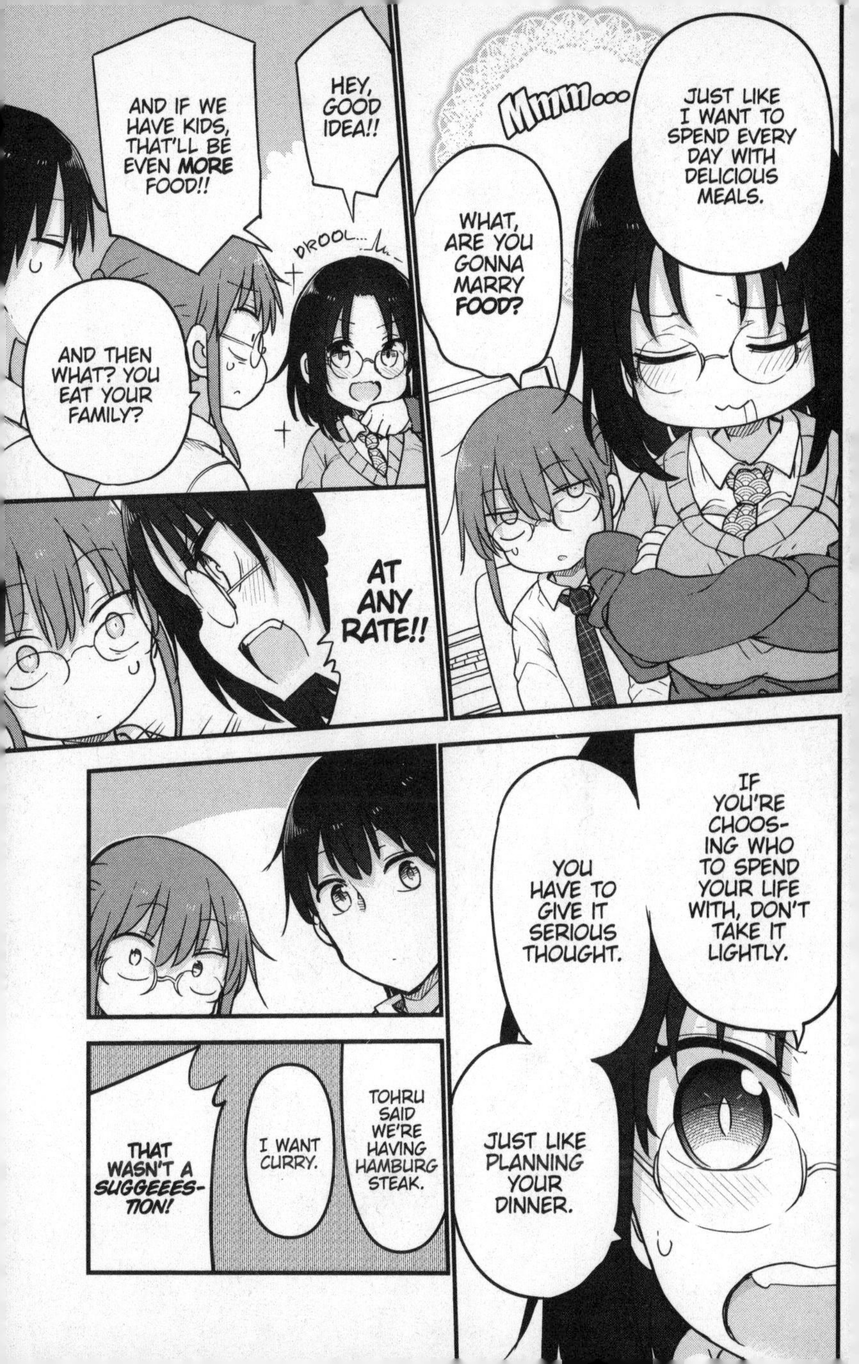
Mmmm...
JUST LIKE I WANT TO SPEND EVERY DAY WITH DELICIOUS MEALS.
WHAT, ARE YOU GONNA MARRY FOOD?
HEY, GOOD IDEA!!
AND IF WE HAVE KIDS, THAT'LL BE EVEN MORE FOOD!!
DROOL...
AND THEN WHAT? YOU EAT YOUR FAMILY?
AT ANY RATE!!
IF YOU'RE CHOOSING WHO TO SPEND YOUR LIFE WITH, DON'T TAKE IT LIGHTLY.
YOU HAVE TO GIVE IT SERIOUS THOUGHT.
JUST LIKE PLANNING YOUR DINNER.
TOHRU SAID WE'RE HAVING HAMBURG STEAK.
I WANT CURRY.
THAT WASN'T A SUGGEEESTION!

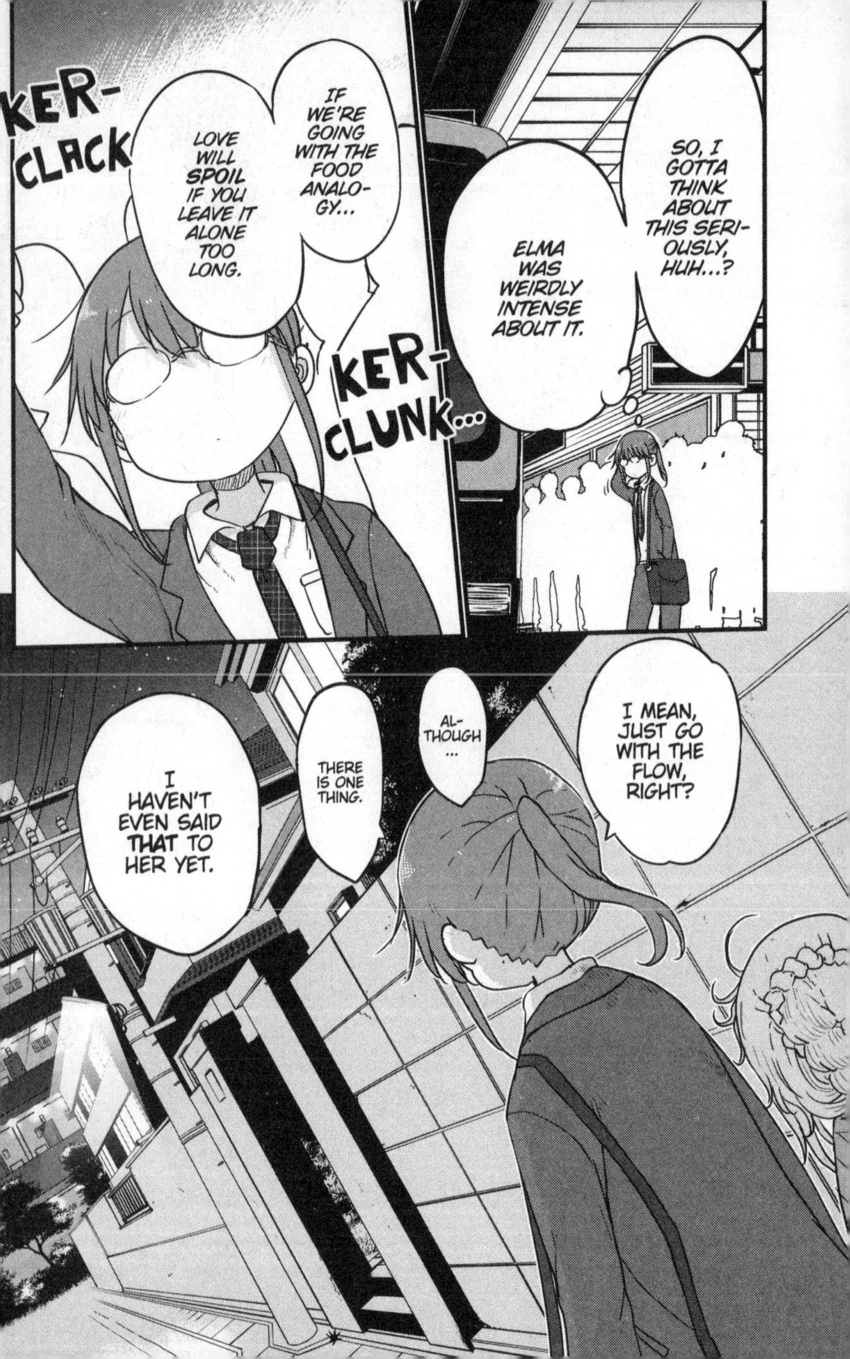
SO, I GOTTA THINK ABOUT THIS SERIOUSLY, HUH...?
ELMA WAS WEIRDLY INTENSE ABOUT IT.
KER-CLUNK...
IF WE'RE GOING WITH THE FOOD ANALOGY...
LOVE WILL SPOIL IF YOU LEAVE IT ALONE TOO LONG.
KER-CLACK
I MEAN, JUST GO WITH THE FLOW, RIGHT?
ALTHOUGH...
THERE IS ONE THING.
I HAVEN'T EVEN SAID THAT TO HER YET.

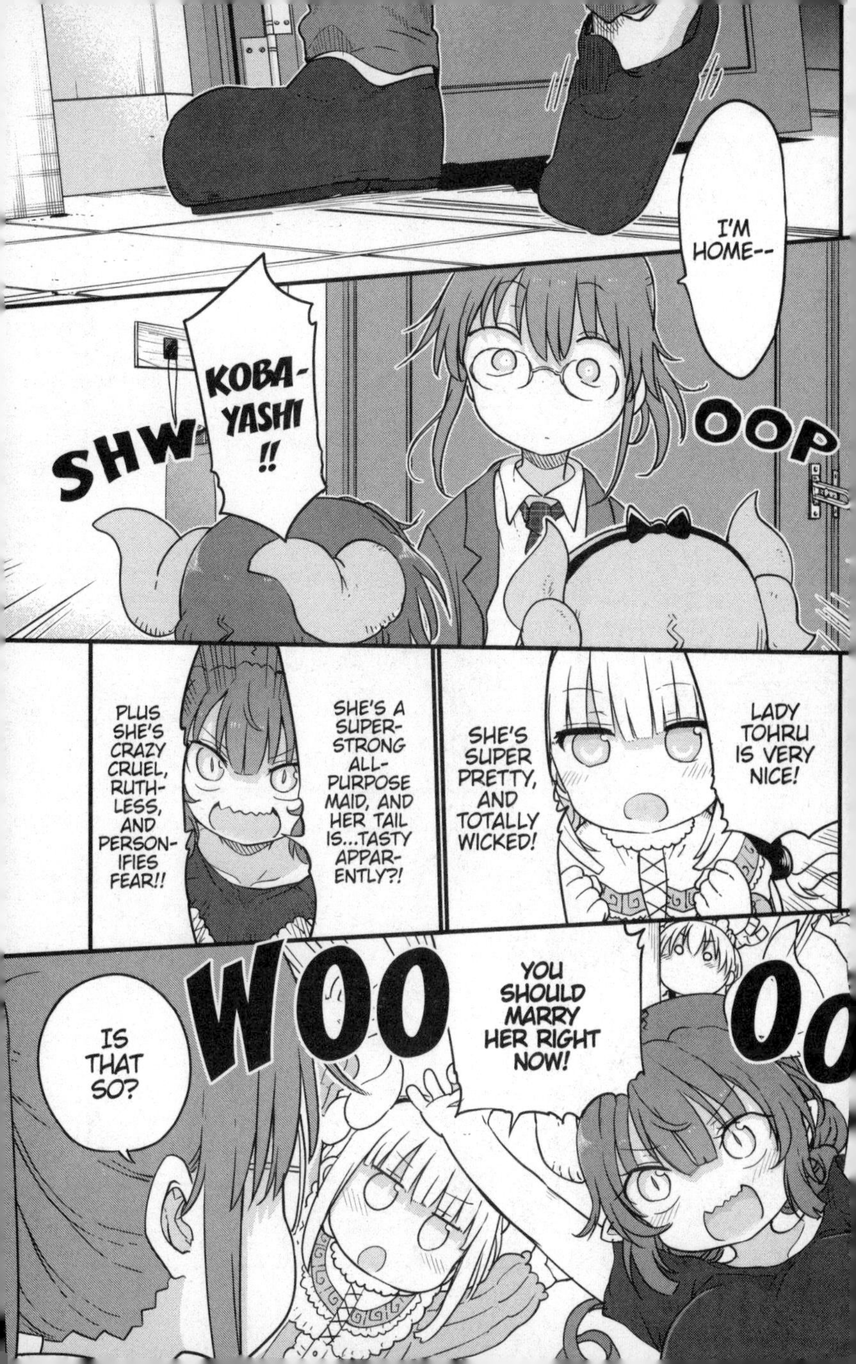
I'M HOME--
KOBA-YASHI!!
SHW
OOP
LADY TOHRU IS VERY NICE!
SHE'S SUPER PRETTY, AND TOTALLY WICKED!
SHE'S A SUPER-STRONG ALL-PURPOSE MAID, AND HER TAIL IS...TASTY APPARENTLY?!
PLUS SHE'S CRAZY CRUEL, RUTHLESS, AND PERSONIFIES FEAR!!
OO
YOU SHOULD MARRY HER RIGHT NOW!
WOO
IS THAT SO?

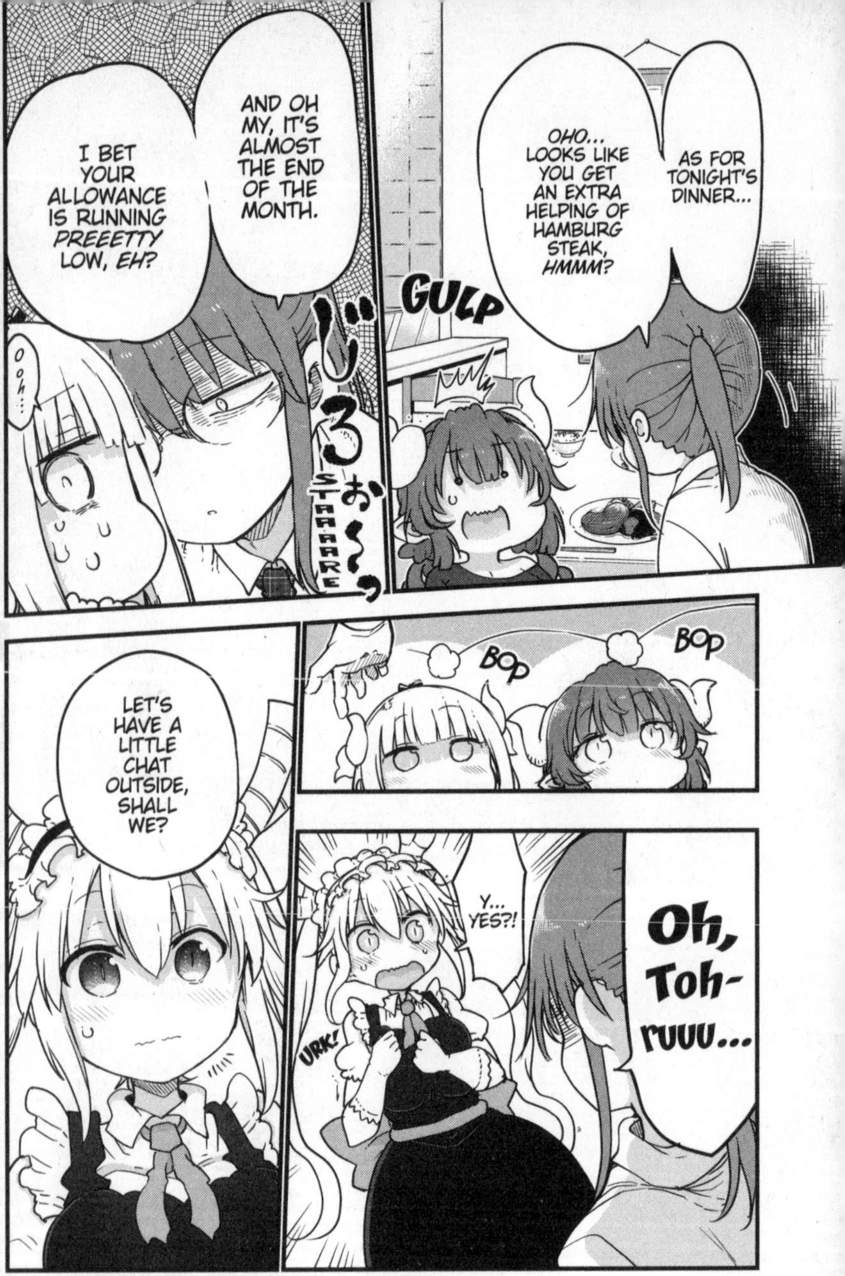
AS FOR TONIGHT'S DINNER...
OHO... LOOKS LIKE YOU GET AN EXTRA HELPING OF HAMBURG STEAK, *HMMM?*
GULP
AND OH MY, IT'S ALMOST THE END OF THE MONTH.
I BET YOUR ALLOWANCE IS RUNNING *PREEETTY* LOW, *EH?*
STAAARE
ooh...
BOP
BOP
Oh, Toh-ruuu...
Y... YES?!
URK!
LET'S HAVE A LITTLE CHAT OUTSIDE, SHALL WE?

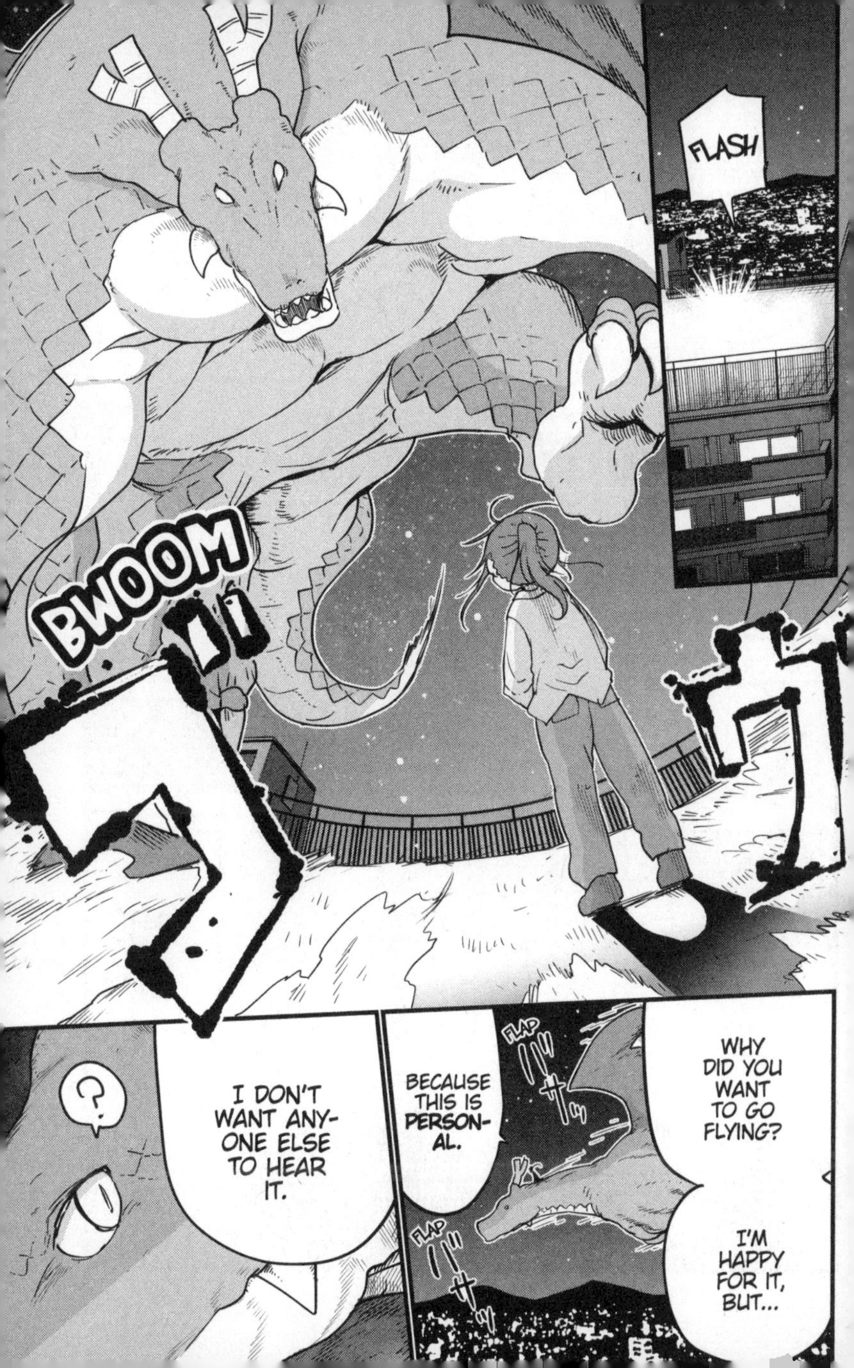
FLASH
BWOOM
WHY DID YOU WANT TO GO FLYING?
I'M HAPPY FOR IT, BUT...
FLAP
FLAP
BECAUSE THIS IS **PERSON-AL.**
?
I DON'T WANT ANY-ONE ELSE TO HEAR IT.

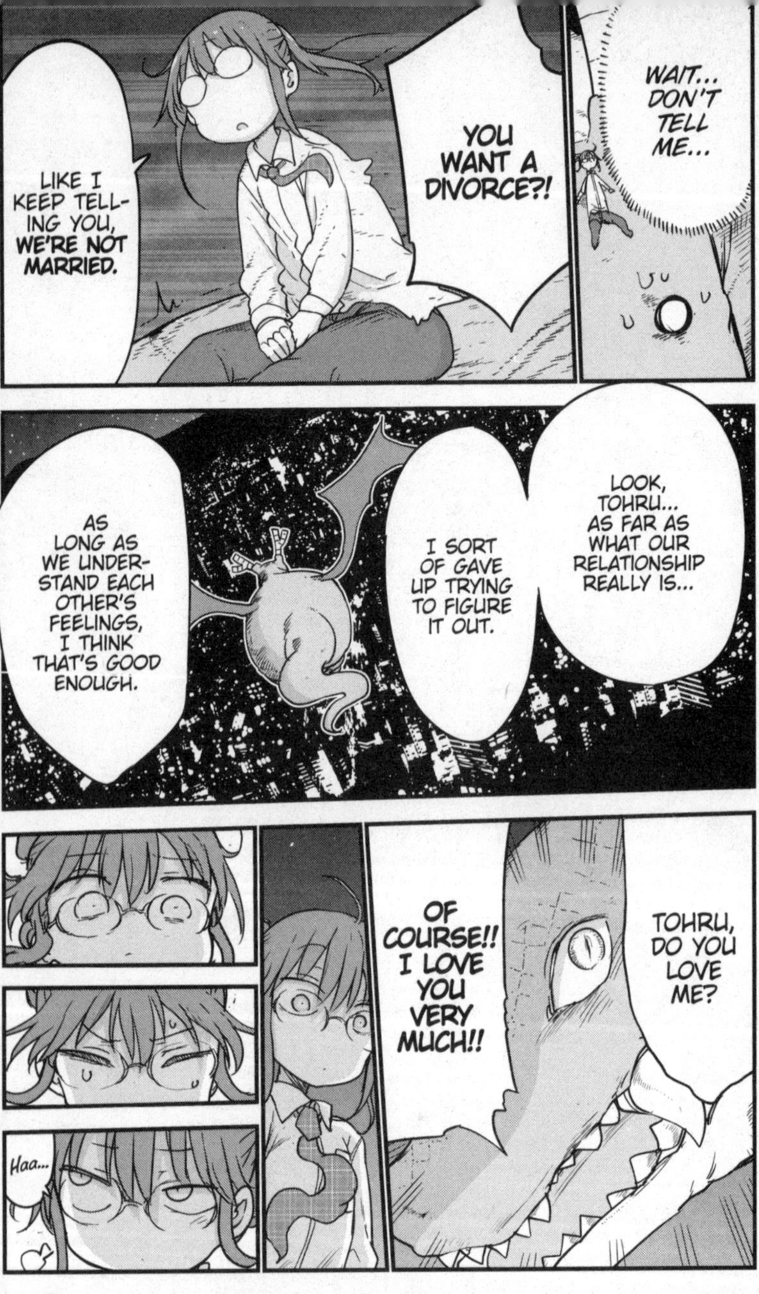
WAIT... DON'T TELL ME...
YOU WANT A DIVORCE?!
LIKE I KEEP TELLING YOU, WE'RE NOT MARRIED.
LOOK, TOHRU... AS FAR AS WHAT OUR RELATIONSHIP REALLY IS...
I SORT OF GAVE UP TRYING TO FIGURE IT OUT.
AS LONG AS WE UNDERSTAND EACH OTHER'S FEELINGS, I THINK THAT'S GOOD ENOUGH.
TOHRU, DO YOU LOVE ME?
OF COURSE!! I LOVE YOU VERY MUCH!!
Haa...

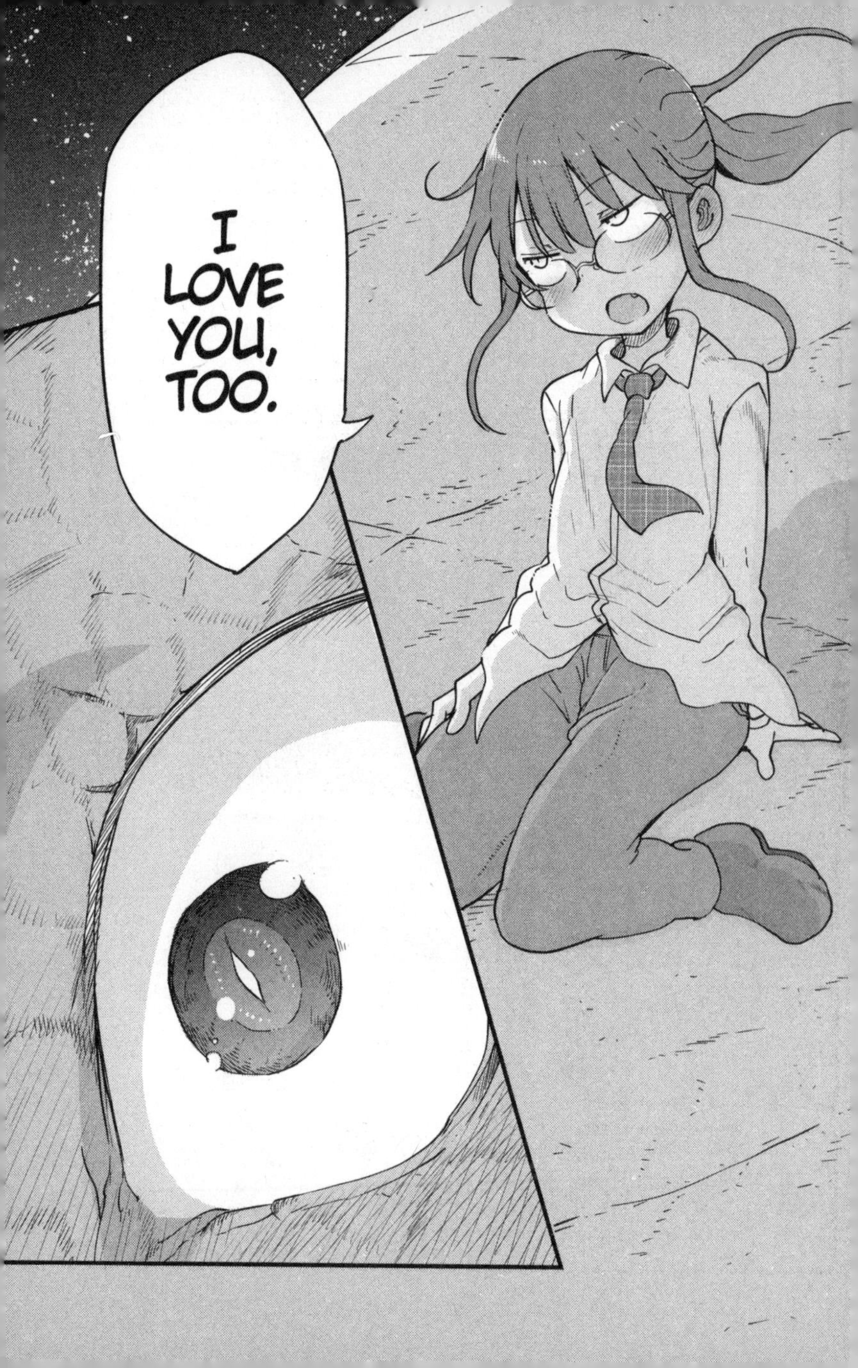
I LOVE YOU, TOO.

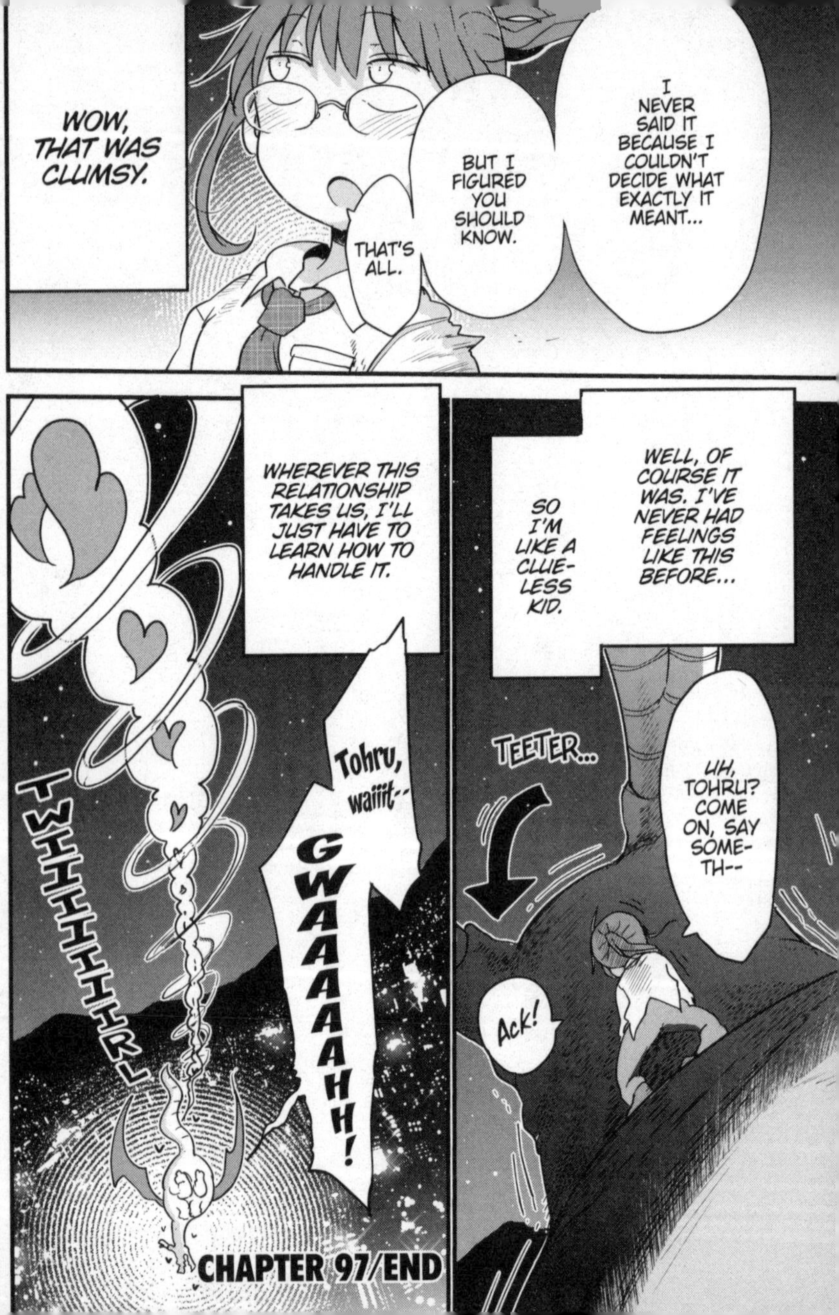
I NEVER SAID IT BECAUSE I COULDN'T DECIDE WHAT EXACTLY IT MEANT...
BUT I FIGURED YOU SHOULD KNOW.
THAT'S ALL.
WOW, THAT WAS CLUMSY.
WELL, OF COURSE IT WAS. I'VE NEVER HAD FEELINGS LIKE THIS BEFORE...
SO I'M LIKE A CLUE-LESS KID.
UH, TOHRU? COME ON, SAY SOMETH--
TEETER...
Ack!
WHEREVER THIS RELATIONSHIP TAKES US, I'LL JUST HAVE TO LEARN HOW TO HANDLE IT.
Tohru, waiiit--
GWAAAAAAHH!
TWHIIIIIIIRL
CHAPTER 97/END

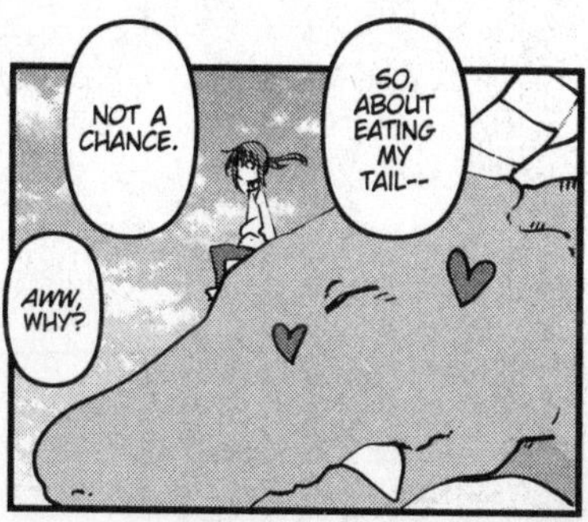
SO, ABOUT EATING MY TAIL--
NOT A CHANCE.
AWW, WHY?

Miss Kobayashi's Dragon Maid

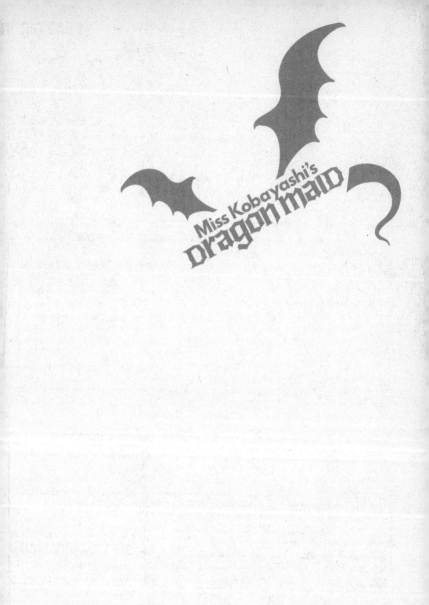

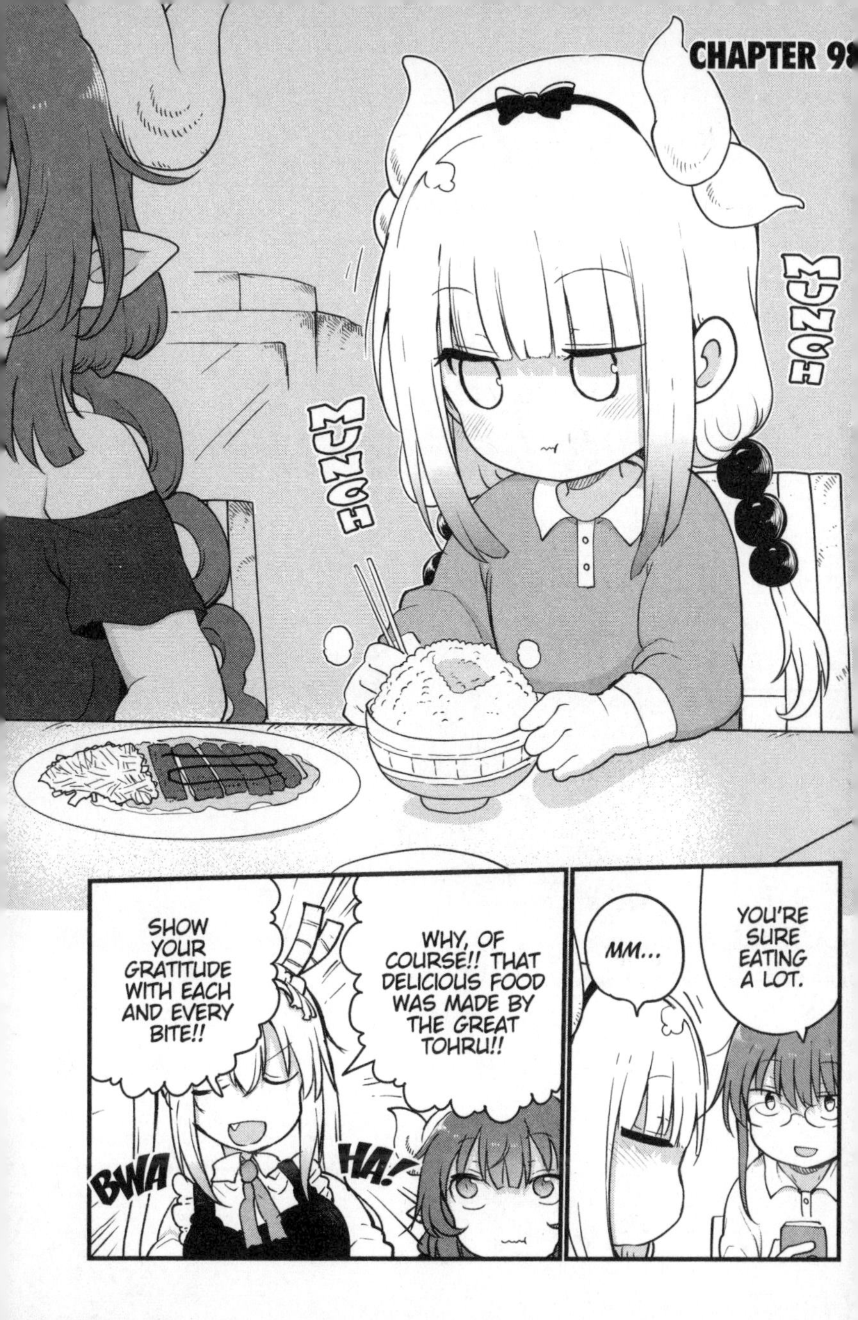
CHAPTER 9
MUNCH
MUNCH
YOU'RE SURE EATING A LOT.
MM...
WHY, OF COURSE!! THAT DELICIOUS FOOD WAS MADE BY THE GREAT TOHRU!!
SHOW YOUR GRATITUDE WITH EACH AND EVERY BITE!!
BWA HA!

CHAPTER 98: TOHRU AND SCHOOL LUNCH

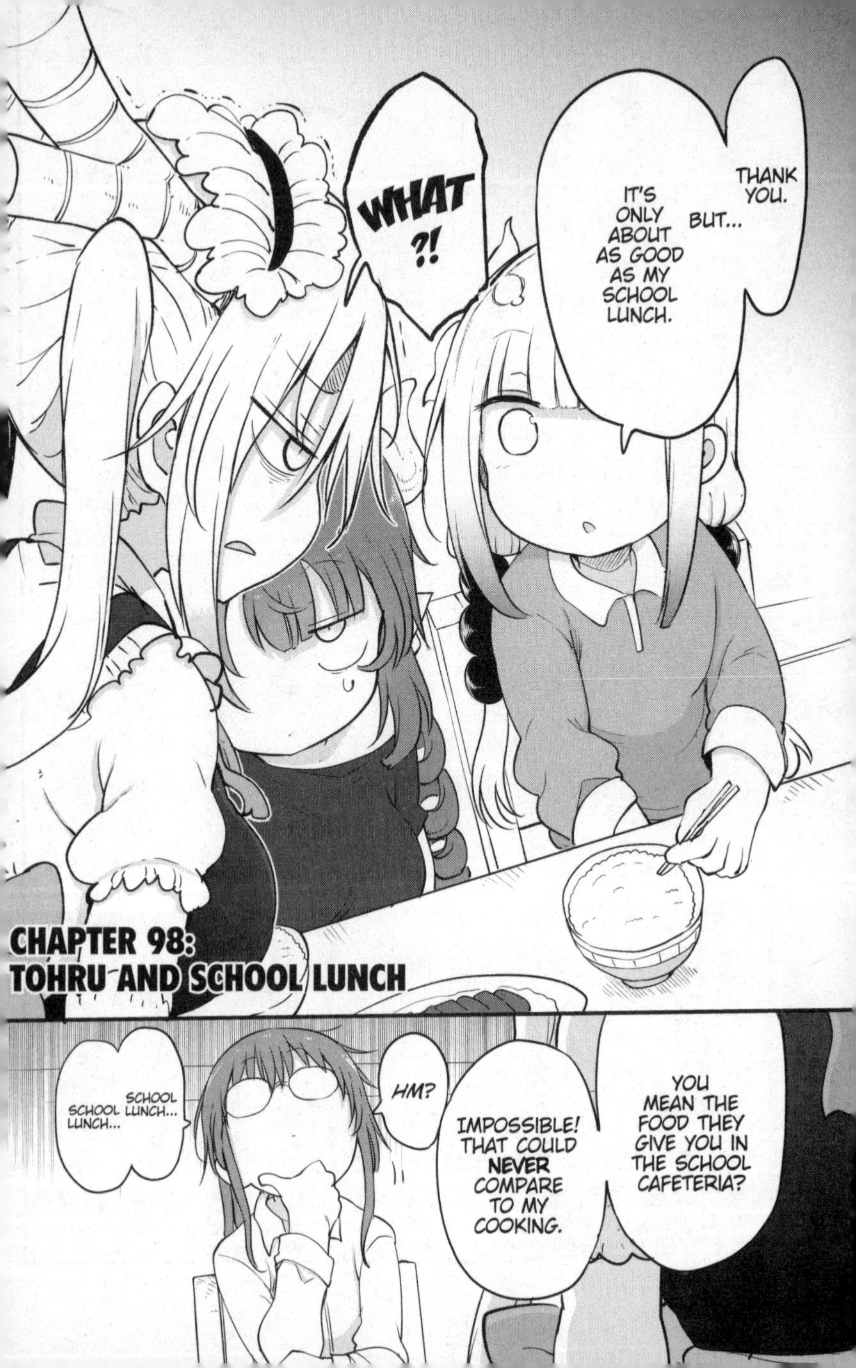
THANK YOU. BUT... IT'S ONLY ABOUT AS GOOD AS MY SCHOOL LUNCH.
WHAT ?!
YOU MEAN THE FOOD THEY GIVE YOU IN THE SCHOOL CAFETERIA?
IMPOSSIBLE! THAT COULD NEVER COMPARE TO MY COOKING.
HM?
SCHOOL LUNCH... SCHOOL LUNCH...

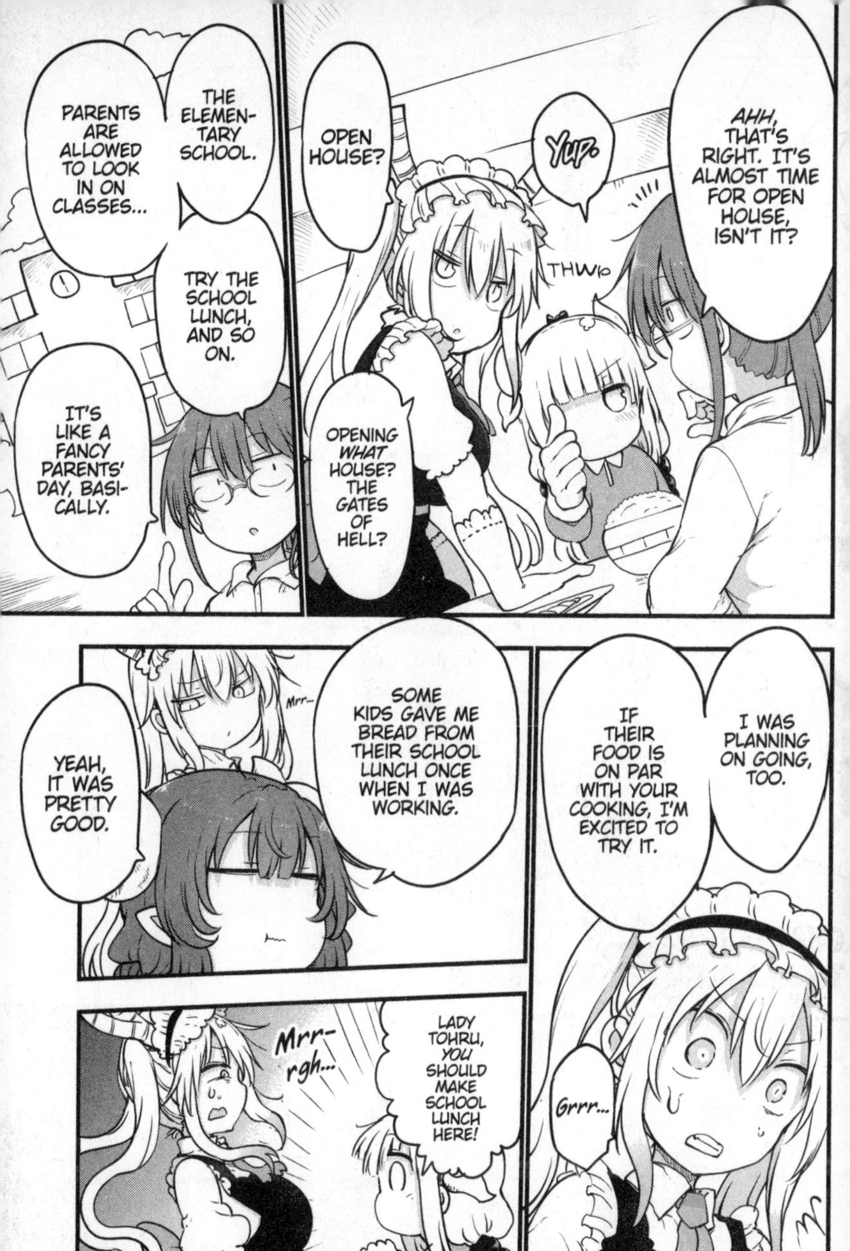
AHH, THAT'S RIGHT. IT'S ALMOST TIME FOR OPEN HOUSE, ISN'T IT?
Yup.
THWIP
OPEN HOUSE?
OPENING *WHAT* HOUSE? THE GATES OF HELL?
THE ELEMENTARY SCHOOL.
PARENTS ARE ALLOWED TO LOOK IN ON CLASSES...
TRY THE SCHOOL LUNCH, AND SO ON.
IT'S LIKE A FANCY PARENTS' DAY, BASICALLY.
I WAS PLANNING ON GOING, TOO.
IF THEIR FOOD IS ON PAR WITH YOUR COOKING, I'M EXCITED TO TRY IT.
Grrr...
SOME KIDS GAVE ME BREAD FROM THEIR SCHOOL LUNCH ONCE WHEN I WAS WORKING.
Mrr...
YEAH, IT WAS PRETTY GOOD.
LADY TOHRU, *YOU* SHOULD MAKE SCHOOL LUNCH HERE!
Mrr-rgh...

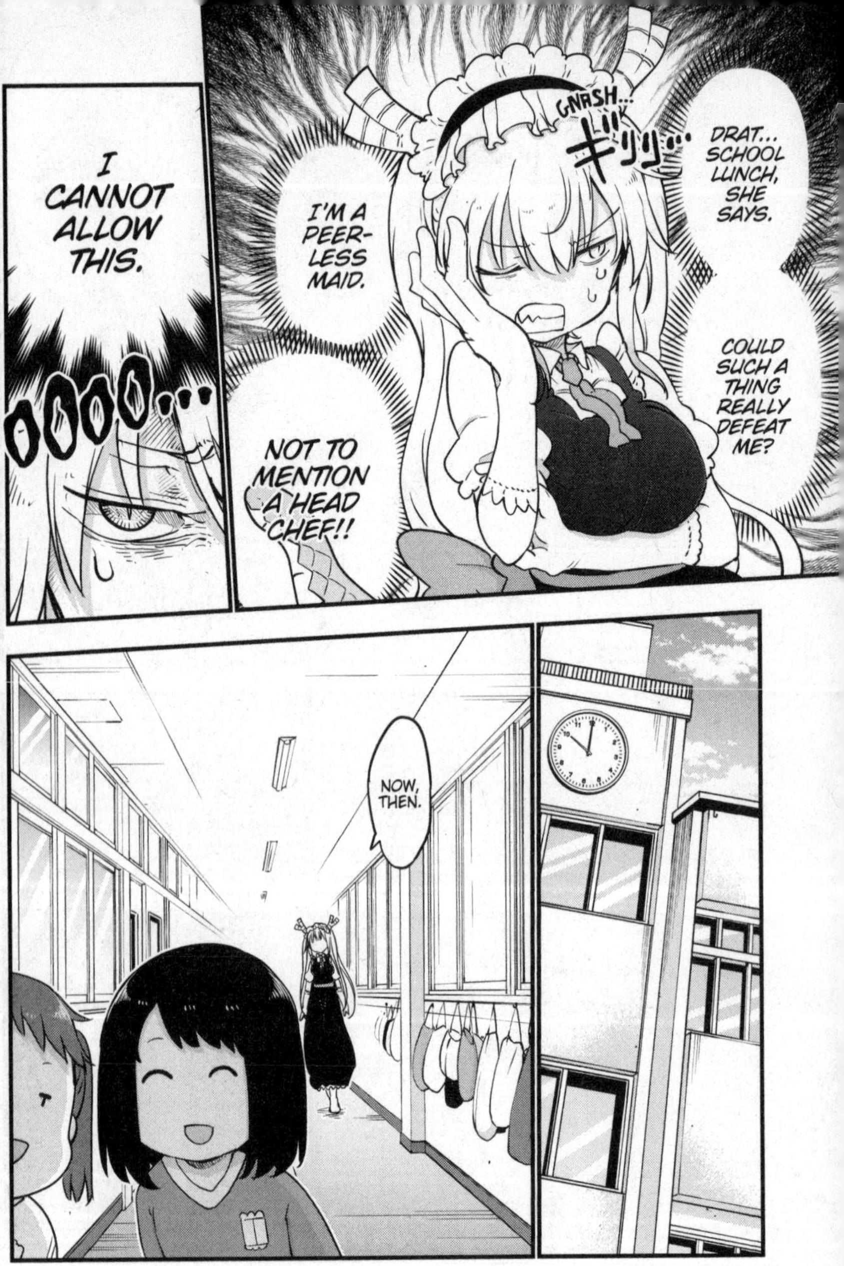
GNASH...
ギリリ…
DRAT... SCHOOL LUNCH, SHE SAYS.
COULD SUCH A THING REALLY DEFEAT ME?
I'M A PEERLESS MAID.
NOT TO MENTION A HEAD CHEF!!
I CANNOT ALLOW THIS.
OOOO...
NOW, THEN.

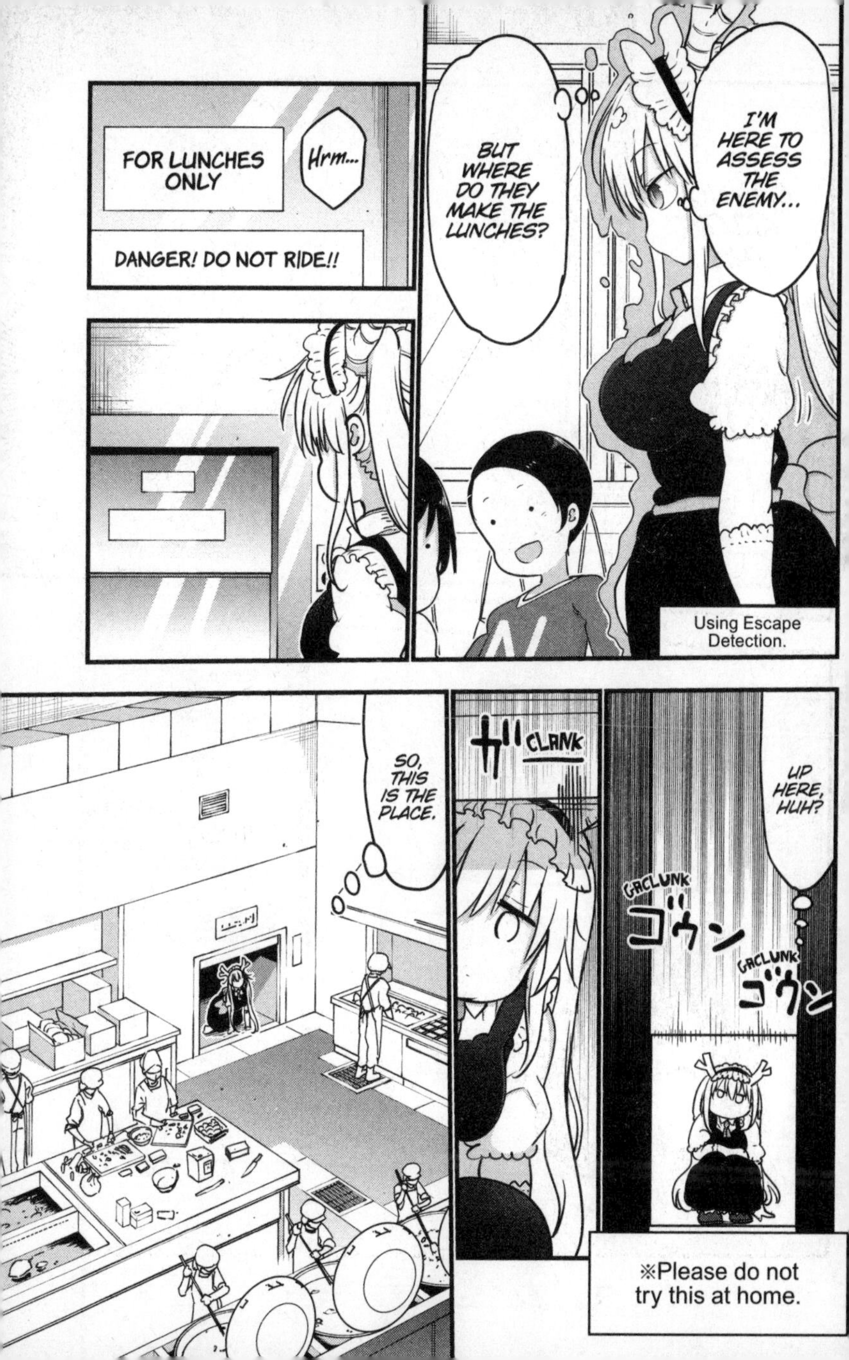
I'M HERE TO ASSESS THE ENEMY...
BUT WHERE DO THEY MAKE THE LUNCHES?
Using Escape Detection.
FOR LUNCHES ONLY
Hrm...
DANGER! DO NOT RIDE!!
UP HERE, HUH?
GACLUNK
ゴウン
GACLUNK
ゴウン
※Please do not try this at home.
ガッ
CLANK
SO, THIS IS THE PLACE.

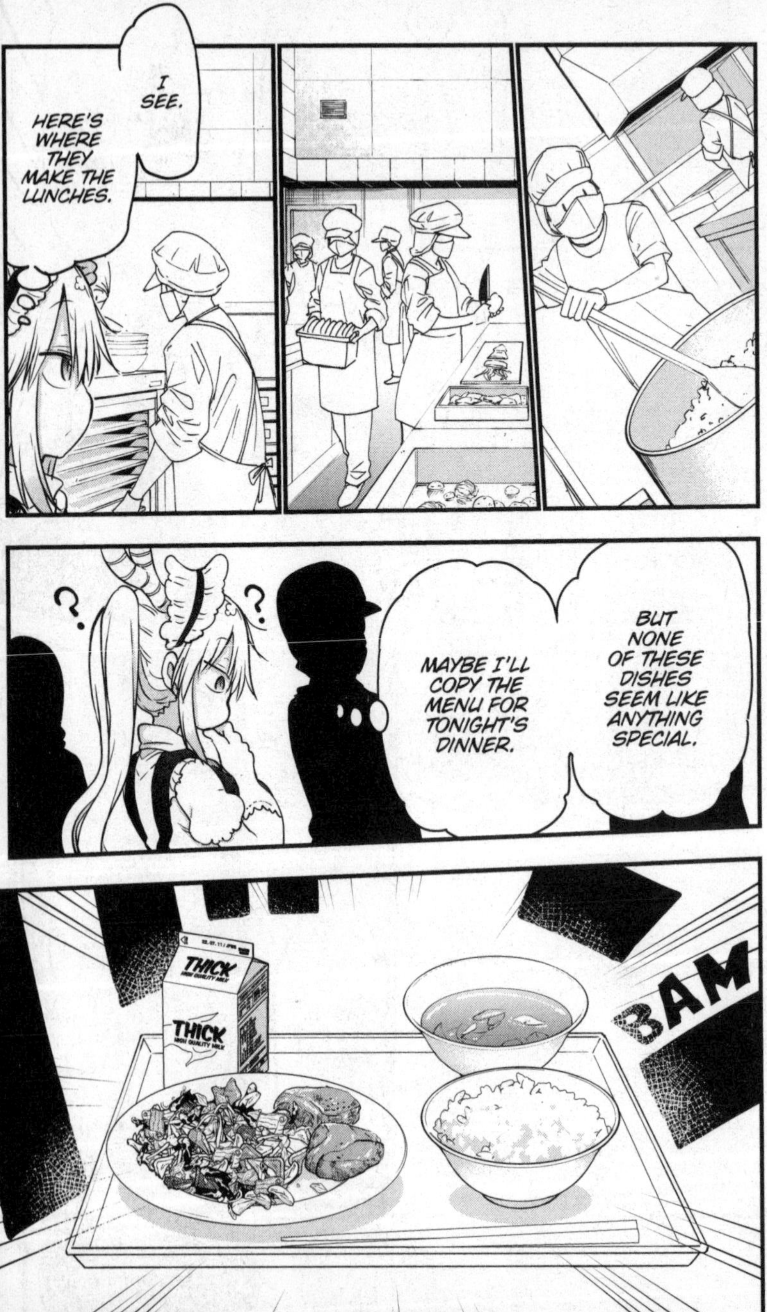
I SEE.
HERE'S WHERE THEY MAKE THE LUNCHES.
BUT NONE OF THESE DISHES SEEM LIKE ANYTHING SPECIAL.
MAYBE I'LL COPY THE MENU FOR TONIGHT'S DINNER.
BAM
THICK
THICK

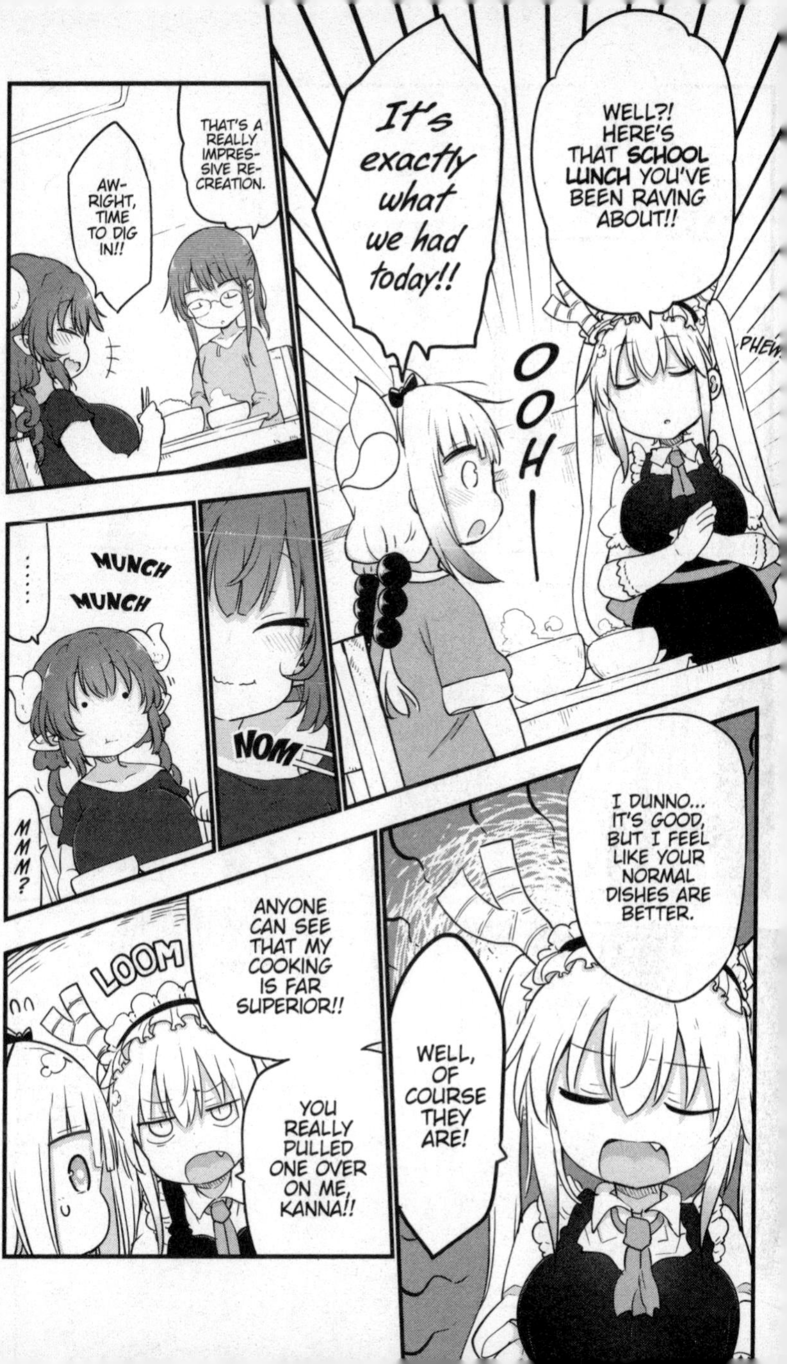
WELL?! HERE'S THAT **SCHOOL LUNCH** YOU'VE BEEN RAVING ABOUT!!
PHEW
It's exactly what we had today!!
OOH
THAT'S A REALLY IMPRESSIVE RE-CREATION.
AW-RIGHT, TIME TO DIG IN!!
NOM
MUNCH
MUNCH
......
MMMM?
I DUNNO... IT'S GOOD, BUT I FEEL LIKE YOUR NORMAL DISHES ARE BETTER.
WELL, OF COURSE THEY ARE!
ANYONE CAN SEE THAT MY COOKING IS FAR SUPERIOR!!
LOOM
YOU REALLY PULLED ONE OVER ON ME, KANNA!!

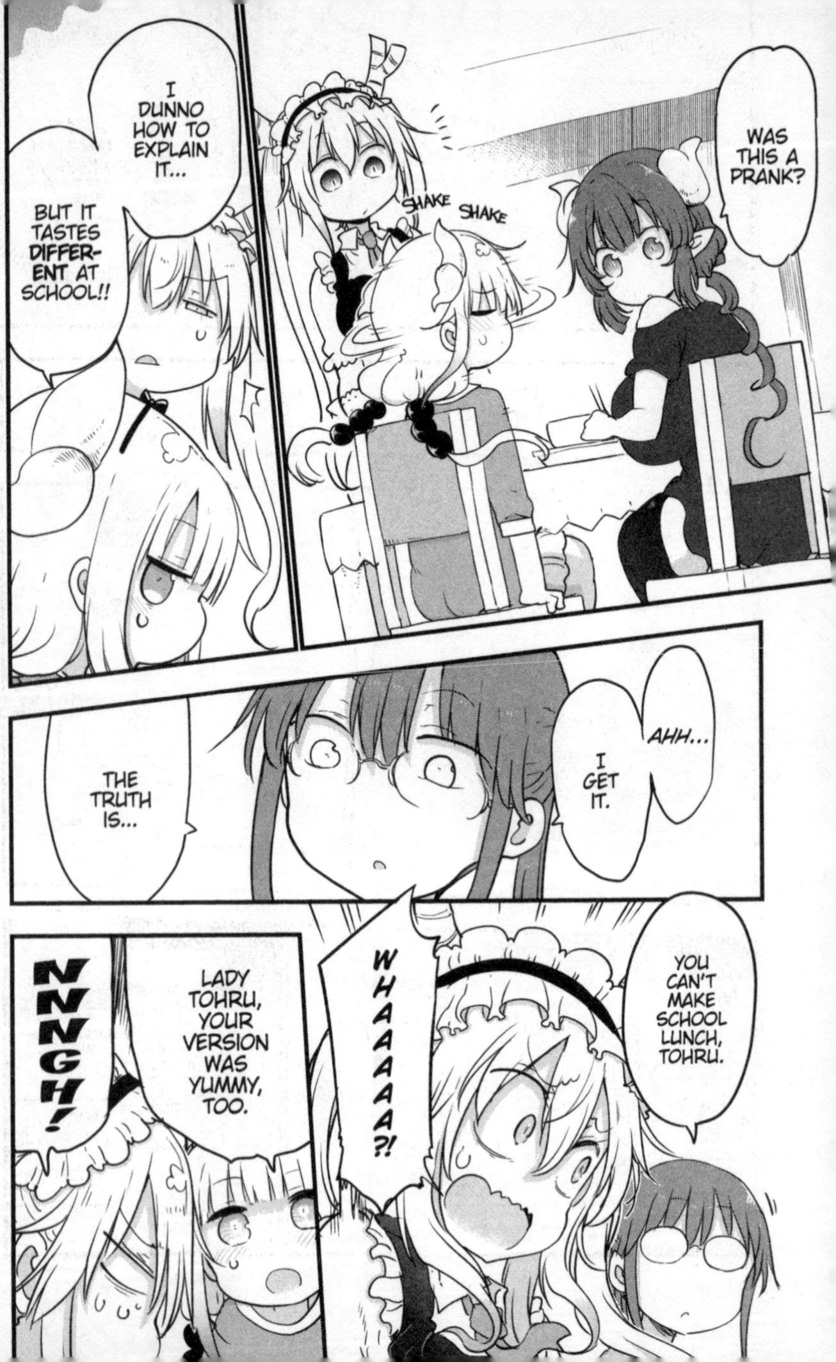
WAS THIS A PRANK?
SHAKE SHAKE
I DUNNO HOW TO EXPLAIN IT...
BUT IT TASTES DIFFERENT AT SCHOOL!!
AHH... I GET IT.
THE TRUTH IS...
YOU CAN'T MAKE SCHOOL LUNCH, TOHRU.
WHAAAAAA?!
LADY TOHRU, YOUR VERSION WAS YUMMY, TOO.
NNNGH!

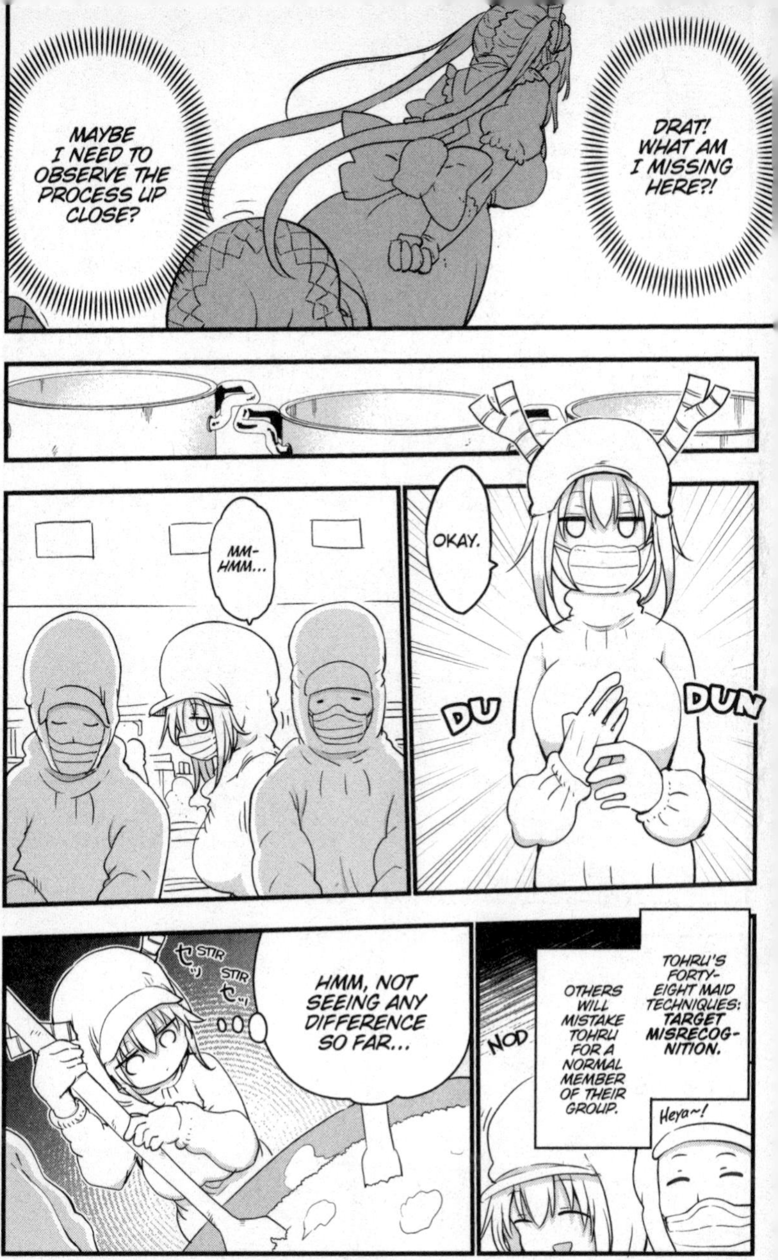
DRAT! WHAT AM I MISSING HERE?!
MAYBE I NEED TO OBSERVE THE PROCESS UP CLOSE?
OKAY.
DU
DUN
MM-HMM...
TOHRU'S FORTY-EIGHT MAID TECHNIQUES: TARGET MISRECOGNITION.
OTHERS WILL MISTAKE TOHRU FOR A NORMAL MEMBER OF THEIR GROUP.
NOD
Heya~!
HMM, NOT SEEING ANY DIFFERENCE SO FAR...
STIR
STIR

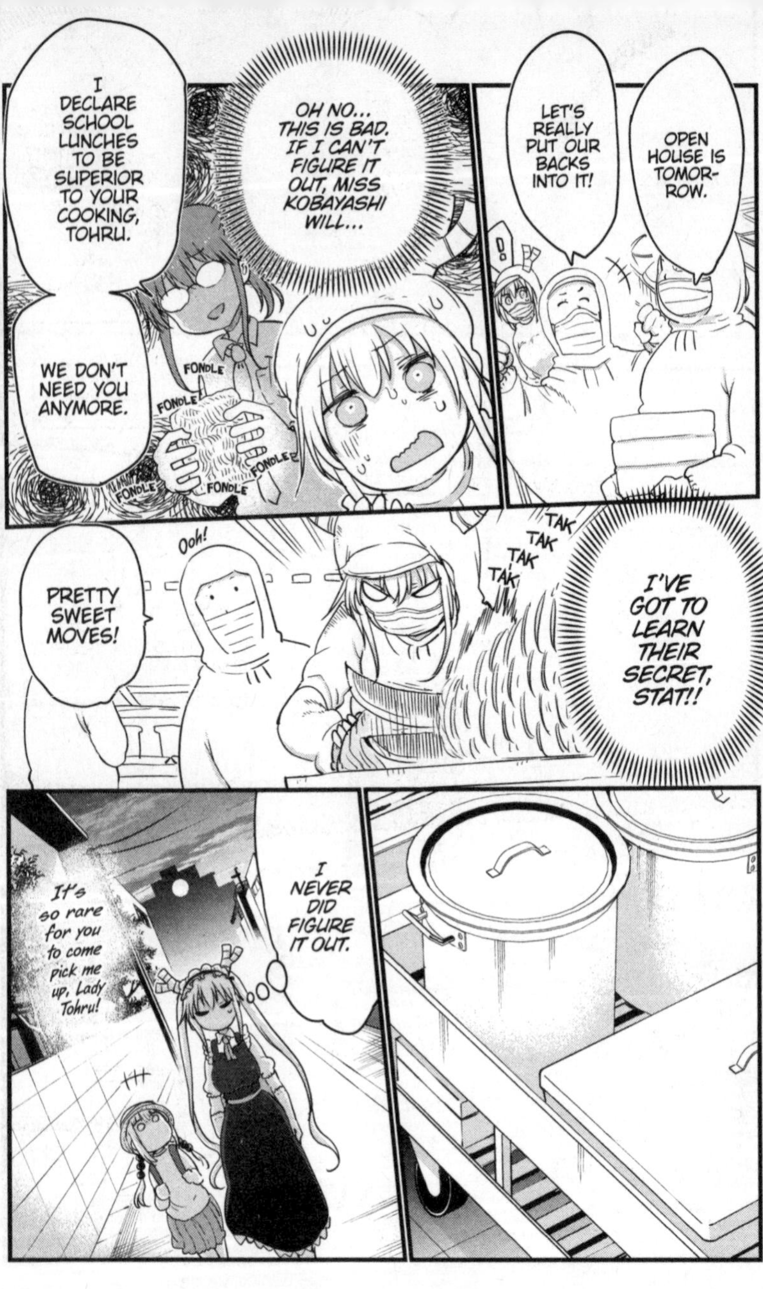
OPEN HOUSE IS TOMORROW.
LET'S REALLY PUT OUR BACKS INTO IT!
!
OH NO... THIS IS BAD. IF I CAN'T FIGURE IT OUT, MISS KOBAYASHI WILL...
I DECLARE SCHOOL LUNCHES TO BE SUPERIOR TO YOUR COOKING, TOHRU.
WE DON'T NEED YOU ANYMORE.
FONDLE FONDLE FONDLE FONDLE FONDLE
I'VE GOT TO LEARN THEIR SECRET, STAT!!
TAK TAK TAK TAK
Ooh!
PRETTY SWEET MOVES!
I NEVER DID FIGURE IT OUT.
It's so rare for you to come pick me up, Lady Tohru!

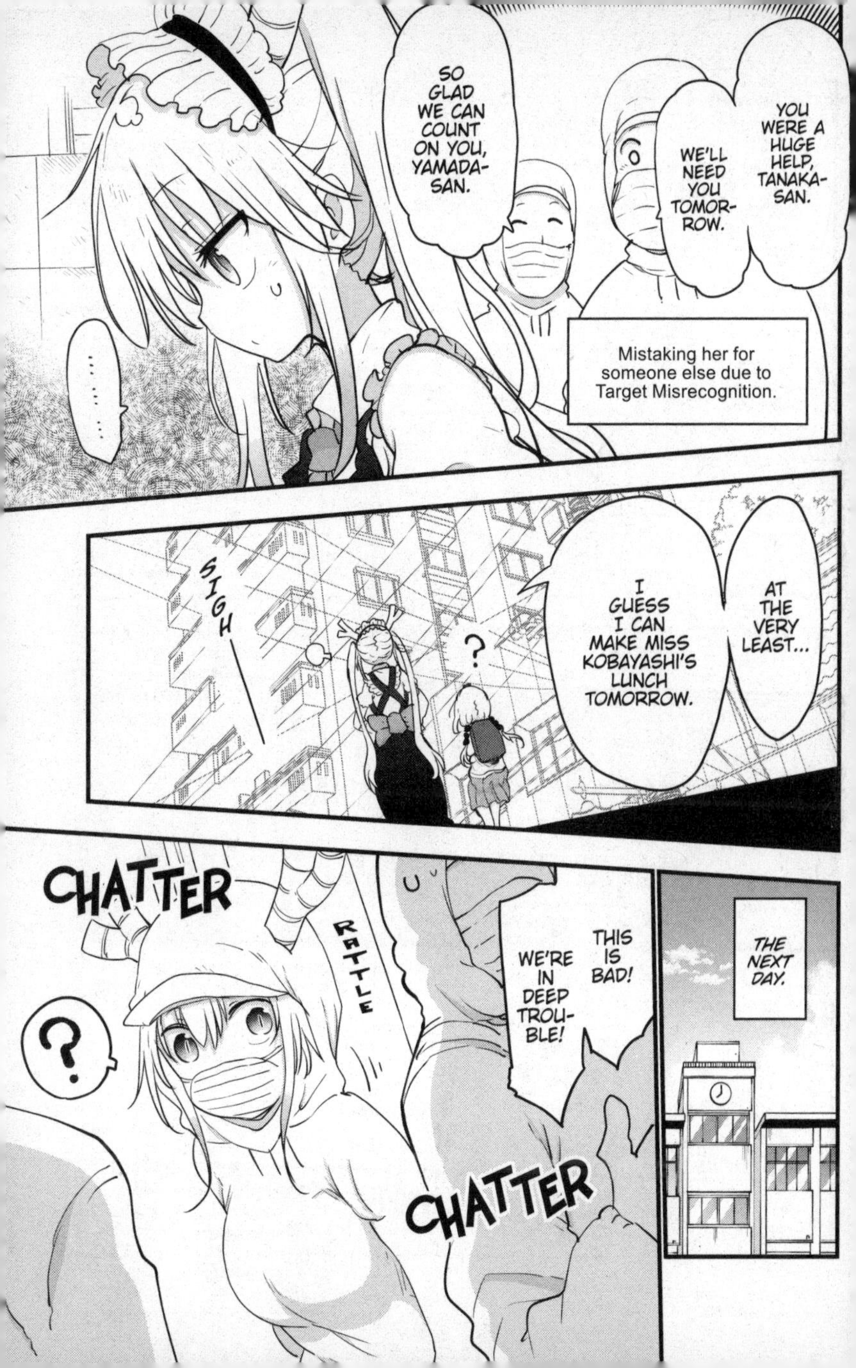
YOU WERE A HUGE HELP, TANAKA-SAN.
WE'LL NEED YOU TOMORROW.
SO GLAD WE CAN COUNT ON YOU, YAMADA-SAN.
Mistaking her for someone else due to Target Misrecognition.
......
AT THE VERY LEAST...
I GUESS I CAN MAKE MISS KOBAYASHI'S LUNCH TOMORROW.
?
SIGH
THE NEXT DAY.
THIS IS BAD!
WE'RE IN DEEP TROUBLE!
RATTLE
CHATTER
CHATTER
?

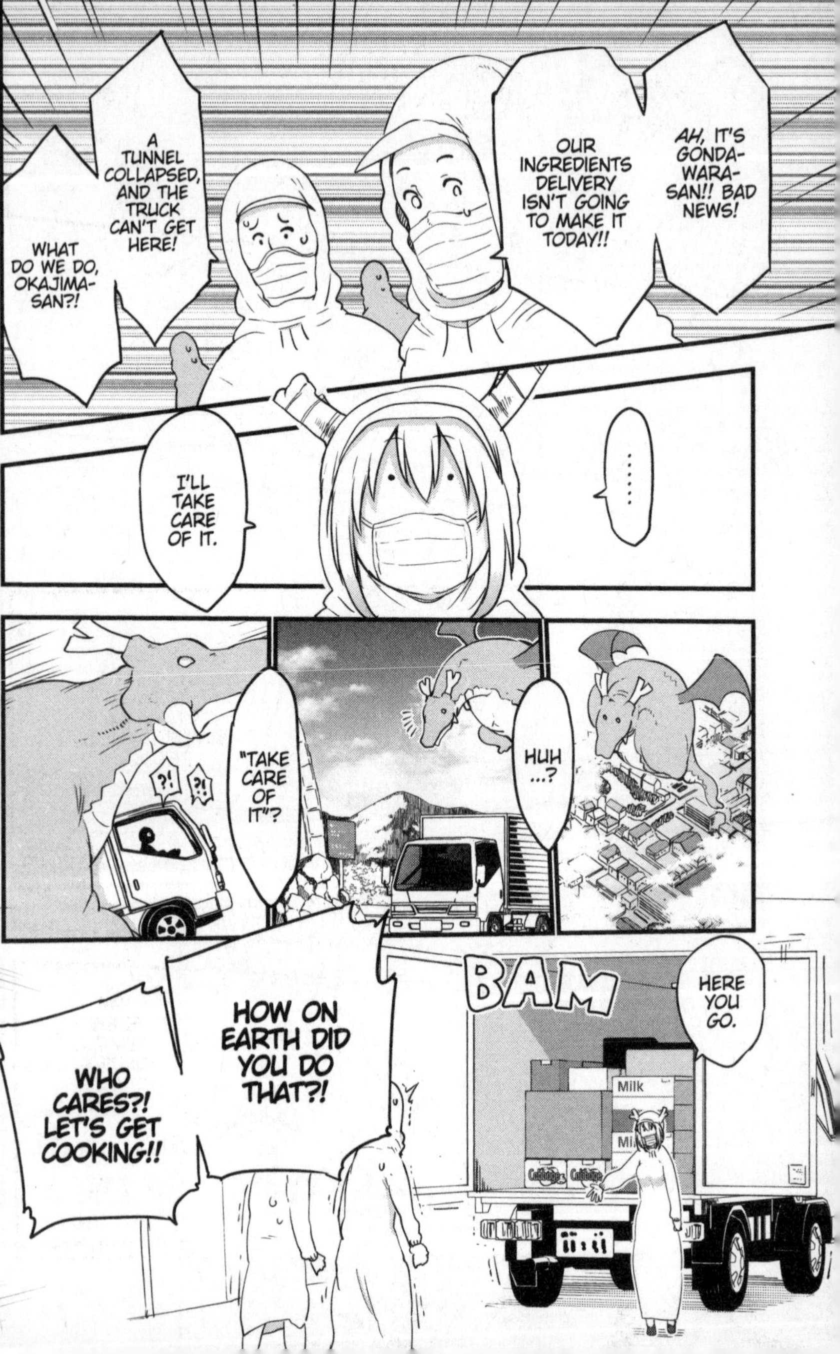
AH, IT'S GONDA-WARA-SAN!! BAD NEWS!
OUR INGREDIENTS DELIVERY ISN'T GOING TO MAKE IT TODAY!!
A TUNNEL COLLAPSED, AND THE TRUCK CAN'T GET HERE!
WHAT DO WE DO, OKAJIMA-SAN?!
......
I'LL TAKE CARE OF IT.
HUH ...?
"TAKE CARE OF IT"?
?!
?!
BAM
HERE YOU GO.
Milk
HOW ON EARTH DID YOU DO THAT?!
WHO CARES?! LET'S GET COOKING!!

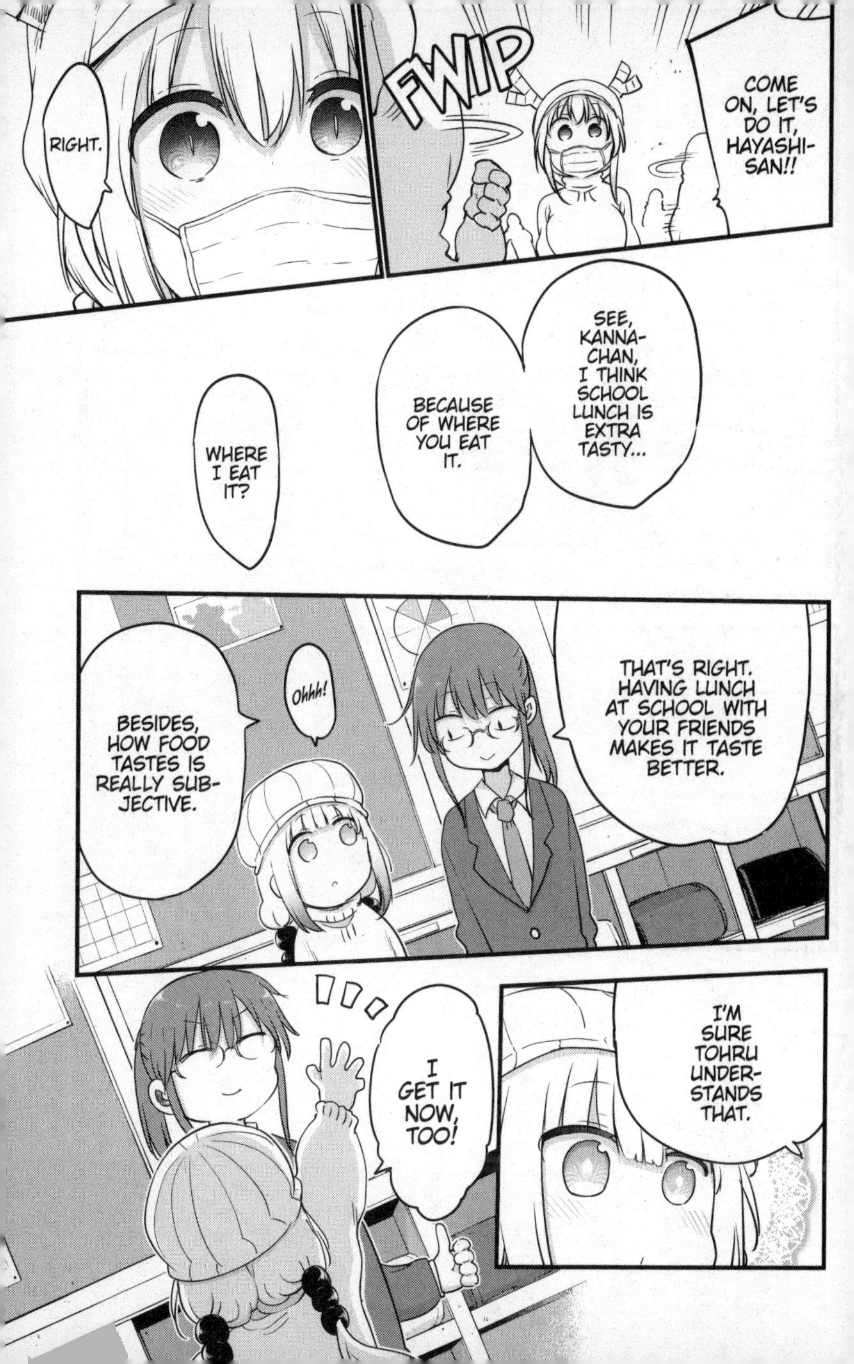
COME ON, LET'S DO IT, HAYASHI-SAN!!
FWIP
RIGHT.
SEE, KANNA-CHAN, I THINK SCHOOL LUNCH IS EXTRA TASTY...
BECAUSE OF WHERE YOU EAT IT.
WHERE I EAT IT?
THAT'S RIGHT. HAVING LUNCH AT SCHOOL WITH YOUR FRIENDS MAKES IT TASTE BETTER.
Ohhh!
BESIDES, HOW FOOD TASTES IS REALLY SUB-JECTIVE.
I'M SURE TOHRU UNDER-STANDS THAT.
I GET IT NOW, TOO!

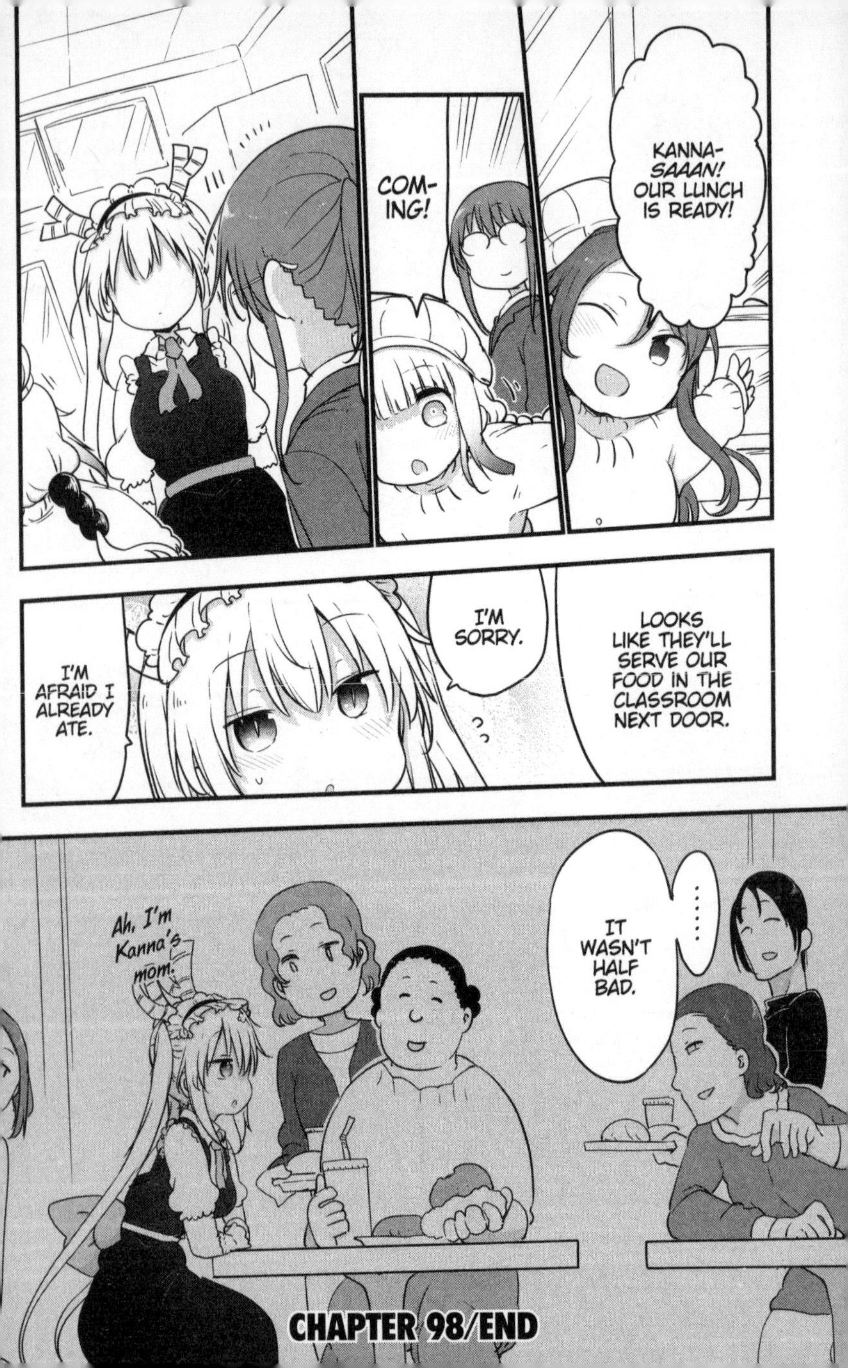
KANNA-SAAAN! OUR LUNCH IS READY!
COM-ING!
LOOKS LIKE THEY'LL SERVE OUR FOOD IN THE CLASSROOM NEXT DOOR.
I'M SORRY.
I'M AFRAID I ALREADY ATE.
......
IT WASN'T HALF BAD.
Ah, I'm Kanna's mom.
CHAPTER 98/END

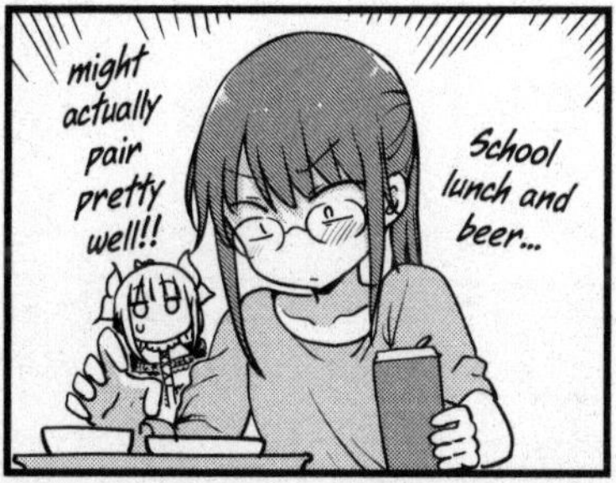
School lunch and beer...
might actually pair pretty well!!

Miss Kobayashi's Dragon Maid

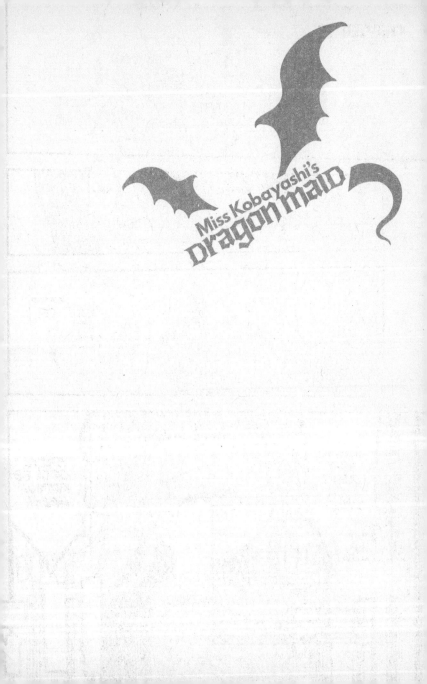

CHAPTER 99

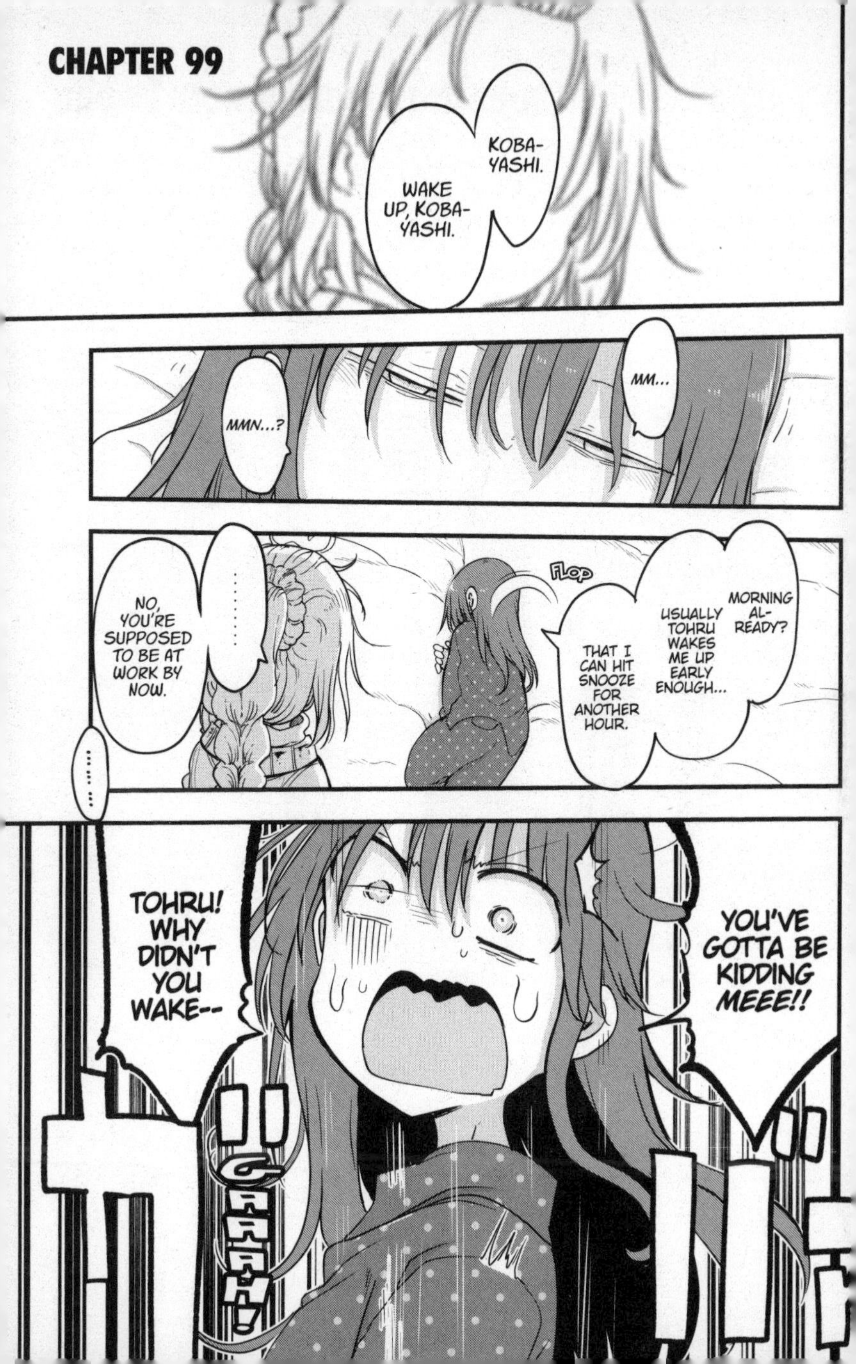
KOBA-YASHI.
WAKE UP, KOBA-YASHI.
MM...
MMN...?
MORNING AL-READY?
USUALLY TOHRU WAKES ME UP EARLY ENOUGH...
THAT I CAN HIT SNOOZE FOR ANOTHER HOUR.
FLOP
......
NO, YOU'RE SUPPOSED TO BE AT WORK BY NOW.
......
YOU'VE GOTTA BE KIDDING MEEE!!
TOHRU! WHY DIDN'T YOU WAKE--

CHAPTER 99: KOBAYASHI AND THE HOLY SWORD

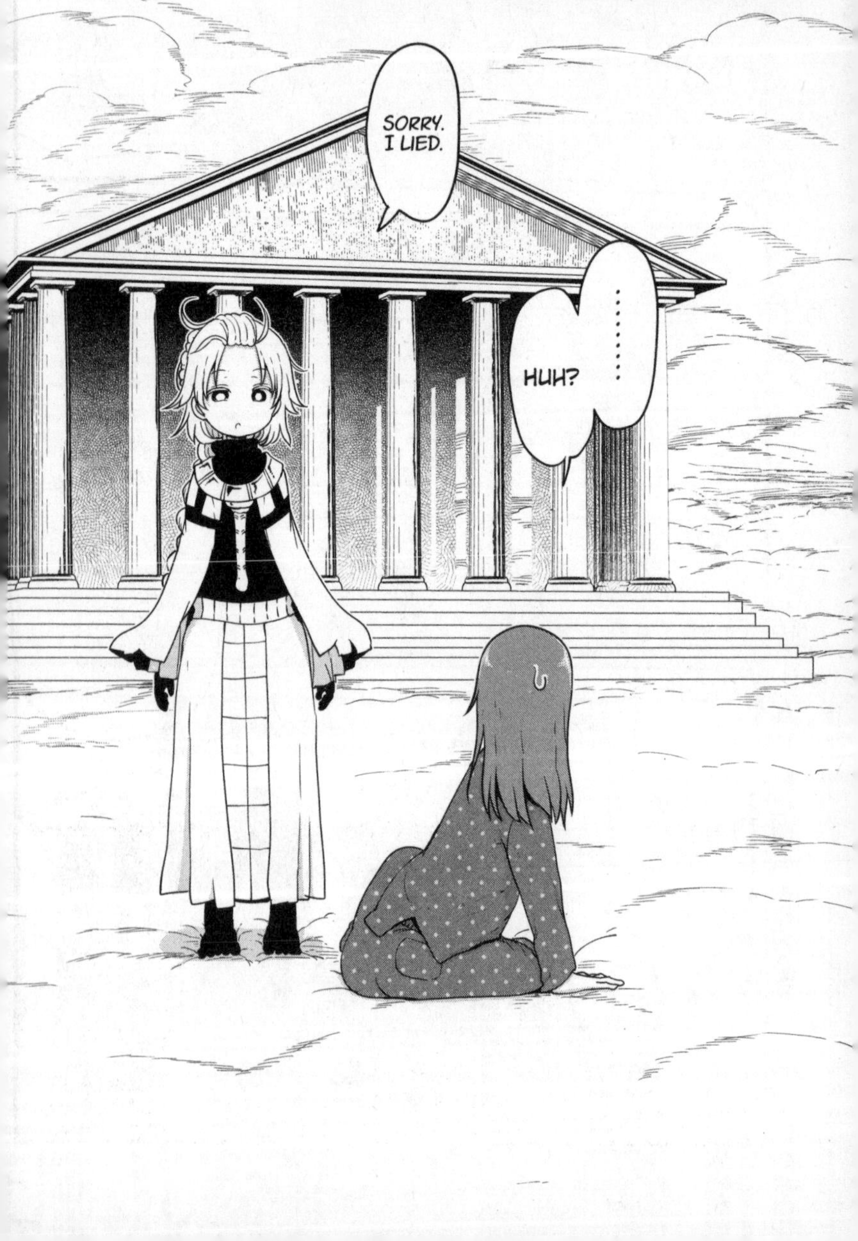
SORRY. I LIED.
...... HUH?

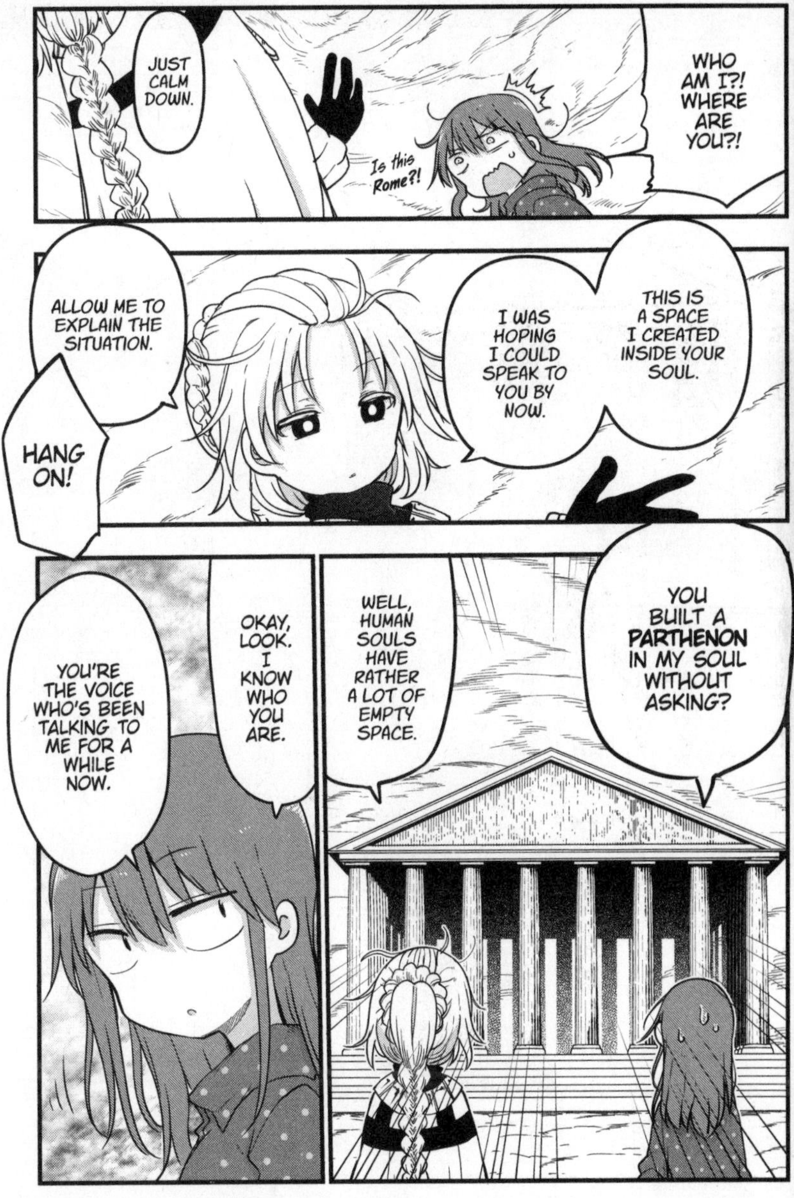
WHO AM I?! WHERE ARE YOU?!
Is this Rome?!
JUST CALM DOWN.
THIS IS A SPACE I CREATED INSIDE YOUR SOUL.
I WAS HOPING I COULD SPEAK TO YOU BY NOW.
ALLOW ME TO EXPLAIN THE SITUATION.
HANG ON!
YOU BUILT A PARTHENON IN MY SOUL WITHOUT ASKING?
WELL, HUMAN SOULS HAVE RATHER A LOT OF EMPTY SPACE.
OKAY, LOOK. I KNOW WHO YOU ARE.
YOU'RE THE VOICE WHO'S BEEN TALKING TO ME FOR A WHILE NOW.

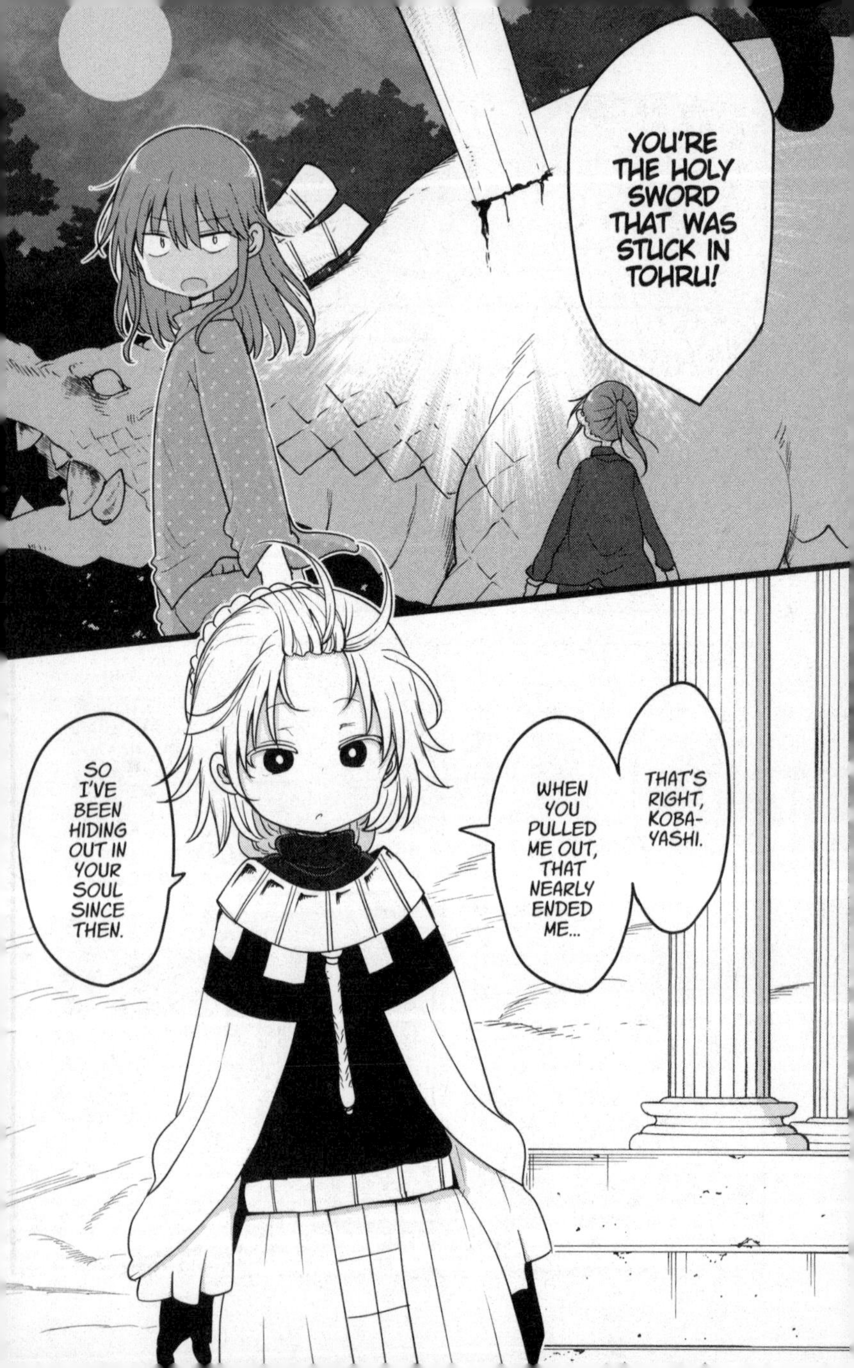
YOU'RE THE HOLY SWORD THAT WAS STUCK IN TOHRU!
THAT'S RIGHT, KOBA-YASHI.
WHEN YOU PULLED ME OUT, THAT NEARLY ENDED ME...
SO I'VE BEEN HIDING OUT IN YOUR SOUL SINCE THEN.

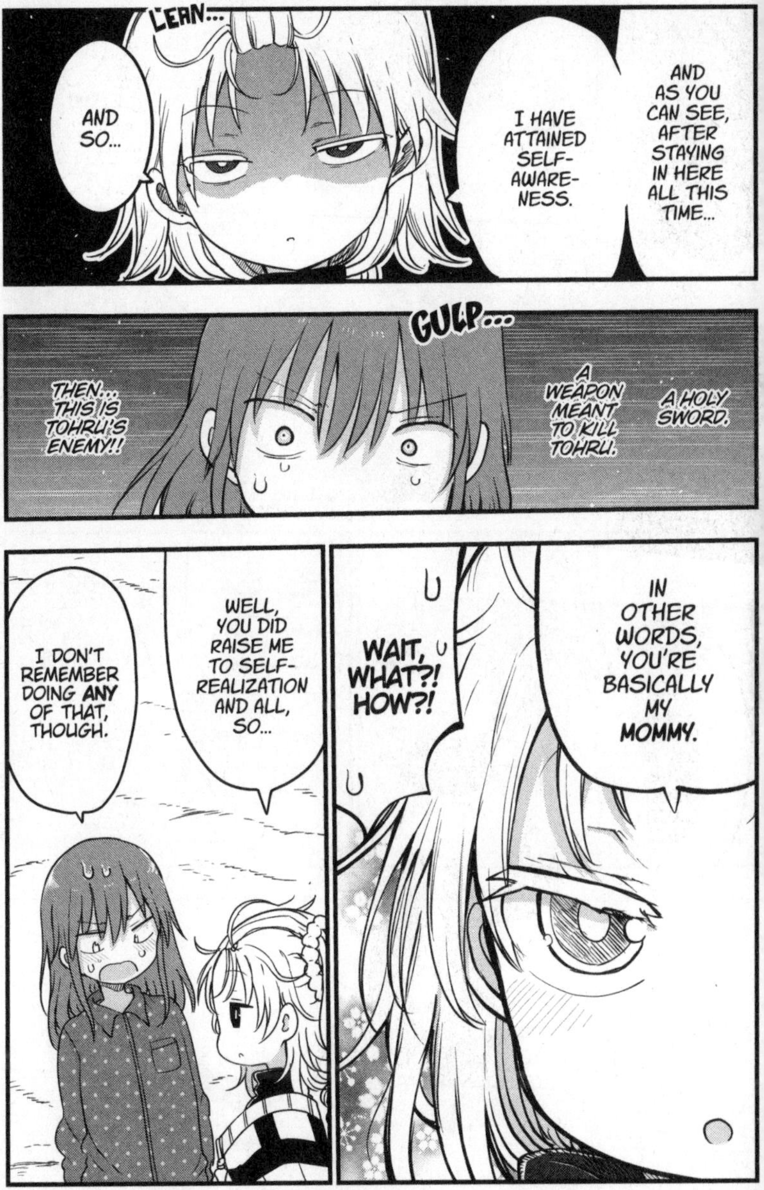
AND AS YOU CAN SEE, AFTER STAYING IN HERE ALL THIS TIME...
I HAVE ATTAINED SELF-AWARENESS.
LEAN...
AND SO...
GULP...
A HOLY SWORD.
A WEAPON MEANT TO KILL TOHRU.
THEN... THIS IS TOHRU'S ENEMY!!
IN OTHER WORDS, YOU'RE BASICALLY MY **MOMMY**.
WAIT, WHAT?! HOW?!
WELL, YOU DID RAISE ME TO SELF-REALIZATION AND ALL, SO...
I DON'T REMEMBER DOING **ANY** OF THAT, THOUGH.

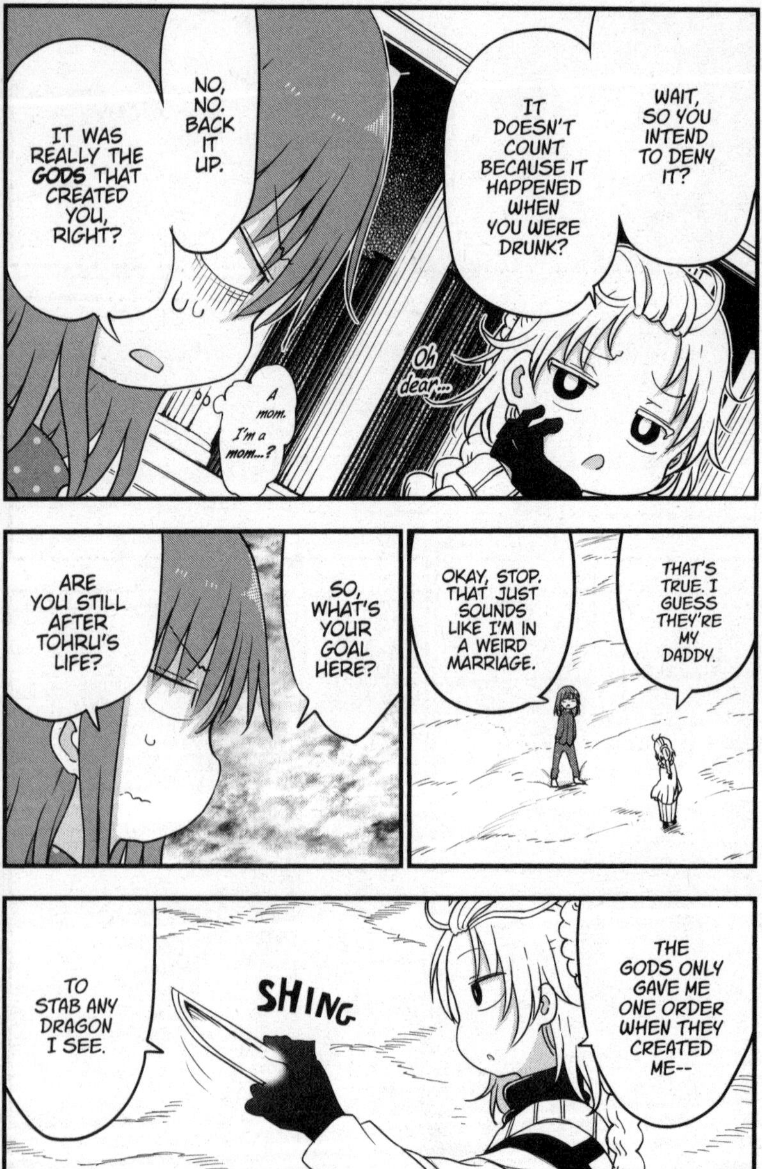
WAIT, SO YOU INTEND TO DENY IT?
IT DOESN'T COUNT BECAUSE IT HAPPENED WHEN YOU WERE DRUNK?
NO, NO. BACK IT UP.
IT WAS REALLY THE **GODS** THAT CREATED YOU, RIGHT?
Oh dear...
A mom. I'm a mom...?
THAT'S TRUE. I GUESS THEY'RE MY DADDY.
OKAY, STOP. THAT JUST SOUNDS LIKE I'M IN A WEIRD MARRIAGE.
SO, WHAT'S YOUR GOAL HERE?
ARE YOU STILL AFTER TOHRU'S LIFE?
THE GODS ONLY GAVE ME ONE ORDER WHEN THEY CREATED ME--
SHING
TO STAB ANY DRAGON I SEE.

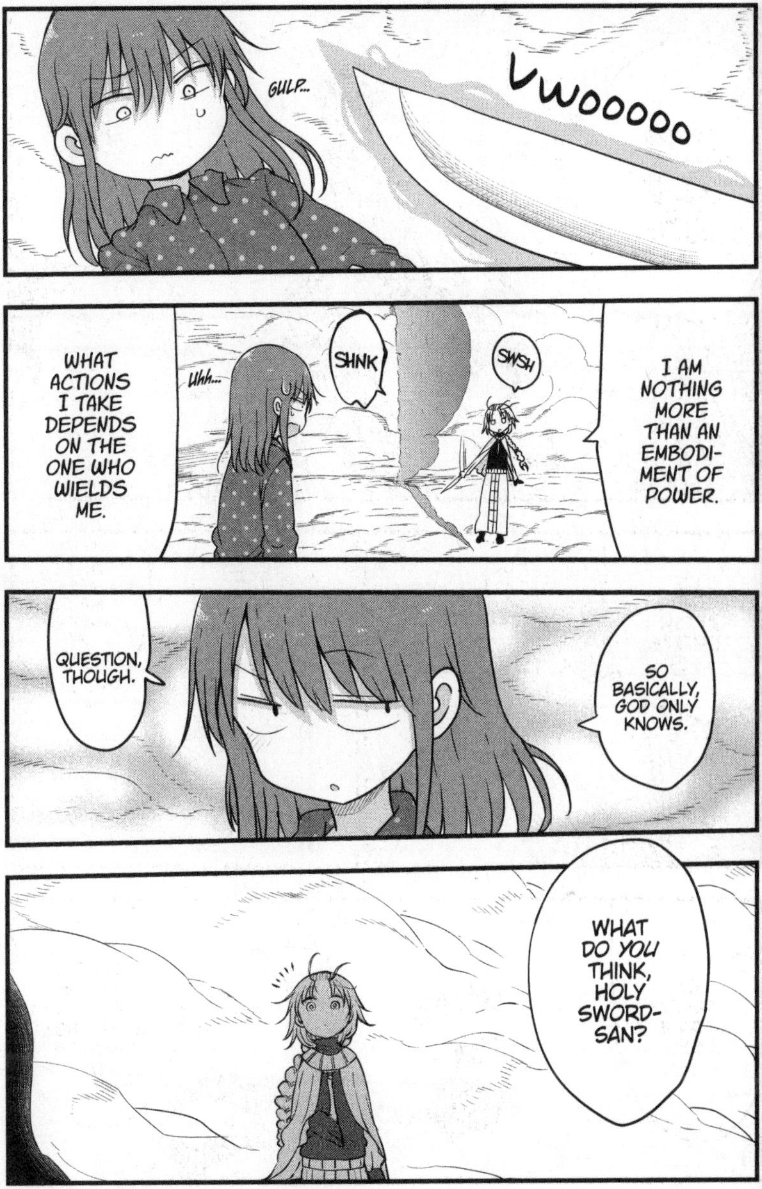
VWOOOOO
GULP...
I AM NOTHING MORE THAN AN EMBODIMENT OF POWER.
SWSH
SHNK
Uhh...
WHAT ACTIONS I TAKE DEPENDS ON THE ONE WHO WIELDS ME.
SO BASICALLY, GOD ONLY KNOWS.
QUESTION, THOUGH.
WHAT DO YOU THINK, HOLY SWORD-SAN?

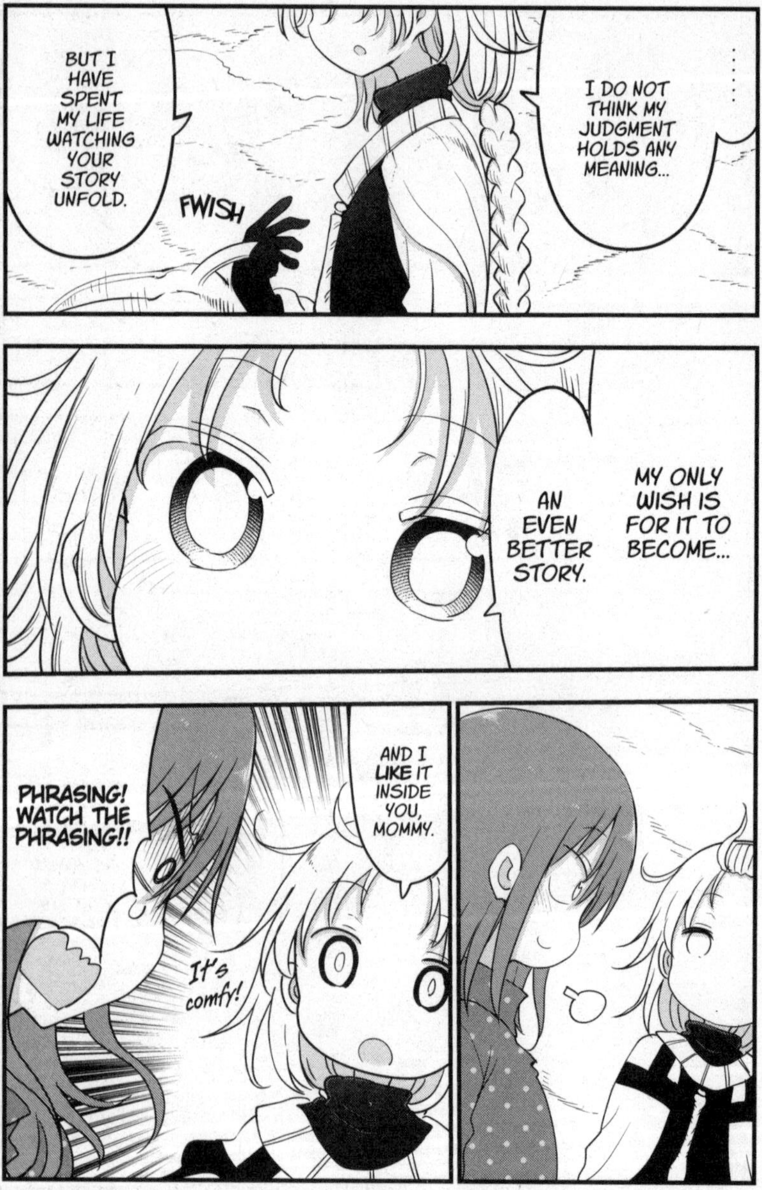
......
I DO NOT THINK MY JUDGMENT HOLDS ANY MEANING...
BUT I HAVE SPENT MY LIFE WATCHING YOUR STORY UNFOLD.
FWISH
MY ONLY WISH IS FOR IT TO BECOME...
AN EVEN BETTER STORY.
AND I LIKE IT INSIDE YOU, MOMMY.
It's comfy!
PHRASING! WATCH THE PHRASING!!

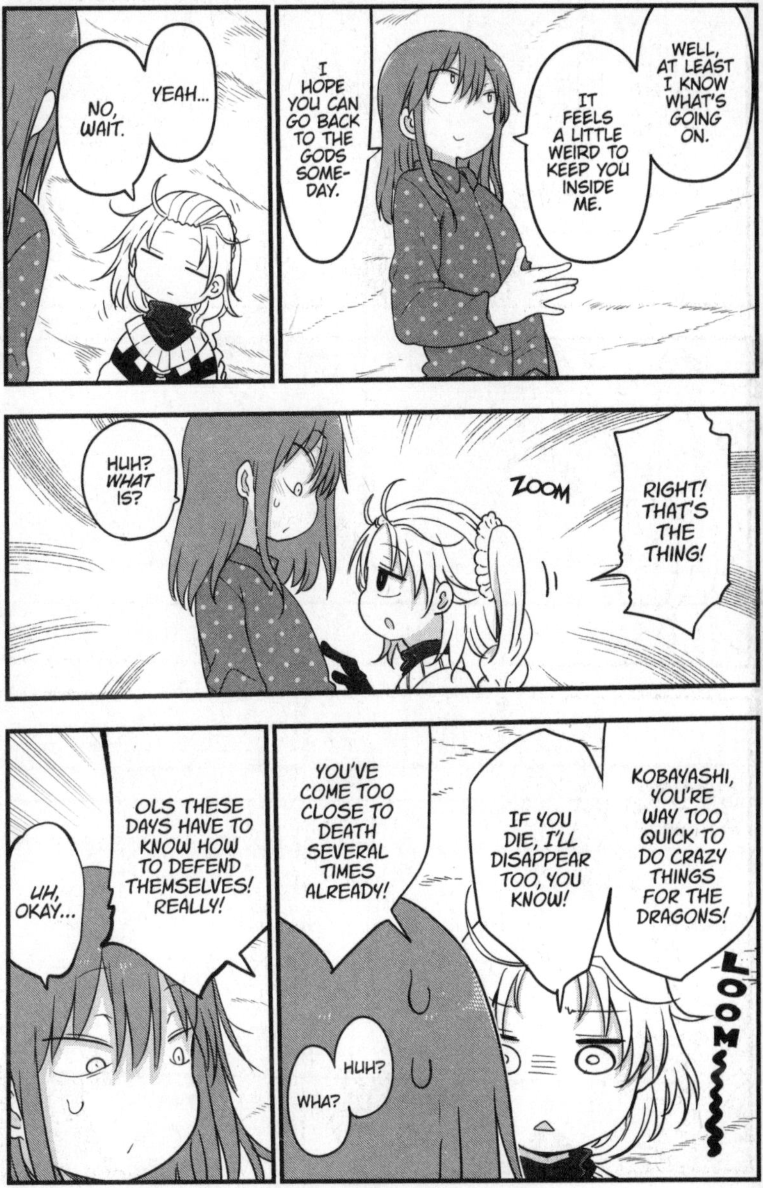
WELL, AT LEAST I KNOW WHAT'S GOING ON.
IT FEELS A LITTLE WEIRD TO KEEP YOU INSIDE ME.
I HOPE YOU CAN GO BACK TO THE GODS SOME-DAY.
YEAH...
NO, WAIT.
RIGHT! THAT'S THE THING!
ZOOM
HUH? WHAT IS?
KOBAYASHI, YOU'RE WAY TOO QUICK TO DO CRAZY THINGS FOR THE DRAGONS!
LOOM
IF YOU DIE, I'LL DISAPPEAR TOO, YOU KNOW!
YOU'VE COME TOO CLOSE TO DEATH SEVERAL TIMES ALREADY!
HUH?
WHA?
OLS THESE DAYS HAVE TO KNOW HOW TO DEFEND THEMSELVES! REALLY!
UH, OKAY...

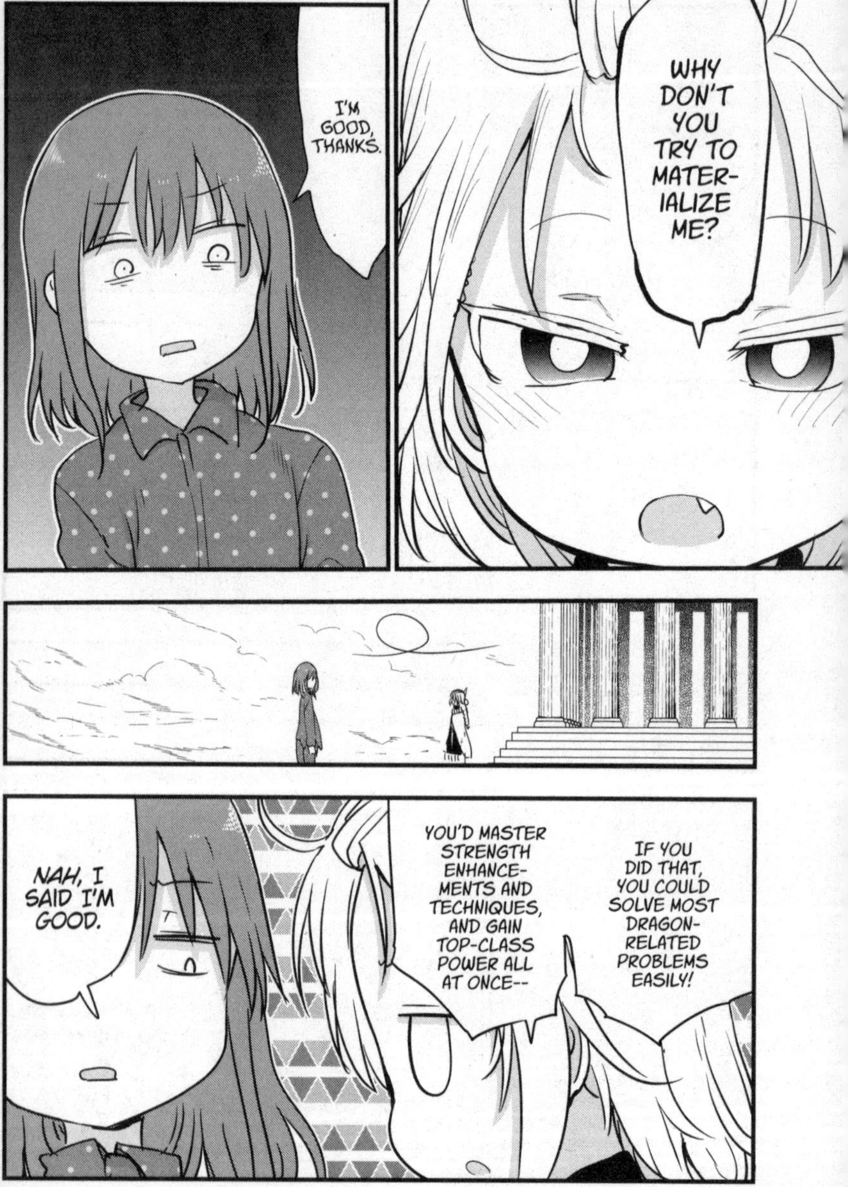
WHY DON'T YOU TRY TO MATERIALIZE ME?
I'M GOOD, THANKS.
IF YOU DID THAT, YOU COULD SOLVE MOST DRAGON-RELATED PROBLEMS EASILY!
YOU'D MASTER STRENGTH ENHANCEMENTS AND TECHNIQUES, AND GAIN TOP-CLASS POWER ALL AT ONCE--
NAH, I SAID I'M GOOD.

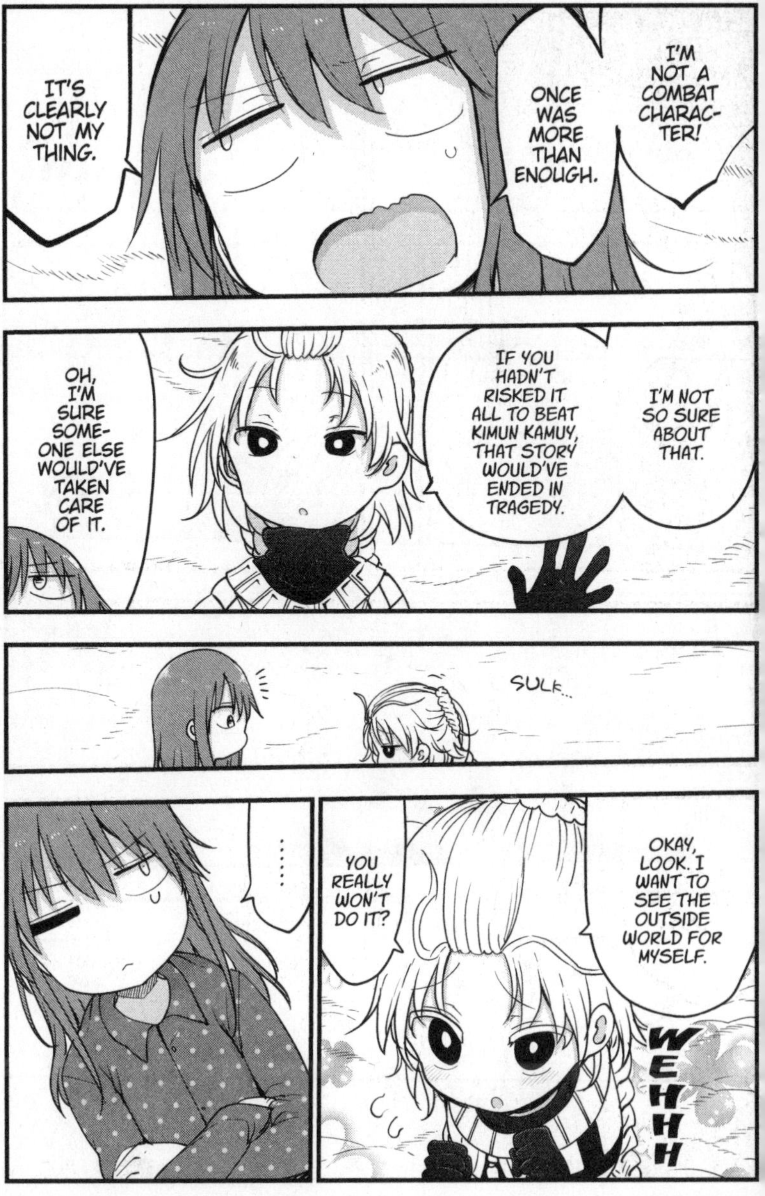
I'M NOT A COMBAT CHARAC-TER!
ONCE WAS MORE THAN ENOUGH.
IT'S CLEARLY NOT MY THING.
I'M NOT SO SURE ABOUT THAT.
IF YOU HADN'T RISKED IT ALL TO BEAT KIMUN KAMUY, THAT STORY WOULD'VE ENDED IN TRAGEDY.
OH, I'M SURE SOME-ONE ELSE WOULD'VE TAKEN CARE OF IT.
SULK...
OKAY, LOOK. I WANT TO SEE THE OUTSIDE WORLD FOR MYSELF.
WEHHH
YOU REALLY WON'T DO IT?
......

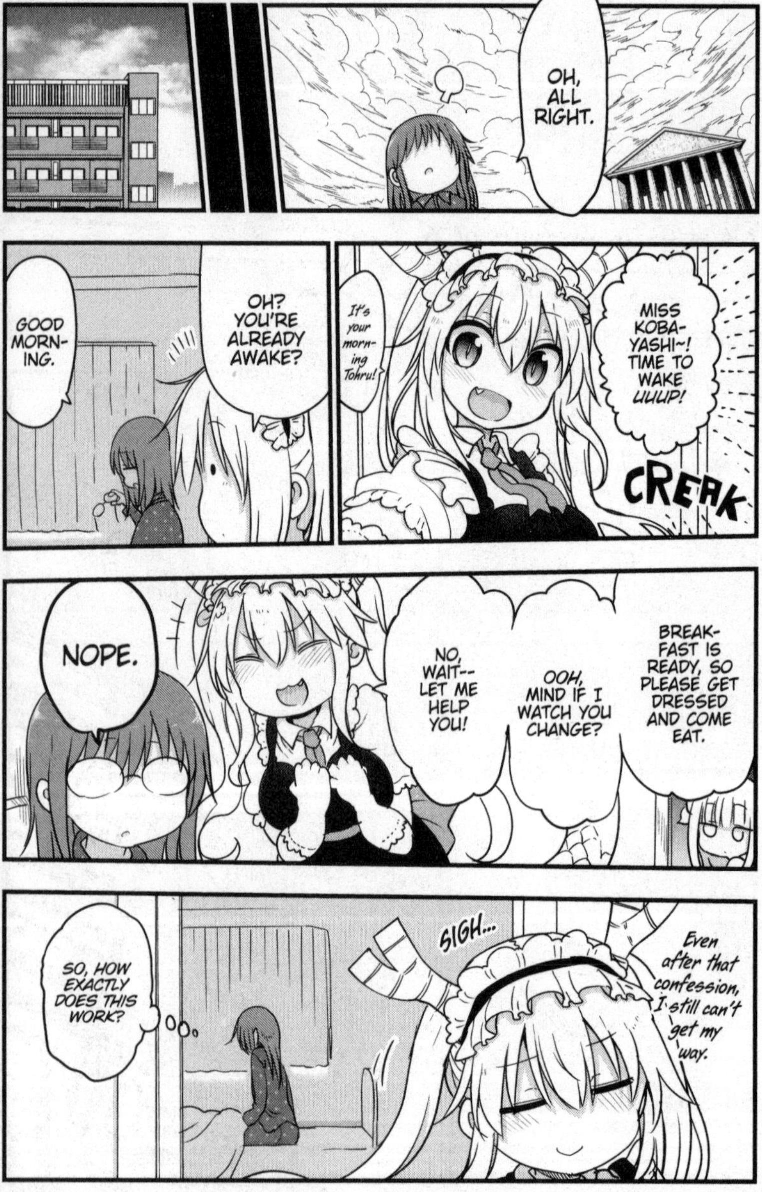
OH, ALL RIGHT.
MISS KOBA-YASHI~! TIME TO WAKE UUUP!
It's your morn-ing Tohru!
CREAK
OH? YOU'RE ALREADY AWAKE?
GOOD MORN-ING.
BREAK-FAST IS READY, SO PLEASE GET DRESSED AND COME EAT.
OOH, MIND IF I WATCH YOU CHANGE?
NO, WAIT-- LET ME HELP YOU!
NOPE.
Even after that confession, I still can't get my way.
SIGH...
SO, HOW EXACTLY DOES THIS WORK?

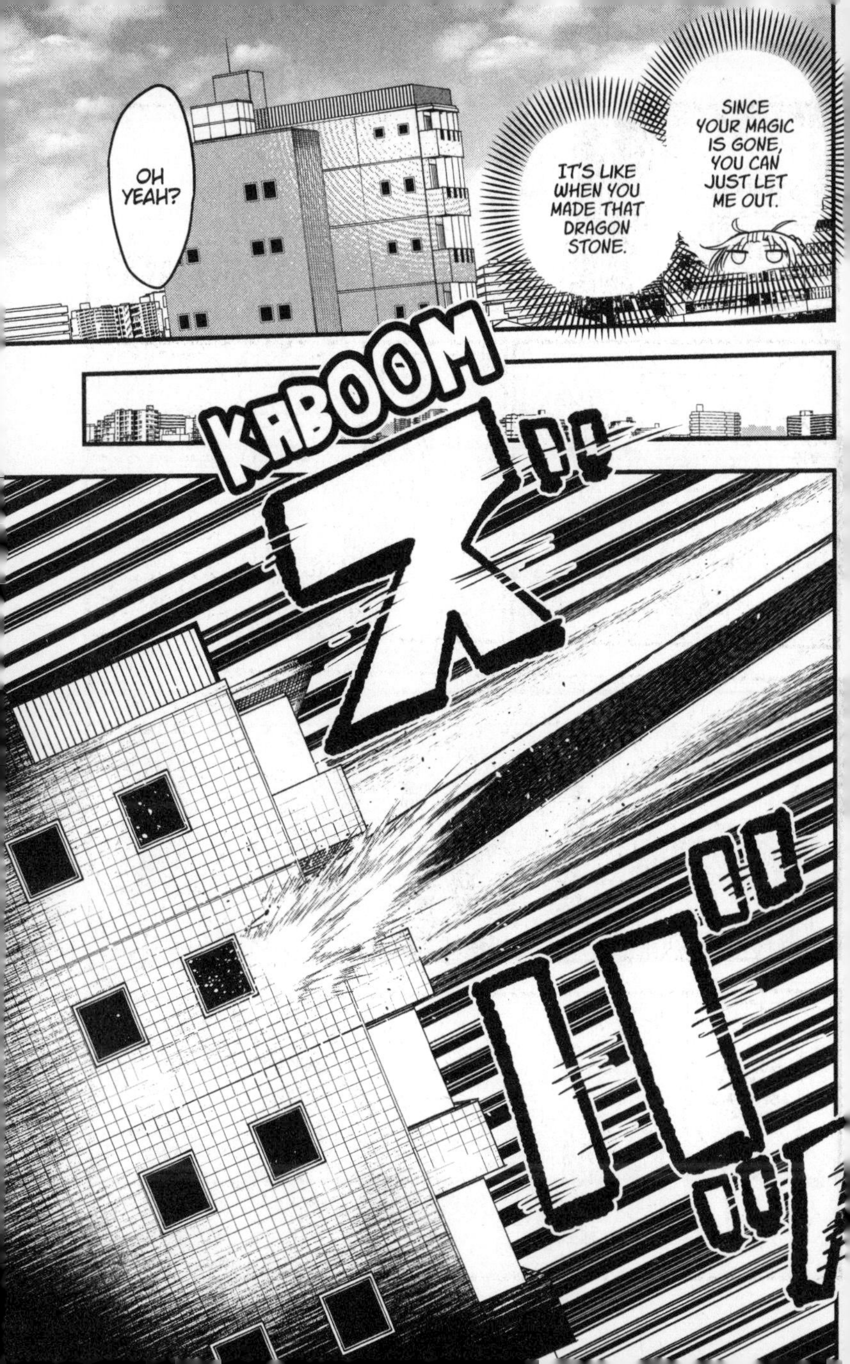
SINCE YOUR MAGIC IS GONE, YOU CAN JUST LET ME OUT.
IT'S LIKE WHEN YOU MADE THAT DRAGON STONE.
OH YEAH?
KABOOM

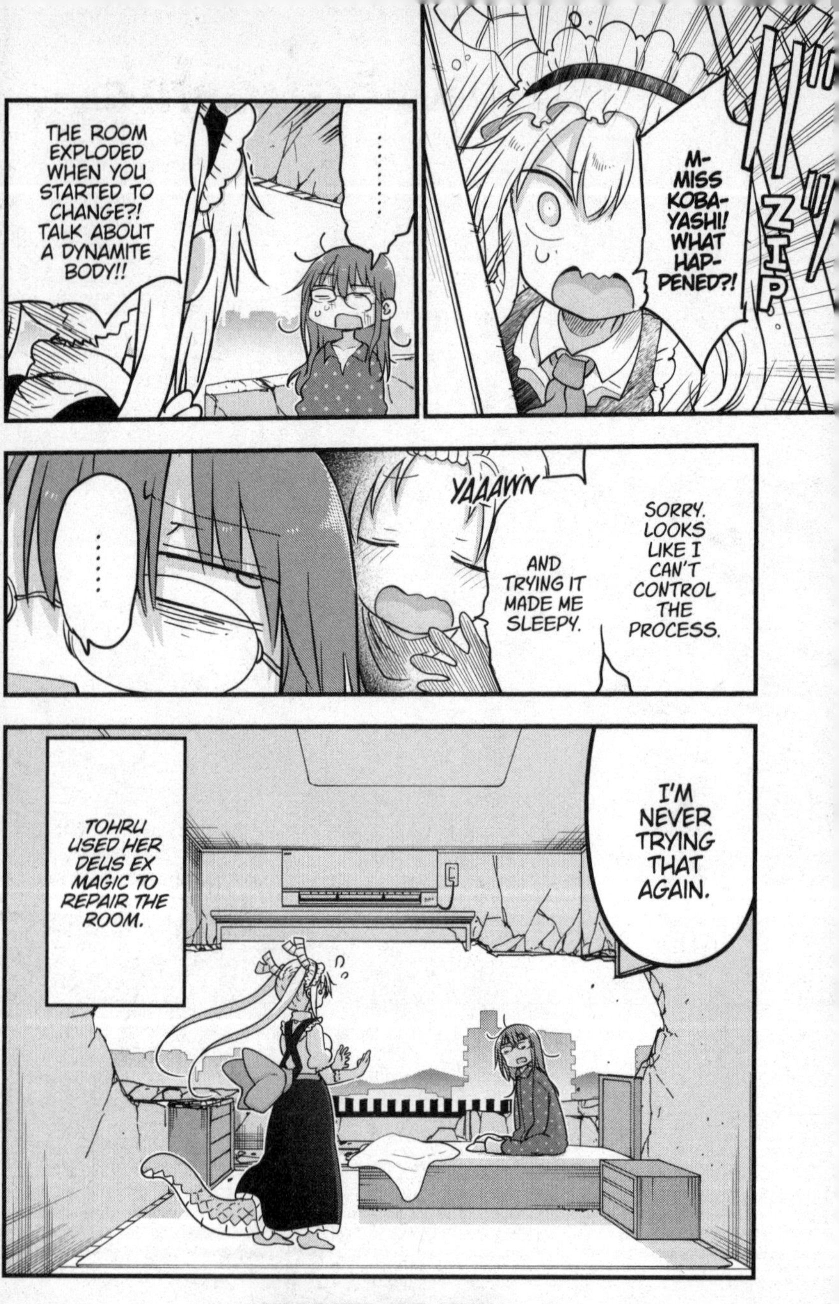
M-MISS KOBAYASHI! WHAT HAPPENED?!
ZIP
...
THE ROOM EXPLODED WHEN YOU STARTED TO CHANGE?! TALK ABOUT A DYNAMITE BODY!!
SORRY. LOOKS LIKE I CAN'T CONTROL THE PROCESS.
AND TRYING IT MADE ME SLEEPY.
YAAAWN
...
I'M NEVER TRYING THAT AGAIN.
TOHRU USED HER DEUS EX MAGIC TO REPAIR THE ROOM.

CHAPTER 99/END

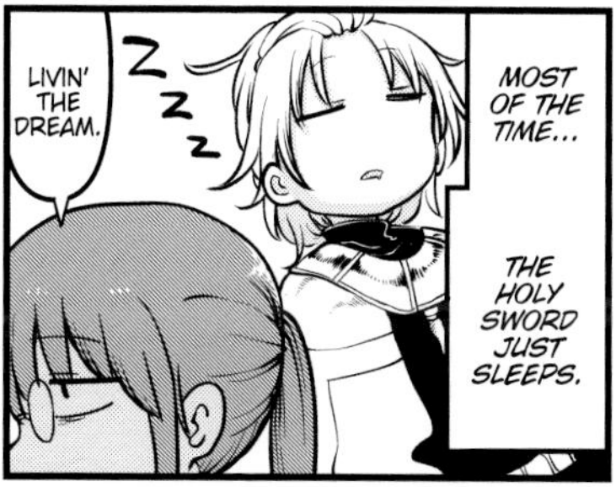

MOST OF THE TIME...
THE HOLY SWORD JUST SLEEPS.
ZZZ
LIVIN' THE DREAM.

Miss Kobayashi's
Dragon Maid

CHAPTER 100

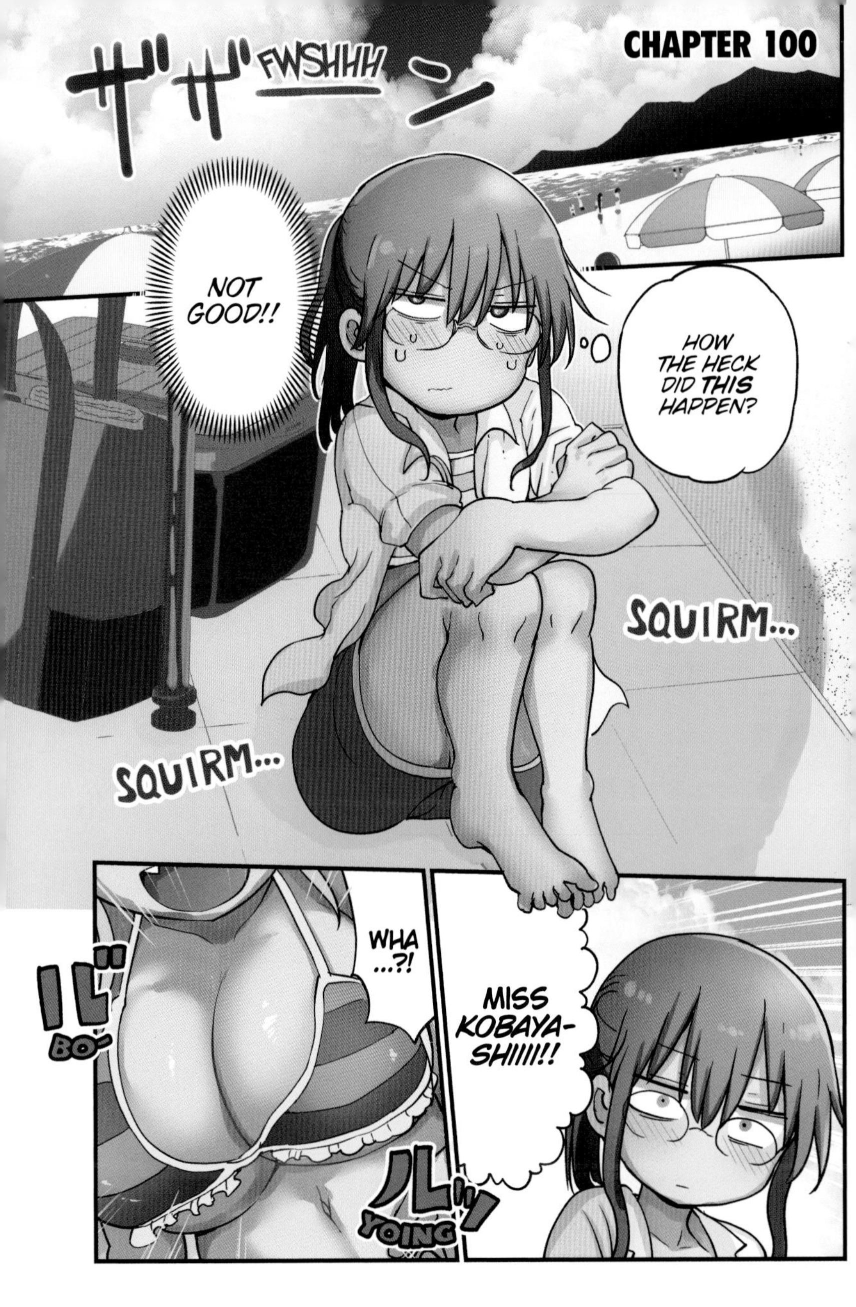

FWSHHH
HOW THE HECK DID THIS HAPPEN?
NOT GOOD!!
SQUIRM...
SQUIRM...
MISS KOBAYA-SHIIIII!!
WHA ...?!
BO-
YOING

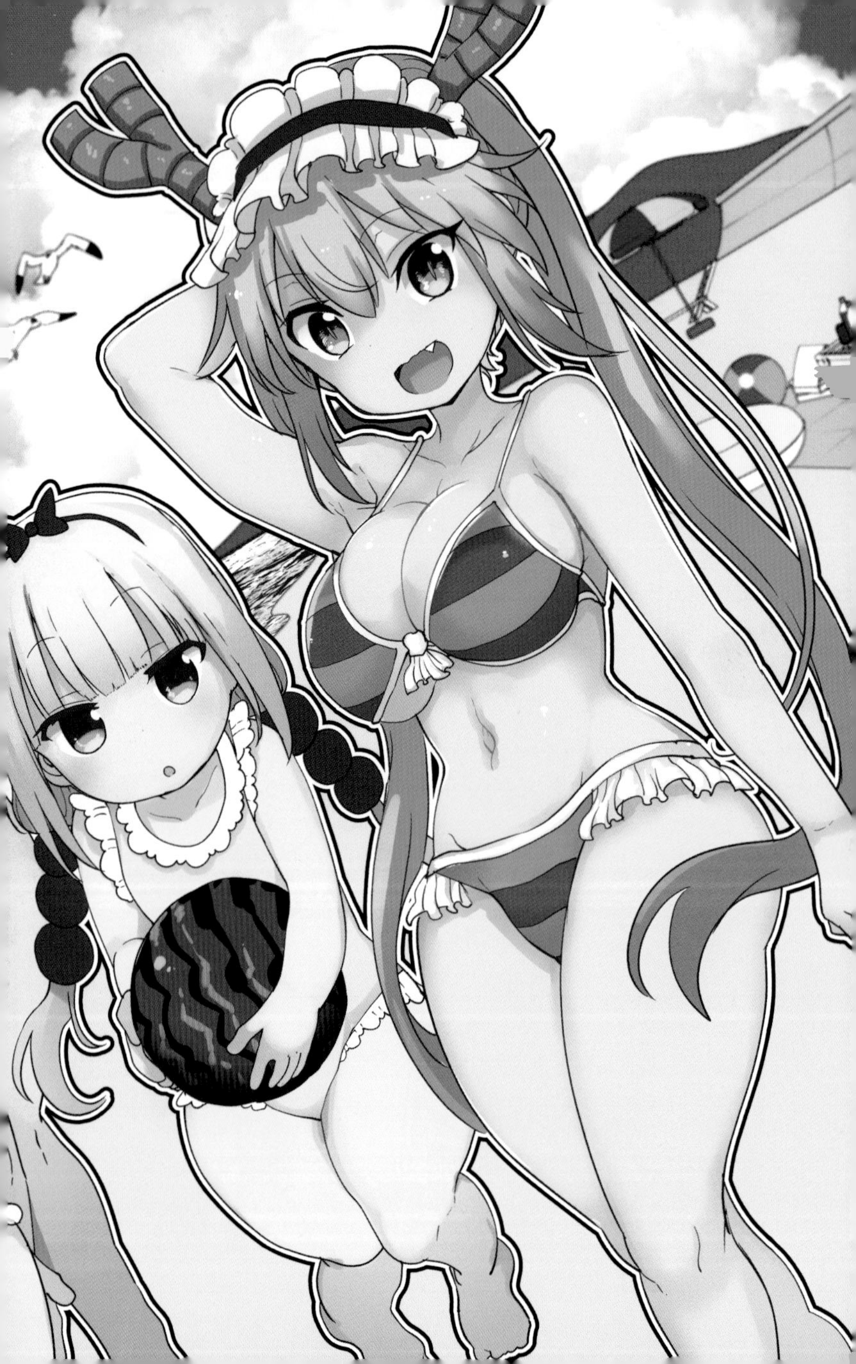

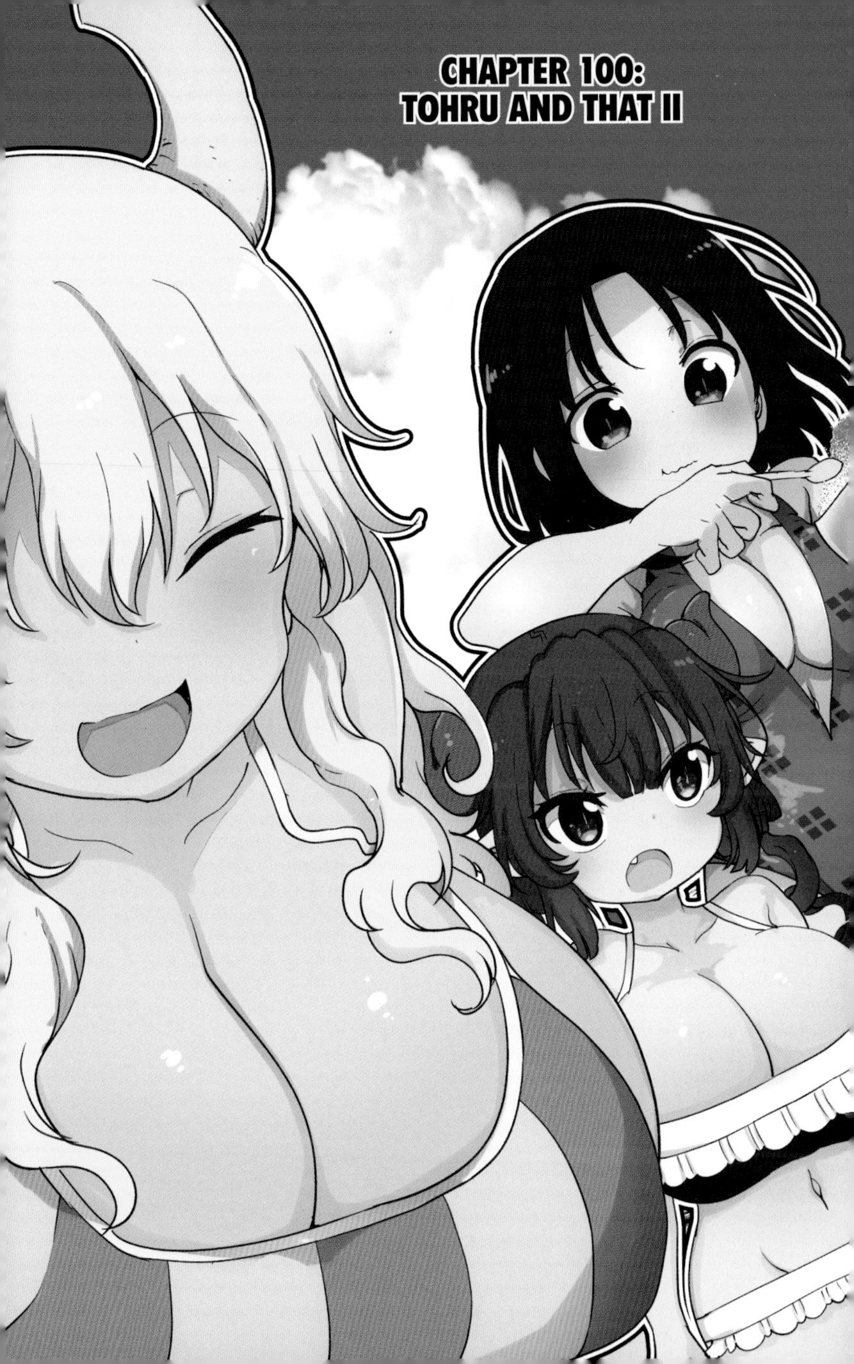
CHAPTER 100:
TOHRU AND THAT II

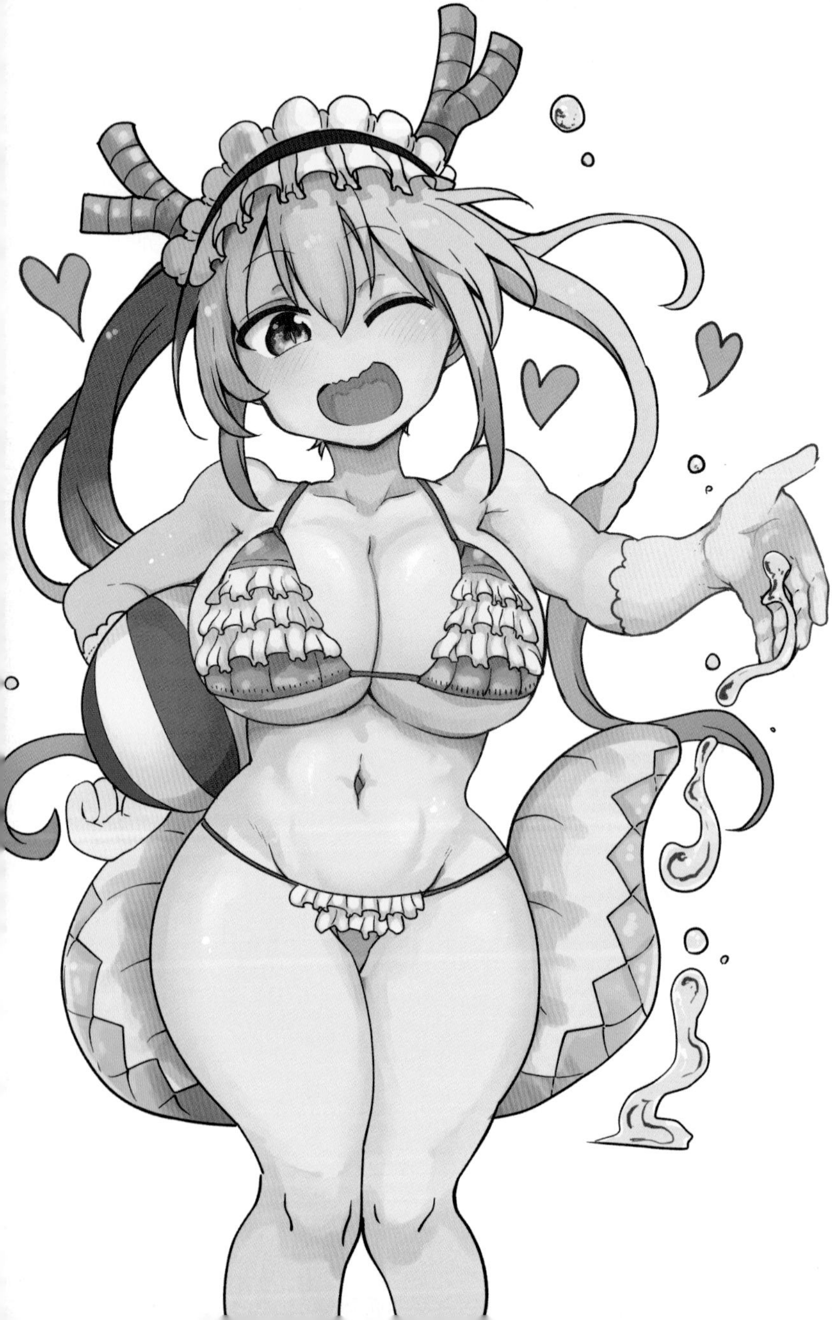

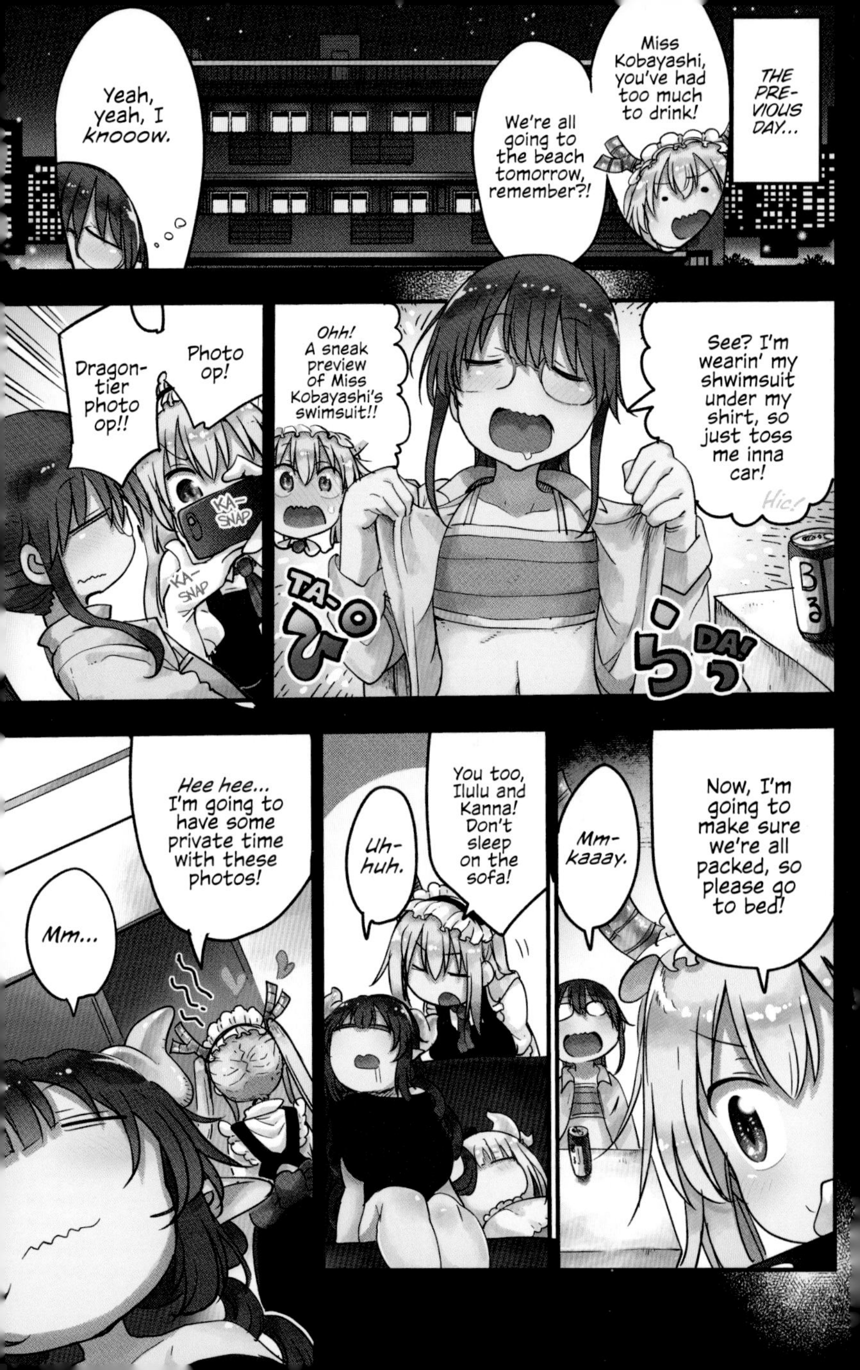
THE PREVIOUS DAY...
Miss Kobayashi, you've had too much to drink!
We're all going to the beach tomorrow, remember?!
Yeah, yeah, I knooow.
See? I'm wearin' my shwimsuit under my shirt, so just toss me inna car!
Hic!
DA!
TA-
Ohh! A sneak preview of Miss Kobayashi's swimsuit!!
Photo op!
Dragon-tier photo op!!
KA-SNAP
KA-SNAP
Now, I'm going to make sure we're all packed, so please go to bed!
Mm-kaaay.
You too, Ilulu and Kanna! Don't sleep on the sofa!
Uh-huh.
Hee hee... I'm going to have some private time with these photos!
Mm...

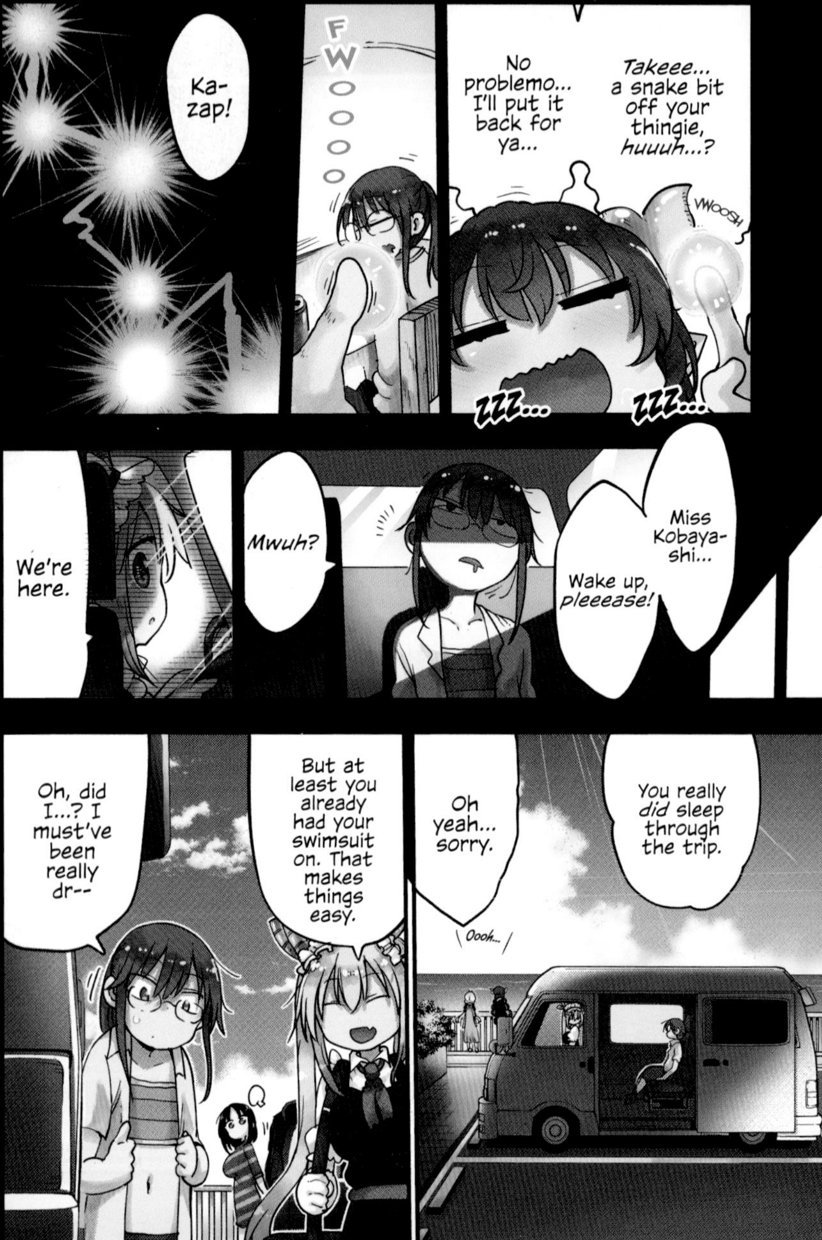
Takeee... a snake bit off your thingie, *huuuh*...?
No problemo... I'll put it back for ya...
VWOOSH
ZZZ...
ZZZ...
FWOOOOO
Ka-zap!
Miss Kobayashi...
Wake up, *pleeease!*
Mwuh?
We're here.
You really *did* sleep through the trip.
Oh yeah... sorry.
Oooh...
But at least you already had your swimsuit on. That makes things easy.
Oh, did I...? I must've been really dr--

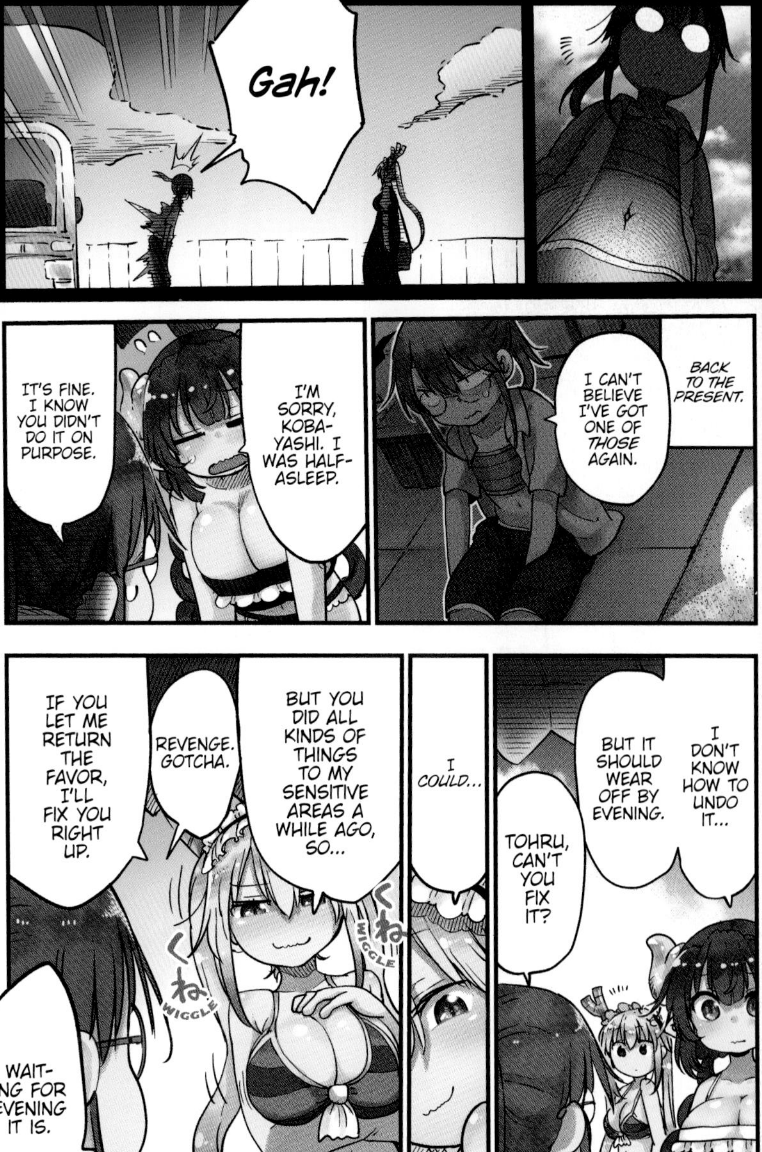
Gah!
BACK TO THE PRESENT.
I CAN'T BELIEVE I'VE GOT ONE OF *THOSE* AGAIN.
I'M SORRY, KOBAYASHI. I WAS HALF-ASLEEP.
IT'S FINE. I KNOW YOU DIDN'T DO IT ON PURPOSE.
I DON'T KNOW HOW TO UNDO IT...
BUT IT SHOULD WEAR OFF BY EVENING.
TOHRU, CAN'T YOU FIX IT?
I *COULD*...
BUT YOU DID ALL KINDS OF THINGS TO MY SENSITIVE AREAS A WHILE AGO, SO...
くね WIGGLE
くね WIGGLE
REVENGE. GOTCHA.
IF YOU LET ME RETURN THE FAVOR, I'LL FIX YOU RIGHT UP.
WAITING FOR EVENING IT IS.

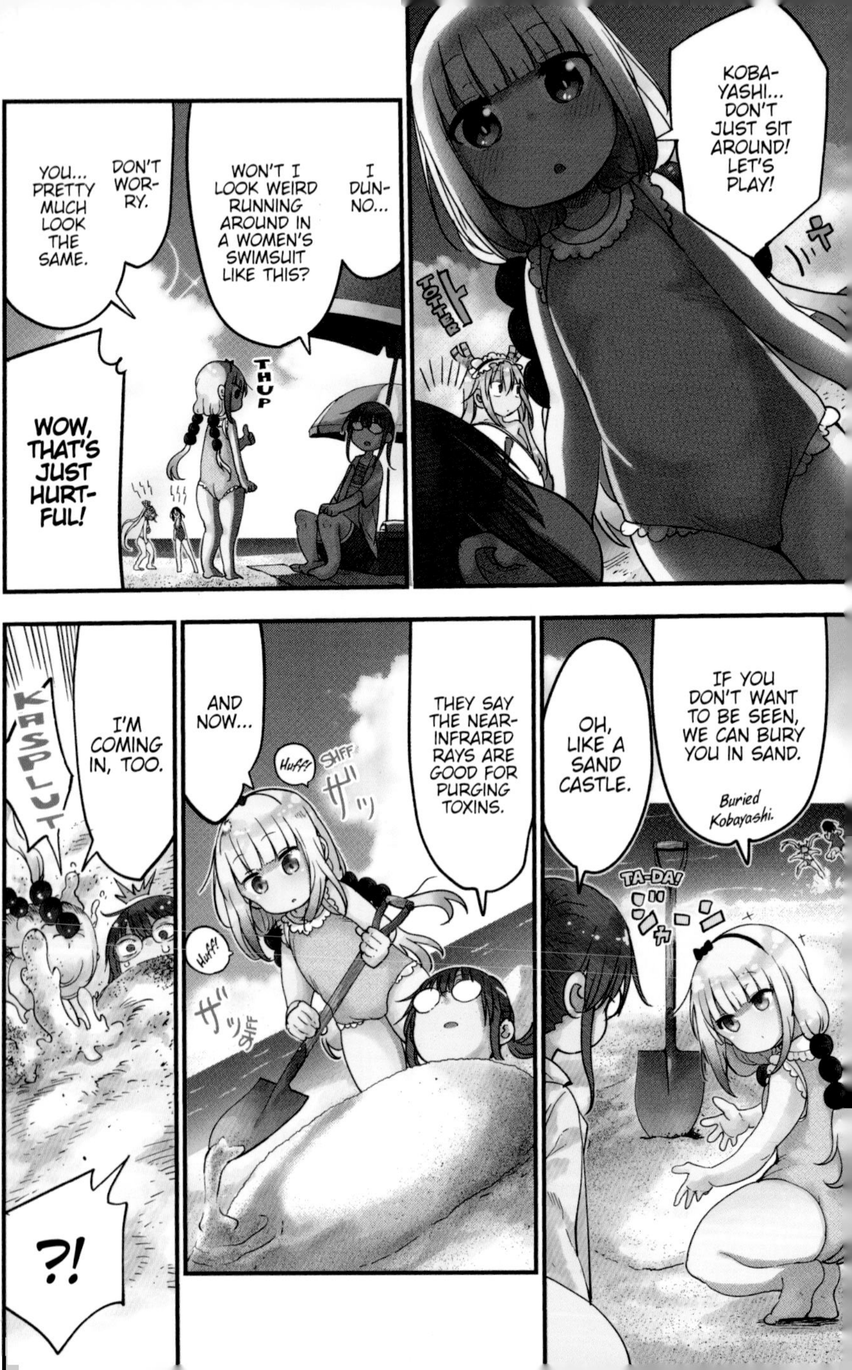
KOBA-YASHI... DON'T JUST SIT AROUND! LET'S PLAY!
TOTTER
I DUN-NO...
WON'T I LOOK WEIRD RUNNING AROUND IN A WOMEN'S SWIMSUIT LIKE THIS?
DON'T WORRY.
YOU... PRETTY MUCH LOOK THE SAME.
THUP
WOW, THAT'S JUST HURTFUL!
IF YOU DON'T WANT TO BE SEEN, WE CAN BURY YOU IN SAND.
Buried Kobayashi.
OH, LIKE A SAND CASTLE.
TA-DA!
THEY SAY THE NEAR-INFRARED RAYS ARE GOOD FOR PURGING TOXINS.
AND NOW...
Huff!
SHFF
Huff!
SHFF
I'M COMING IN, TOO.
KASPLUT
?!

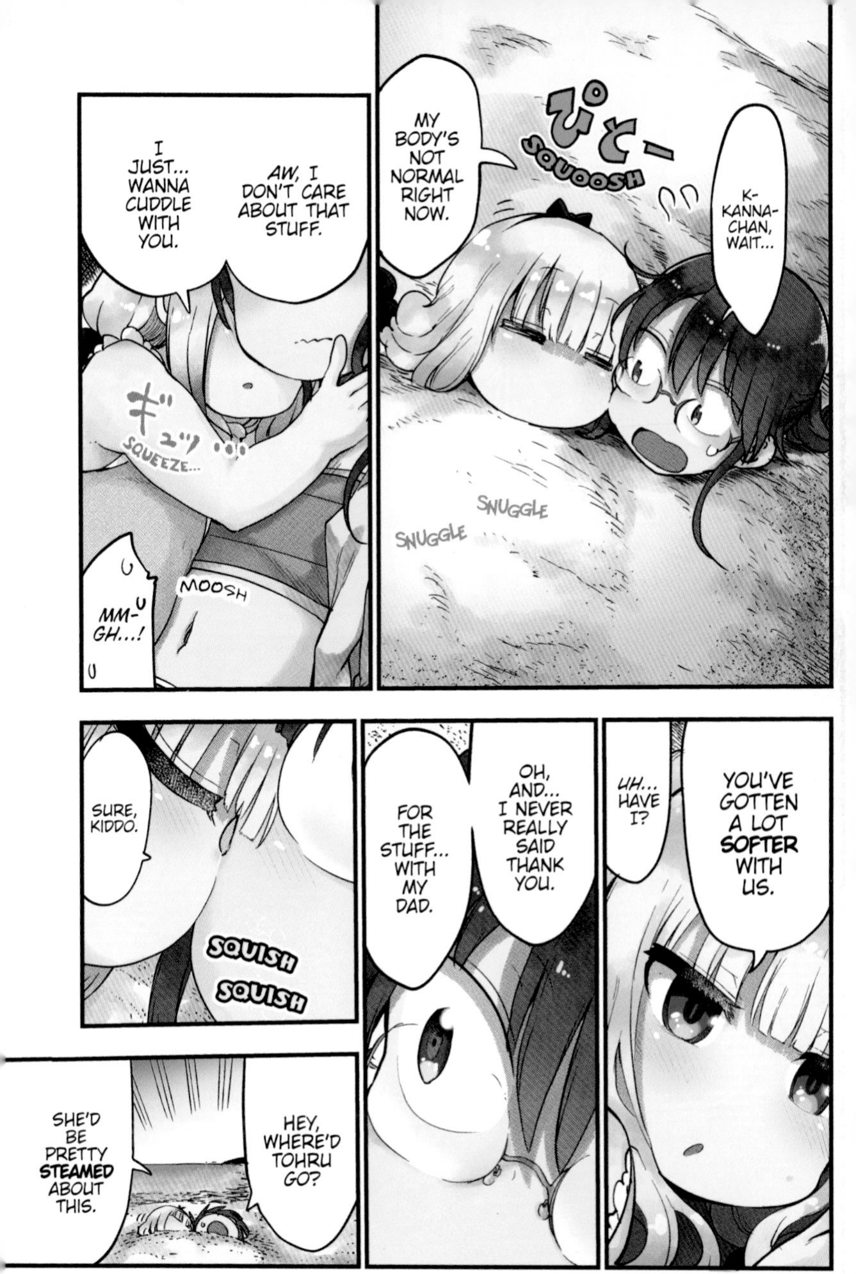
K-KANNA-CHAN, WAIT...
ぴとー
SQUOOOSH
MY BODY'S NOT NORMAL RIGHT NOW.
SNUGGLE
SNUGGLE
AW, I DON'T CARE ABOUT THAT STUFF.
I JUST... WANNA CUDDLE WITH YOU.
ギュッ
SQUEEZE...
MOOSH
MM-GH...!
YOU'VE GOTTEN A LOT SOFTER WITH US.
UH... HAVE I?
OH, AND... I NEVER REALLY SAID THANK YOU.
FOR THE STUFF... WITH MY DAD.
SURE, KIDDO.
SQUISH
SQUISH
HEY, WHERE'D TOHRU GO?
SHE'D BE PRETTY STEAMED ABOUT THIS.

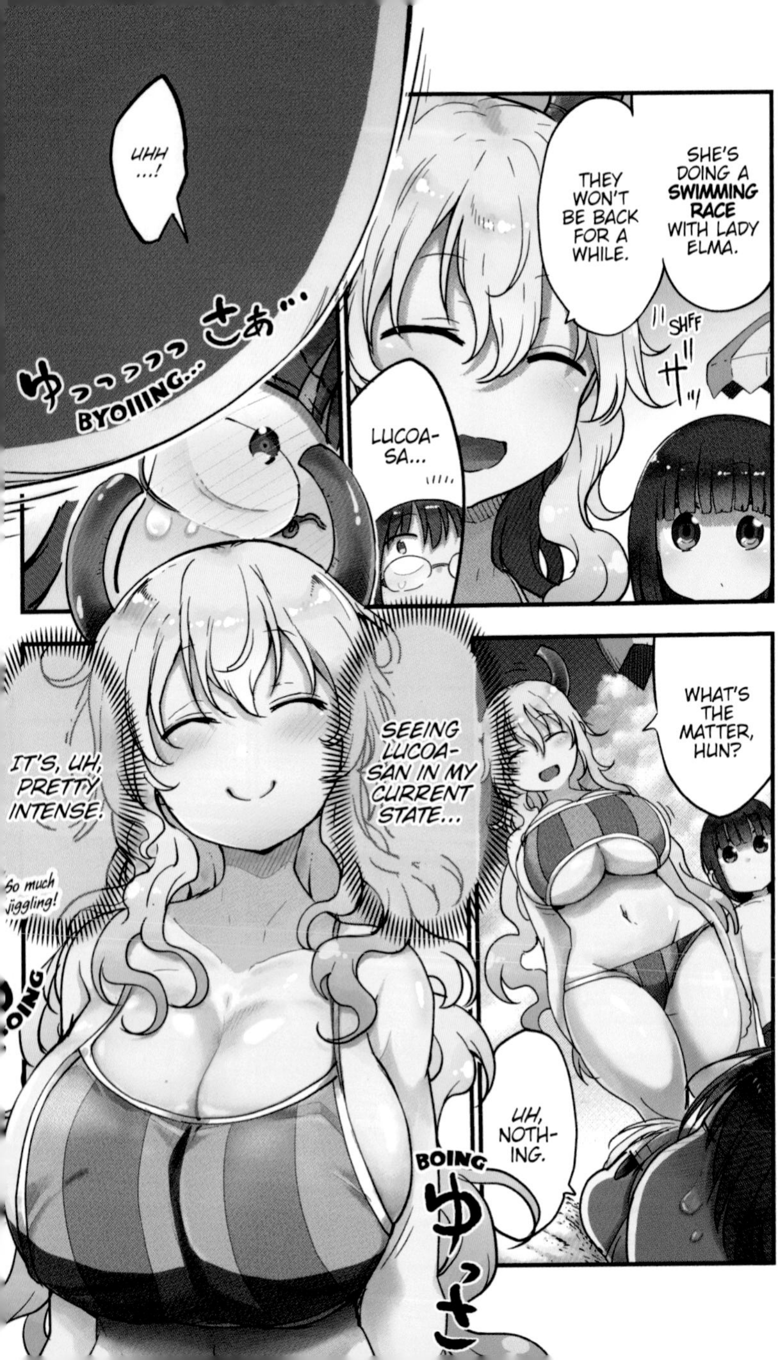
SHE'S DOING A SWIMMING RACE WITH LADY ELMA.
THEY WON'T BE BACK FOR A WHILE.
SHFF
ザッ
LUCOA-SA...
UHH ...!
ゆっっっっっ さあ…
BYOIIING...
WHAT'S THE MATTER, HUN?
UH, NOTHING.
BOING
ゆっさ
SEEING LUCOA-SAN IN MY CURRENT STATE...
IT'S, UH, PRETTY INTENSE.
So much jiggling!
BOING

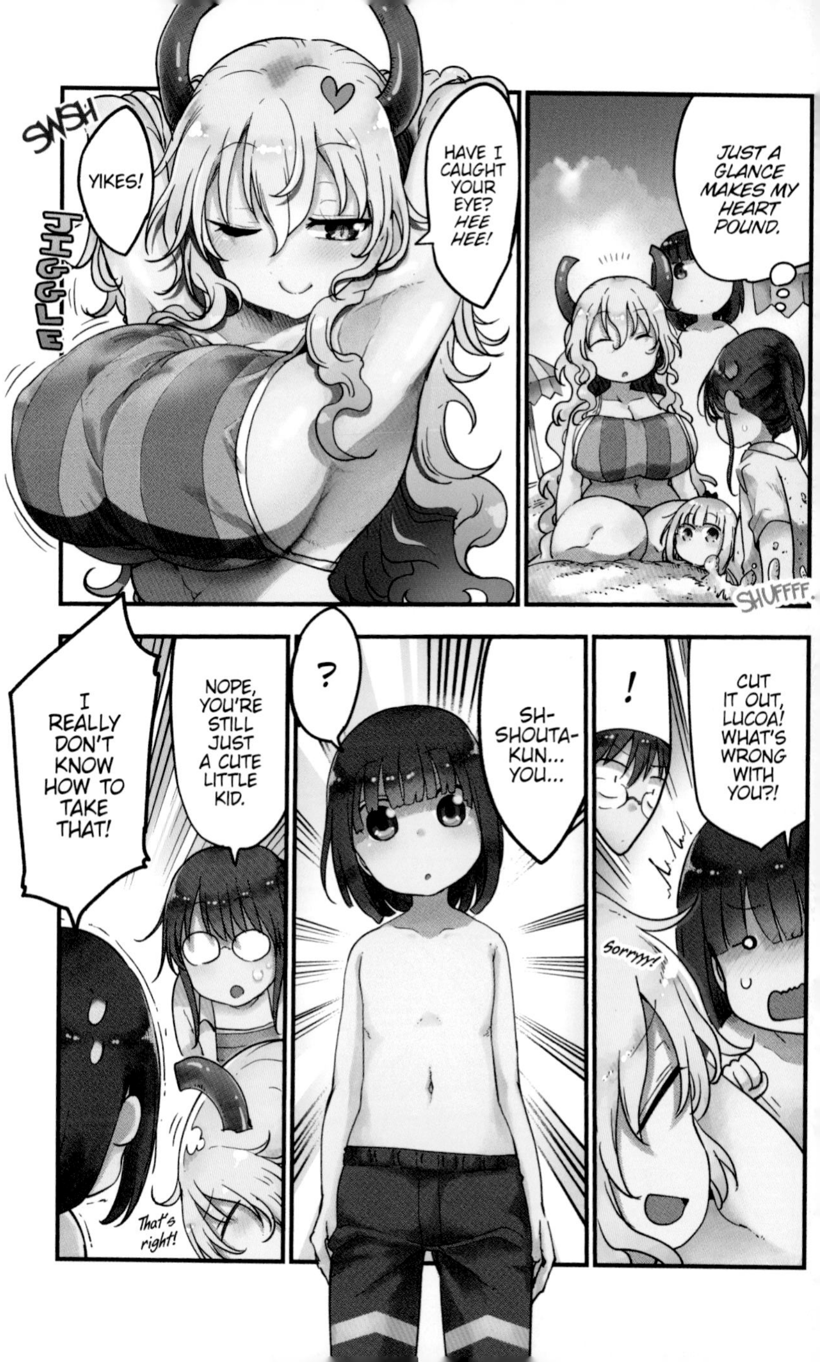
JUST A GLANCE MAKES MY HEART POUND.
SHUFFFF.
HAVE I CAUGHT YOUR EYE? HEE HEE!
SWSH
YIKES!
JIGGLE
CUT IT OUT, LUCOA! WHAT'S WRONG WITH YOU?!
!
Sorryyy!
SH-SHOUTA-KUN... YOU...
?
NOPE, YOU'RE STILL JUST A CUTE LITTLE KID.
I REALLY DON'T KNOW HOW TO TAKE THAT!
That's right!

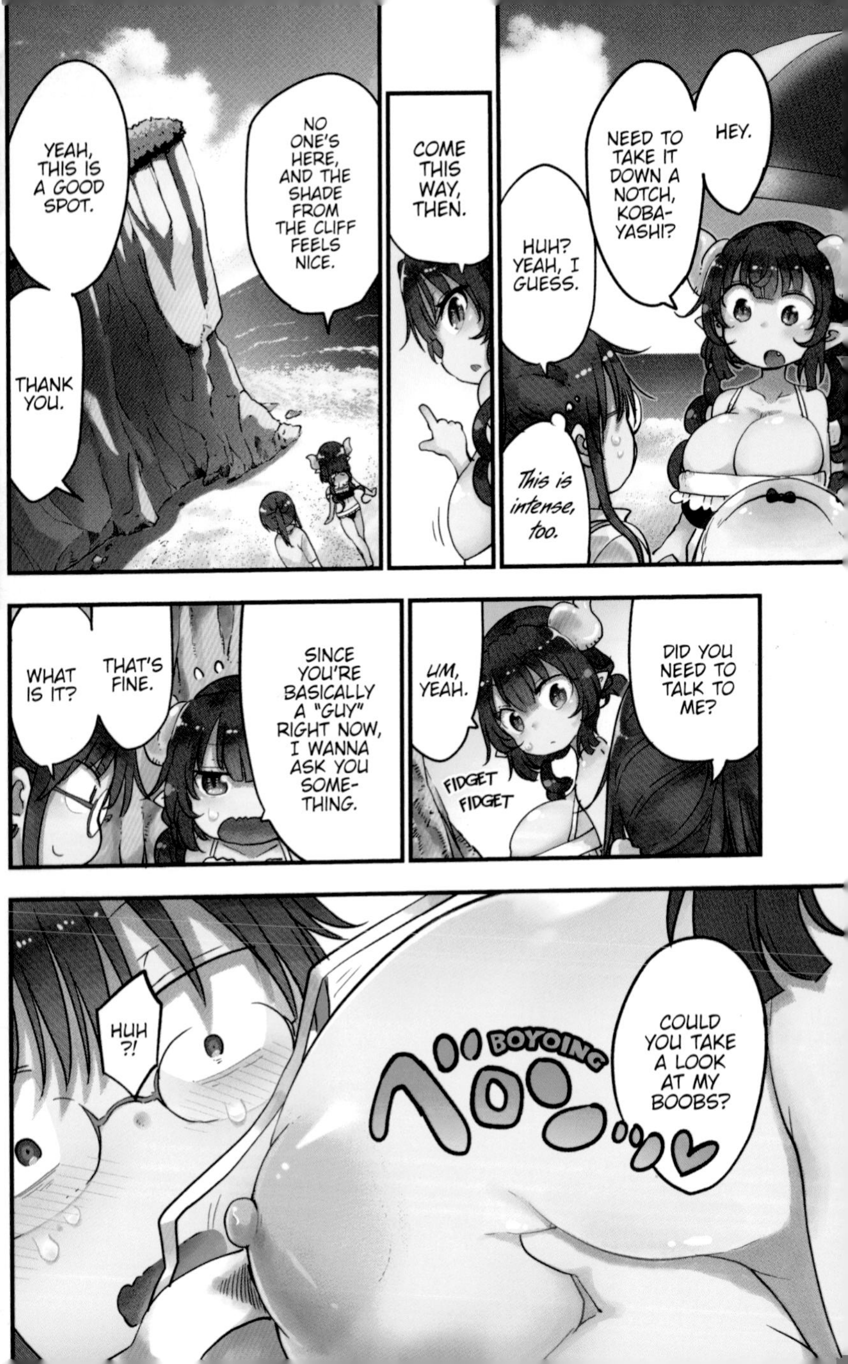
HEY.
NEED TO TAKE IT DOWN A NOTCH, KOBAYASHI?
HUH? YEAH, I GUESS.
This is intense, too.
COME THIS WAY, THEN.
NO ONE'S HERE, AND THE SHADE FROM THE CLIFF FEELS NICE.
YEAH, THIS IS A GOOD SPOT.
THANK YOU.
DID YOU NEED TO TALK TO ME?
UM, YEAH.
FIDGET FIDGET
SINCE YOU'RE BASICALLY A "GUY" RIGHT NOW, I WANNA ASK YOU SOMETHING.
THAT'S FINE.
WHAT IS IT?
COULD YOU TAKE A LOOK AT MY BOOBS?
BOYOING
HUH ?!

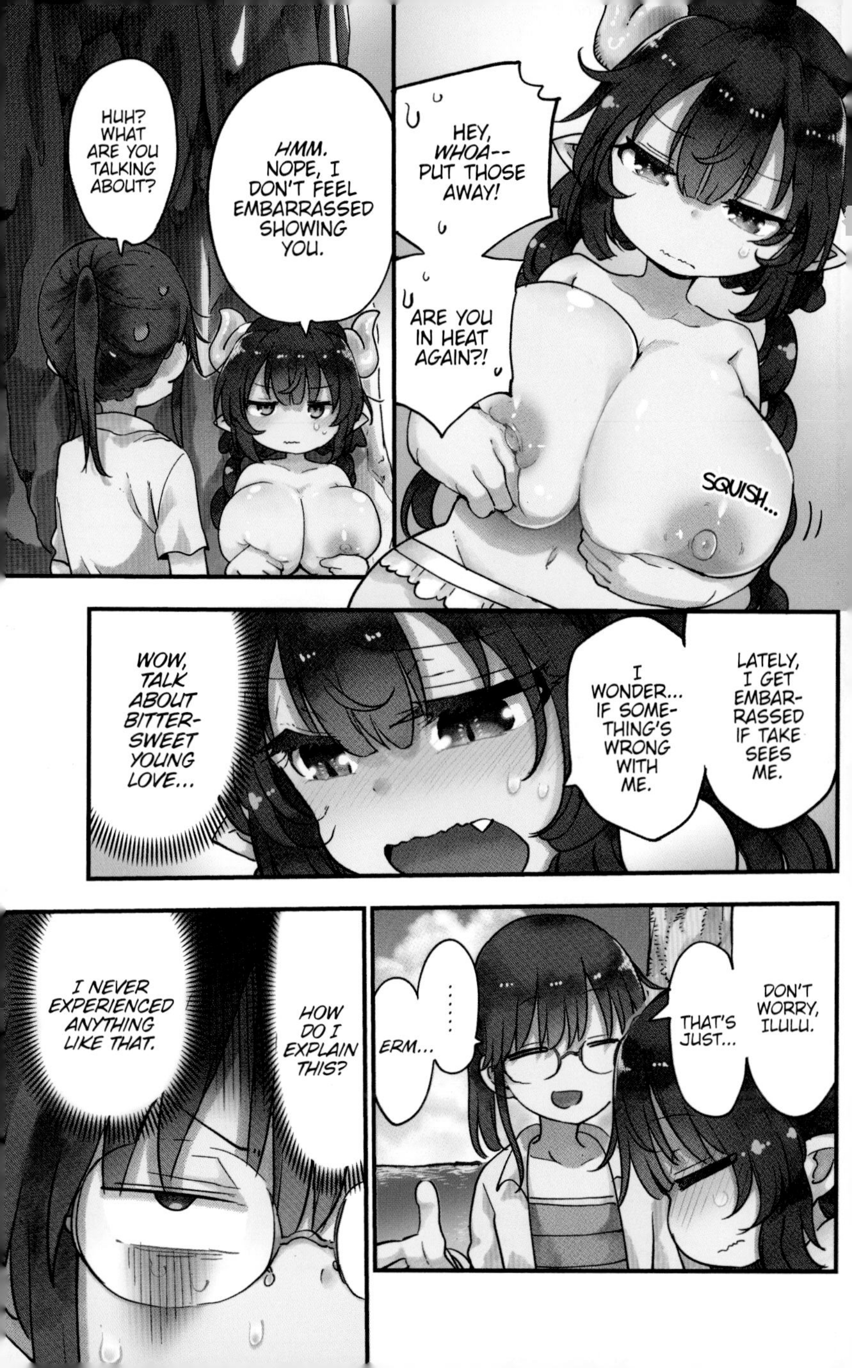
HEY, WHOA-- PUT THOSE AWAY!
ARE YOU IN HEAT AGAIN?!
SQUISH...
HMM. NOPE, I DON'T FEEL EMBARRASSED SHOWING YOU.
HUH? WHAT ARE YOU TALKING ABOUT?
LATELY, I GET EMBARRASSED IF TAKE SEES ME.
I WONDER... IF SOMETHING'S WRONG WITH ME.
WOW, TALK ABOUT BITTERSWEET YOUNG LOVE...
DON'T WORRY, ILULU.
THAT'S JUST...
......
ERM...
HOW DO I EXPLAIN THIS?
I NEVER EXPERIENCED ANYTHING LIKE THAT.

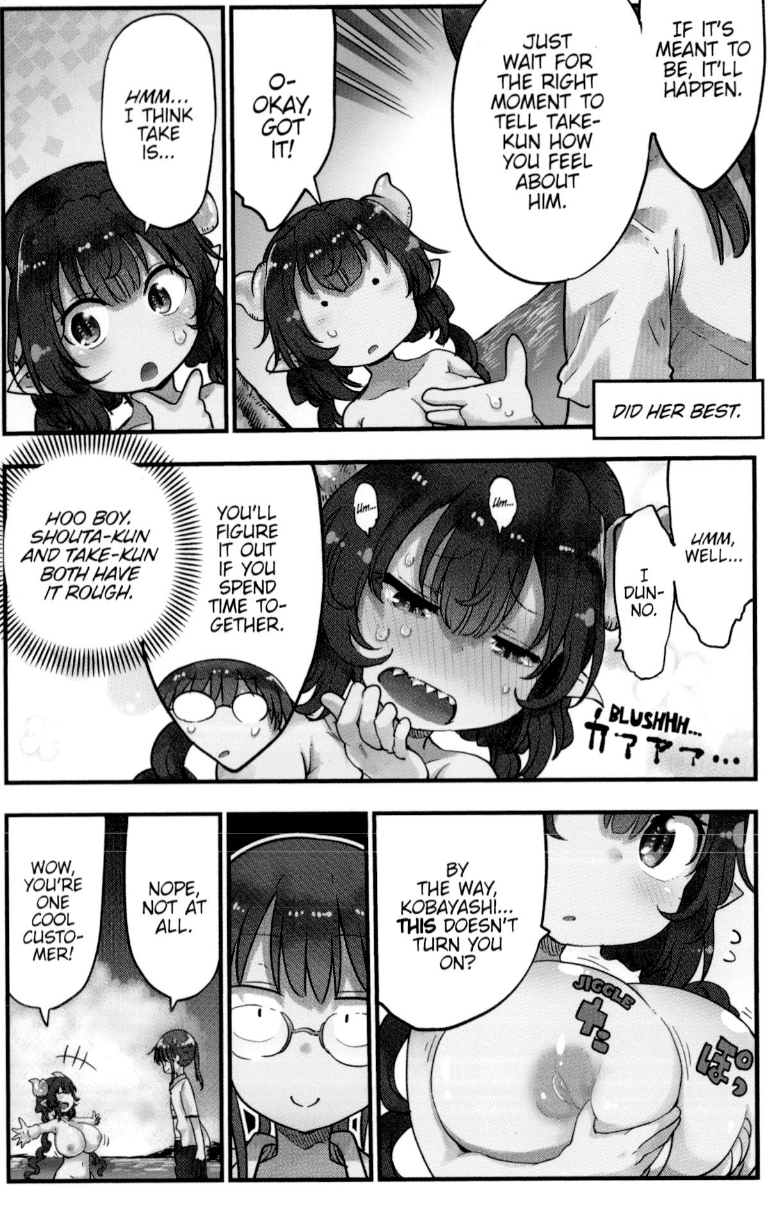
IF IT'S MEANT TO BE, IT'LL HAPPEN.
JUST WAIT FOR THE RIGHT MOMENT TO TELL TAKE-KUN HOW YOU FEEL ABOUT HIM.
DID HER BEST.
O-OKAY, GOT IT!
HMM... I THINK TAKE IS...
UMM, WELL...
I DUNNO.
Um...
Um...
BLUSHHH...
ガァァァ...
YOU'LL FIGURE IT OUT IF YOU SPEND TIME TOGETHER.
HOO BOY. SHOUTA-KUN AND TAKE-KUN BOTH HAVE IT ROUGH.
BY THE WAY, KOBAYASHI... THIS DOESN'T TURN YOU ON?
JIGGLE
NOPE, NOT AT ALL.
WOW, YOU'RE ONE COOL CUSTOMER!

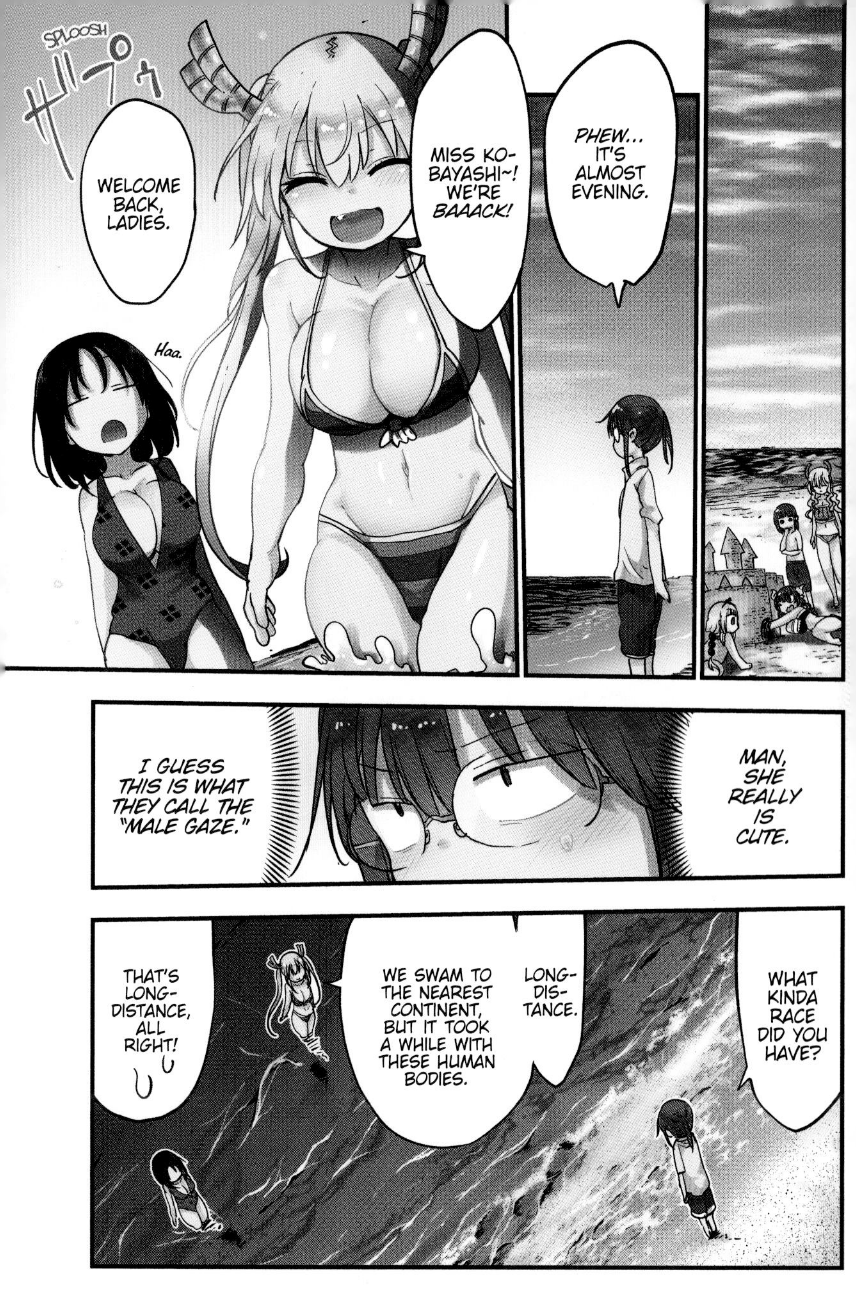
PHEW... IT'S ALMOST EVENING.
MISS KO-BAYASHI~! WE'RE BAAACK!
SPLOOSH
WELCOME BACK, LADIES.
Haa.
MAN, SHE REALLY IS CUTE.
I GUESS THIS IS WHAT THEY CALL THE "MALE GAZE."
WHAT KINDA RACE DID YOU HAVE?
LONG-DISTANCE.
WE SWAM TO THE NEAREST CONTINENT, BUT IT TOOK A WHILE WITH THESE HUMAN BODIES.
THAT'S LONG-DISTANCE, ALL RIGHT!

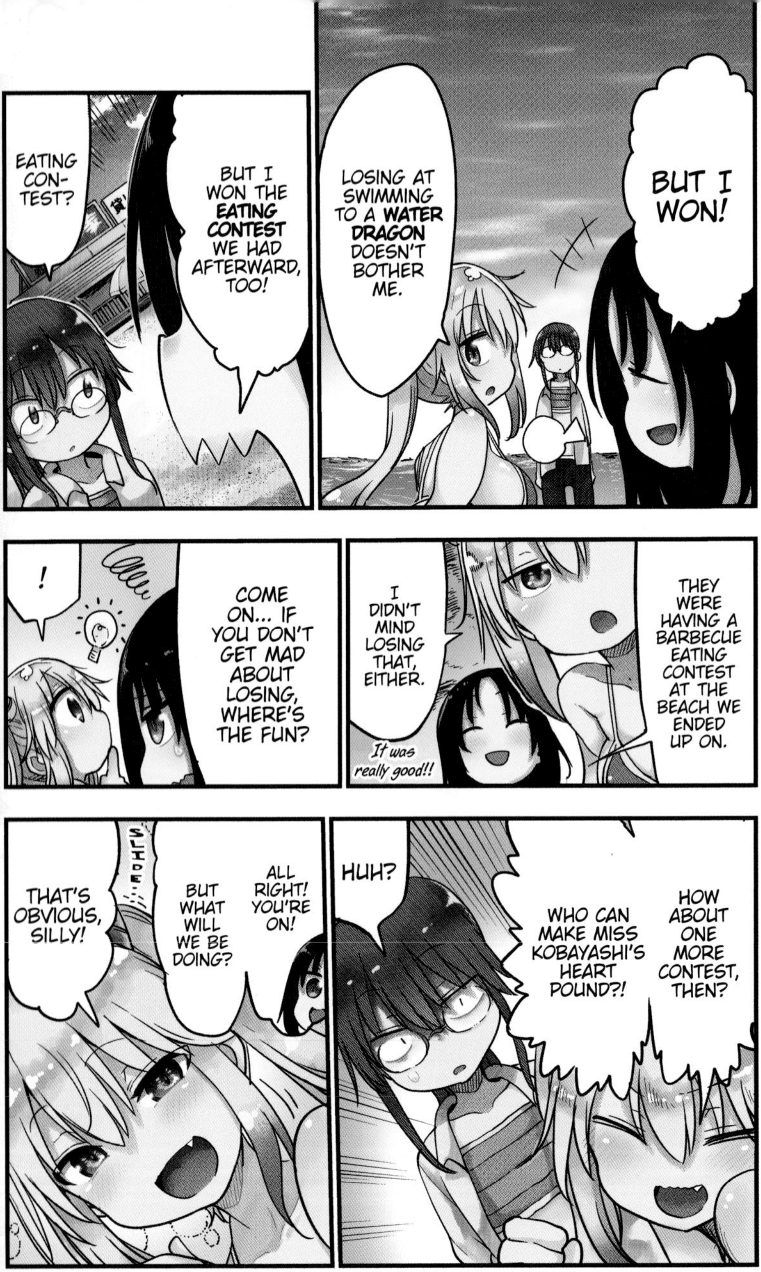
BUT I WON!
LOSING AT SWIMMING TO A **WATER DRAGON** DOESN'T BOTHER ME.
BUT I WON THE **EATING CONTEST** WE HAD AFTERWARD, TOO!
EATING CON-TEST?
THEY WERE HAVING A BARBECUE EATING CONTEST AT THE BEACH WE ENDED UP ON.
I DIDN'T MIND LOSING THAT, EITHER.
It was really good!!
COME ON... IF YOU DON'T GET MAD ABOUT LOSING, WHERE'S THE FUN?
!
HOW ABOUT ONE MORE CONTEST, THEN?
WHO CAN MAKE MISS KOBAYASHI'S HEART POUND?!
HUH?
ALL RIGHT! YOU'RE ON!
BUT WHAT WILL WE BE DOING?
SLIDE...
THAT'S OBVIOUS, SILLY!

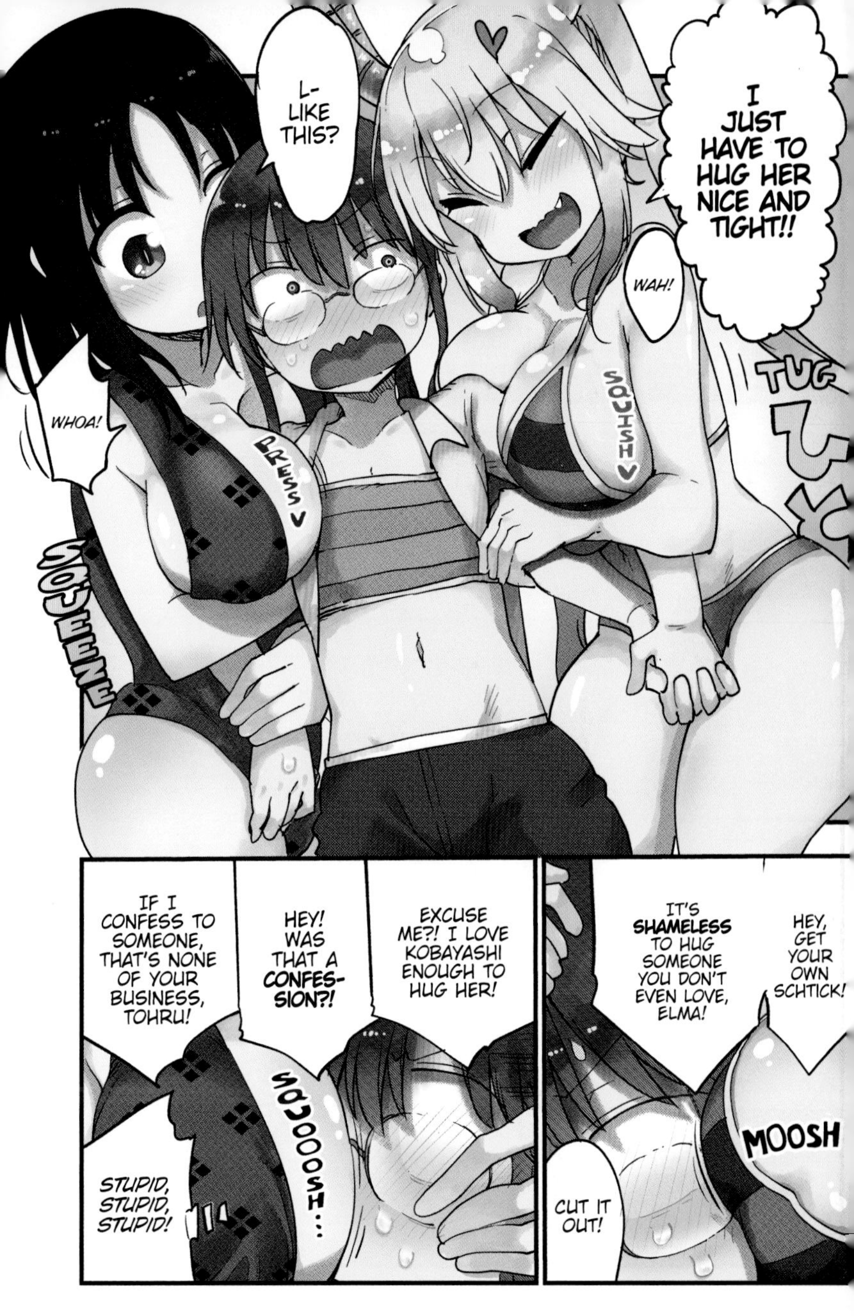
I JUST HAVE TO HUG HER NICE AND TIGHT!!
L-LIKE THIS?
WAH!
TUG
SQUISH♥
PRESS♥
WHOA!
SQUEEZE
HEY, GET YOUR OWN SCHTICK!
IT'S SHAMELESS TO HUG SOMEONE YOU DON'T EVEN LOVE, ELMA!
MOOSH
CUT IT OUT!
EXCUSE ME?! I LOVE KOBAYASHI ENOUGH TO HUG HER!
HEY! WAS THAT A CONFESSION?!
IF I CONFESS TO SOMEONE, THAT'S NONE OF YOUR BUSINESS, TOHRU!
SQUOOOSH...
STUPID, STUPID, STUPID!

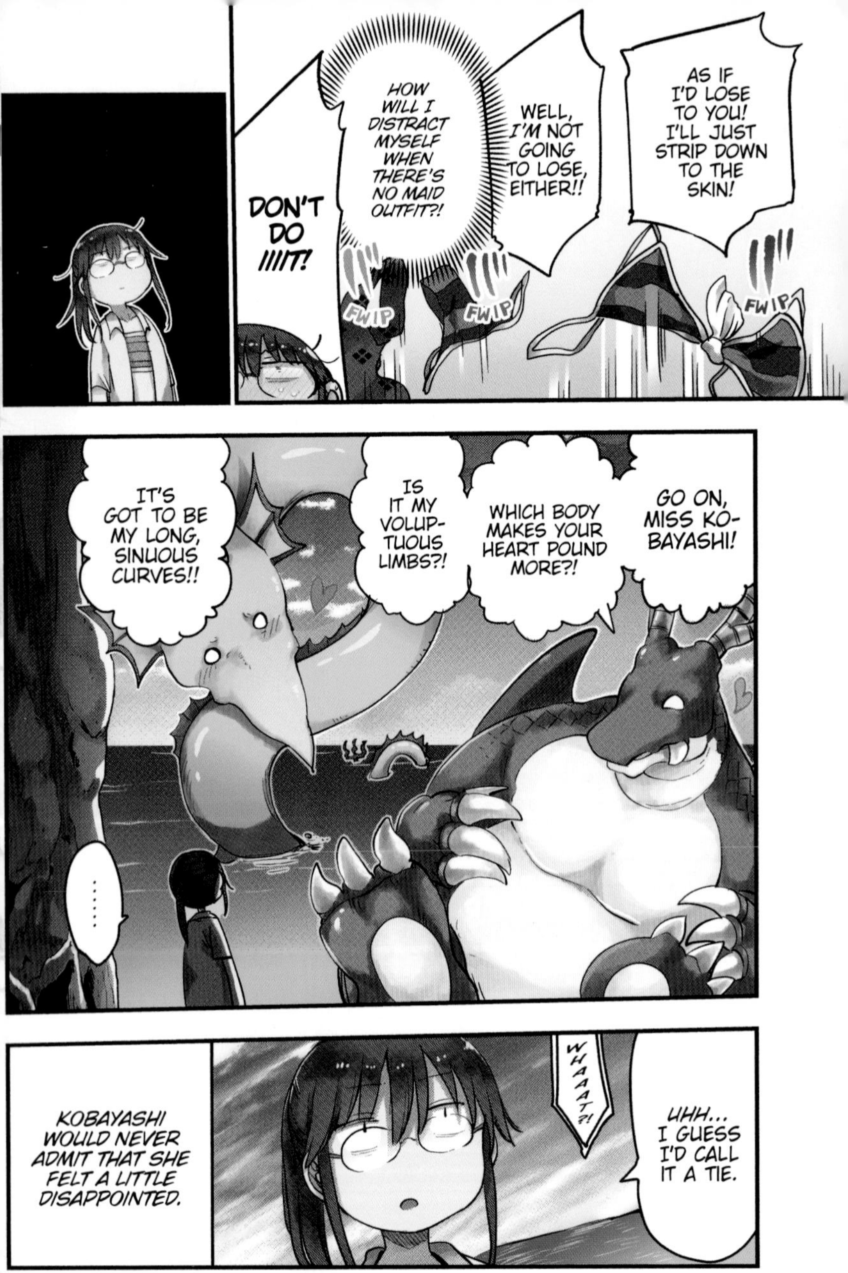
AS IF I'D LOSE TO YOU! I'LL JUST STRIP DOWN TO THE SKIN!
WELL, I'M NOT GOING TO LOSE, EITHER!!
HOW WILL I DISTRACT MYSELF WHEN THERE'S NO MAID OUTFIT?!
FWIP
FWIP
FWIP
DON'T DO IIIIT!
GO ON, MISS KOBAYASHI!
WHICH BODY MAKES YOUR HEART POUND MORE?!
IS IT MY VOLUPTUOUS LIMBS?!
IT'S GOT TO BE MY LONG, SINUOUS CURVES!!
......
UHH... I GUESS I'D CALL IT A TIE.
WHAAAAT?!
KOBAYASHI WOULD NEVER ADMIT THAT SHE FELT A LITTLE DISAPPOINTED.

CHAPTER 100/END

CHAPTER 101

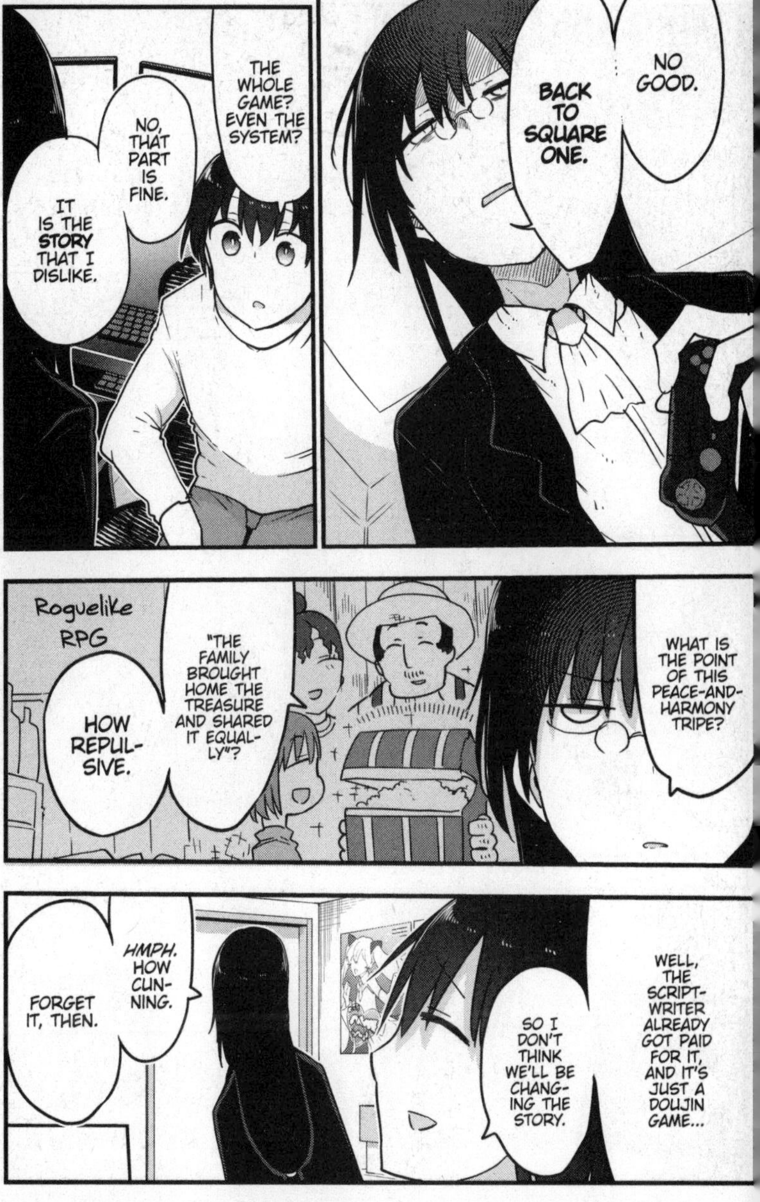
NO GOOD.
BACK TO SQUARE ONE.
THE WHOLE GAME? EVEN THE SYSTEM?
NO, THAT PART IS FINE.
IT IS THE STORY THAT I DISLIKE.
WHAT IS THE POINT OF THIS PEACE-AND-HARMONY TRIPE?
"THE FAMILY BROUGHT HOME THE TREASURE AND SHARED IT EQUALLY"?
Roguelike RPG
HOW REPULSIVE.
WELL, THE SCRIPTWRITER ALREADY GOT PAID FOR IT, AND IT'S JUST A DOUJIN GAME...
SO I DON'T THINK WE'LL BE CHANGING THE STORY.
HMPH. HOW CUNNING.
FORGET IT, THEN.

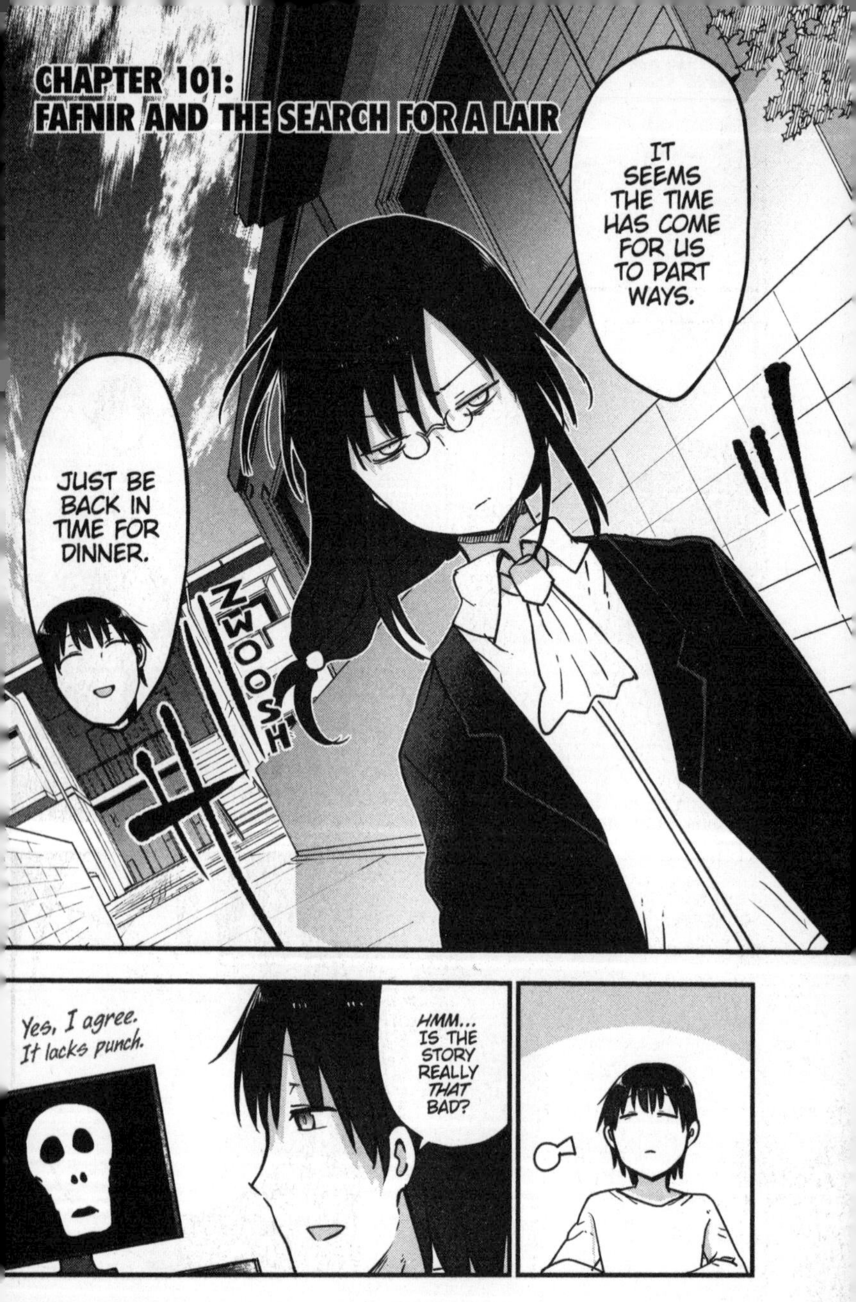
CHAPTER 101:
FAFNIR AND THE SEARCH FOR A LAIR
IT SEEMS THE TIME HAS COME FOR US TO PART WAYS.
JUST BE BACK IN TIME FOR DINNER.
NWOOSH
HMM... IS THE STORY REALLY *THAT* BAD?
Yes, I agree. It lacks punch.

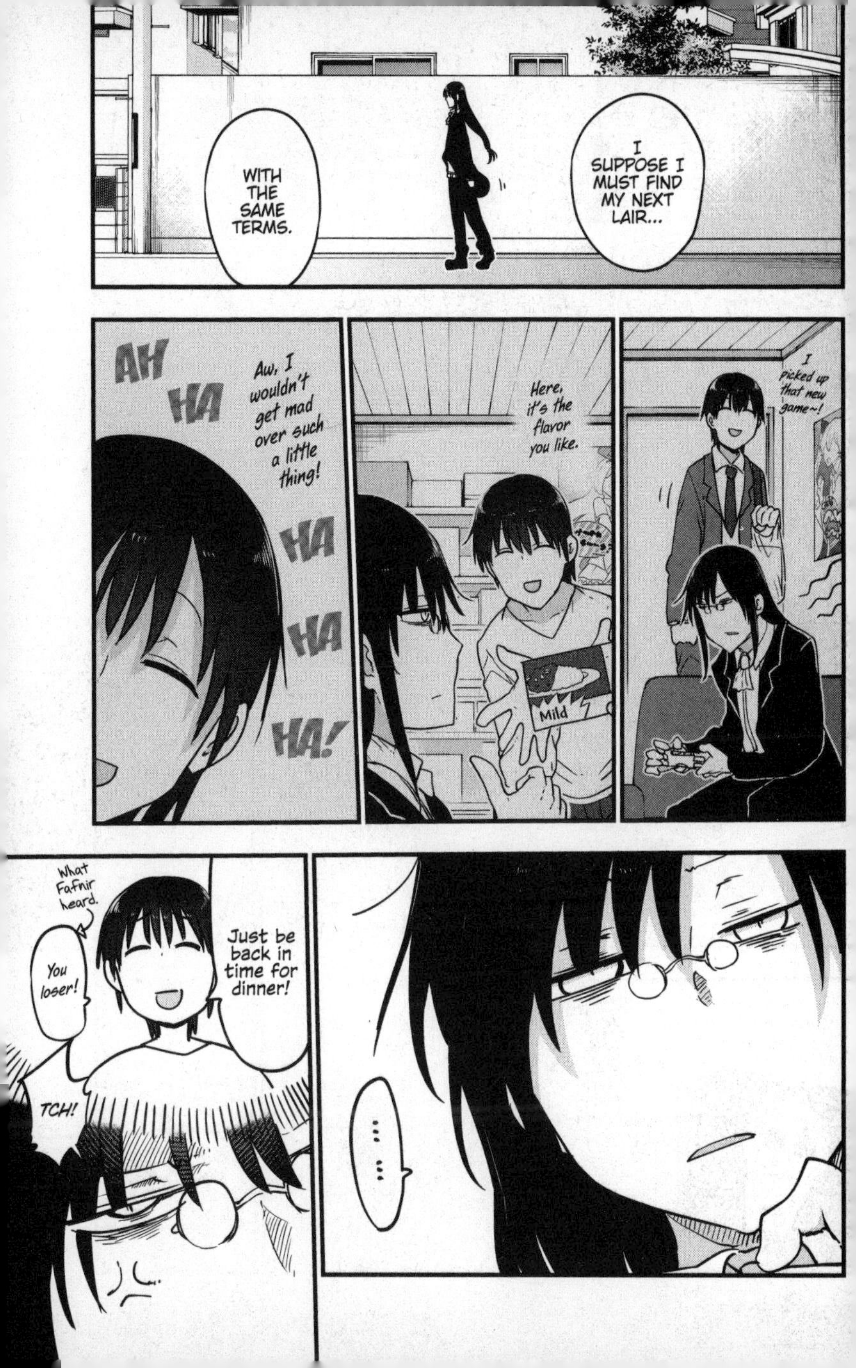
I SUPPOSE I MUST FIND MY NEXT LAIR...
WITH THE SAME TERMS.
I picked up that new game~!
Here, it's the flavor you like.
Mild
AH HA
Aw, I wouldn't get mad over such a little thing!
HA HA HA!
... ...
Just be back in time for dinner!
What Fafnir heard.
You loser!
TCH!

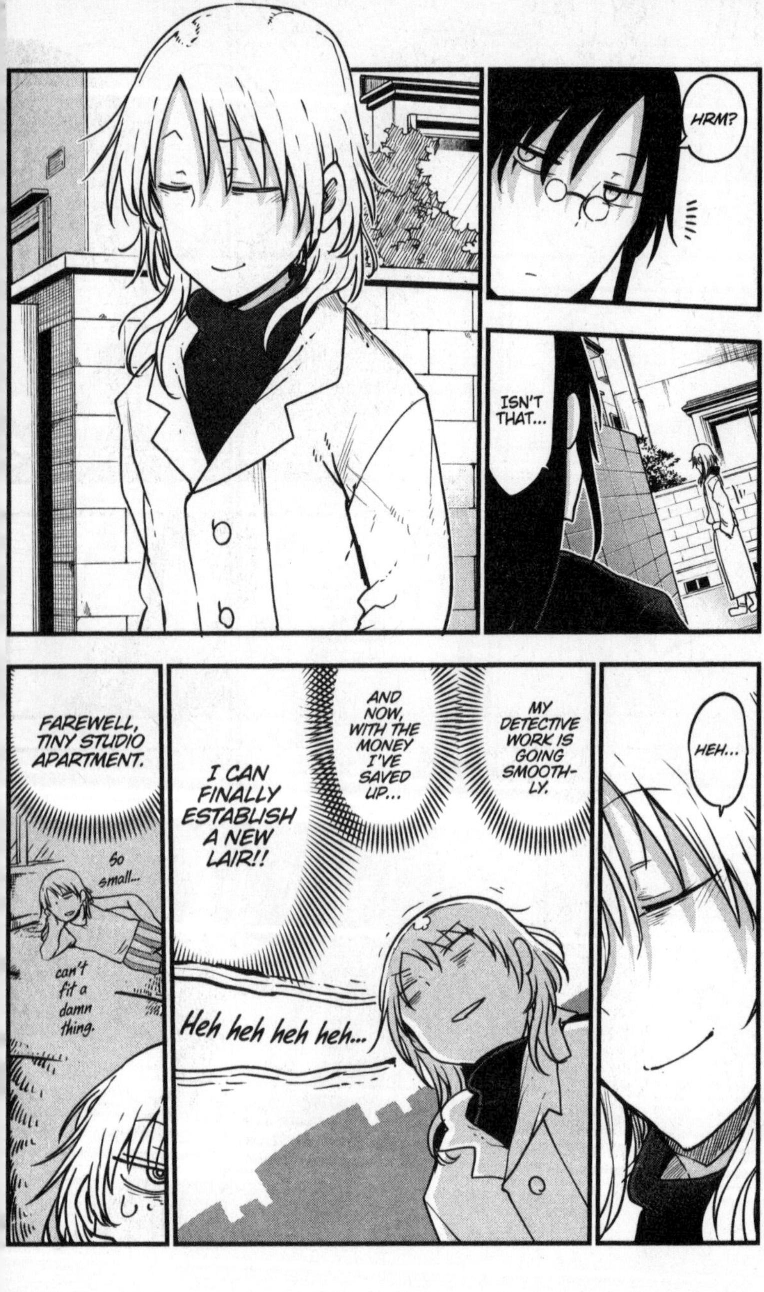
HRM?
ISN'T THAT...
HEH...
MY DETECTIVE WORK IS GOING SMOOTHLY.
AND NOW, WITH THE MONEY I'VE SAVED UP...
I CAN FINALLY ESTABLISH A NEW LAIR!!
Heh heh heh heh...
FAREWELL, TINY STUDIO APARTMENT.
So small... can't fit a damn thing.

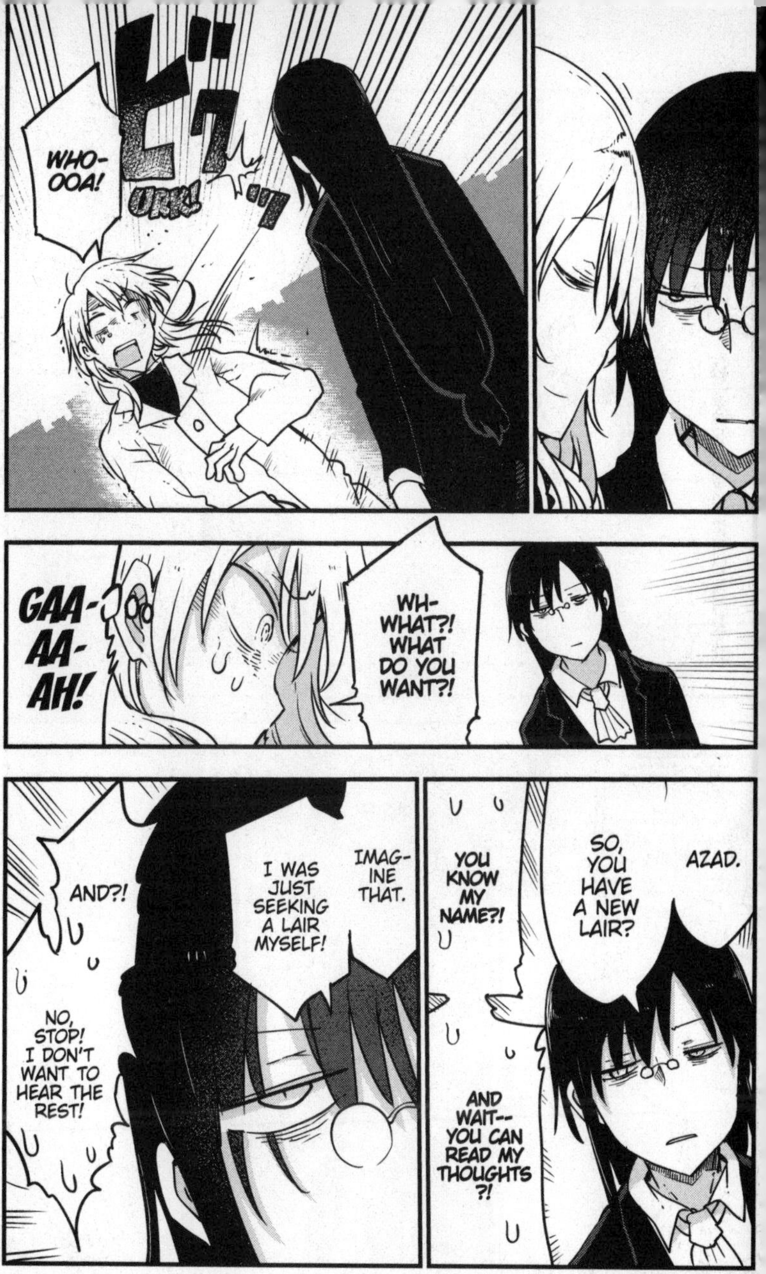
URK!
WHO-OOA!
WH-WHAT?! WHAT DO YOU WANT?!
GAA-AA-AH!
AZAD.
SO, YOU HAVE A NEW LAIR?
YOU KNOW MY NAME?!
AND WAIT-- YOU CAN READ MY THOUGHTS?!
IMAG-INE THAT.
I WAS JUST SEEKING A LAIR MYSELF!
AND?!
NO, STOP! I DON'T WANT TO HEAR THE REST!

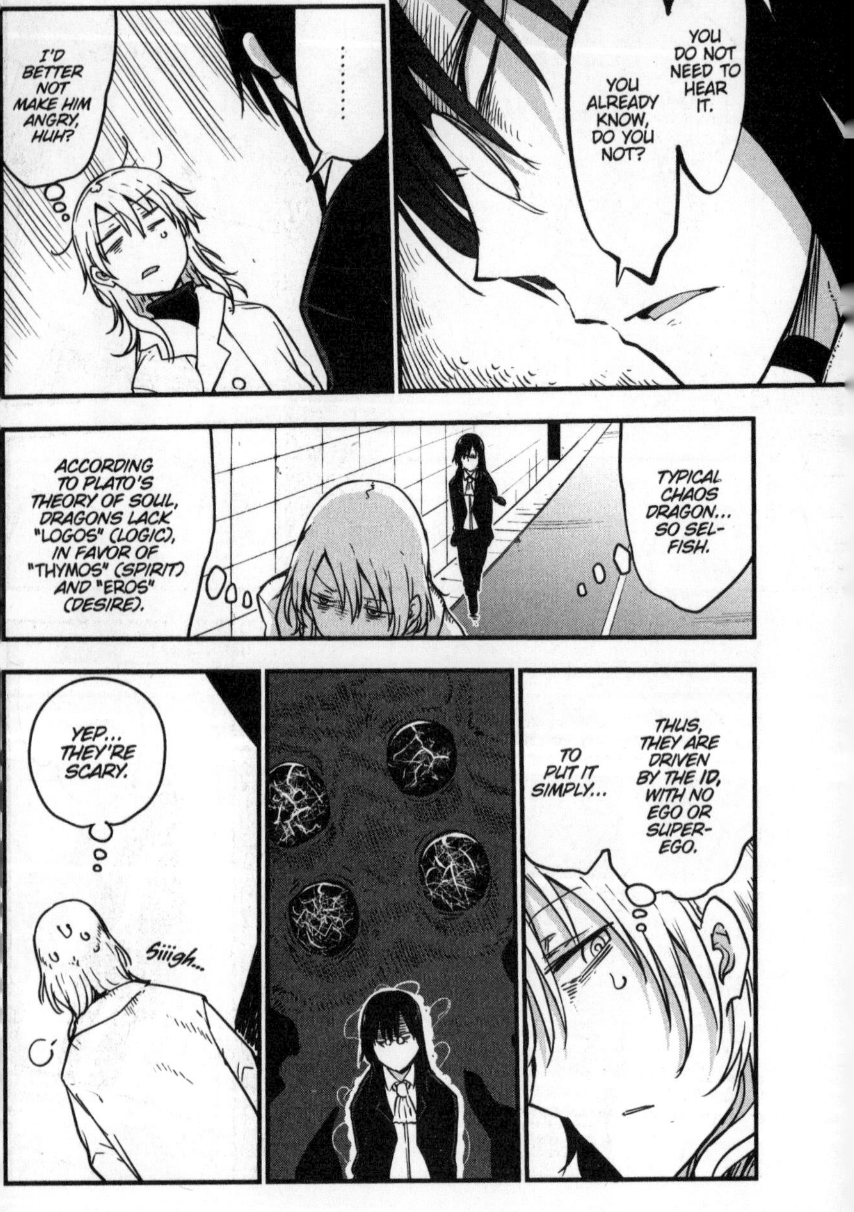

YOU DO NOT NEED TO HEAR IT.
YOU ALREADY KNOW, DO YOU NOT?
......
I'D BETTER NOT MAKE HIM ANGRY, HUH?
TYPICAL CHAOS DRAGON... SO SEL-FISH.
ACCORDING TO PLATO'S THEORY OF SOUL, DRAGONS LACK "LOGOS" (LOGIC), IN FAVOR OF "THYMOS" (SPIRIT) AND "EROS" (DESIRE).
THUS, THEY ARE DRIVEN BY THE ID, WITH NO EGO OR SUPER-EGO.
TO PUT IT SIMPLY...
YEP... THEY'RE SCARY.
Siiigh...

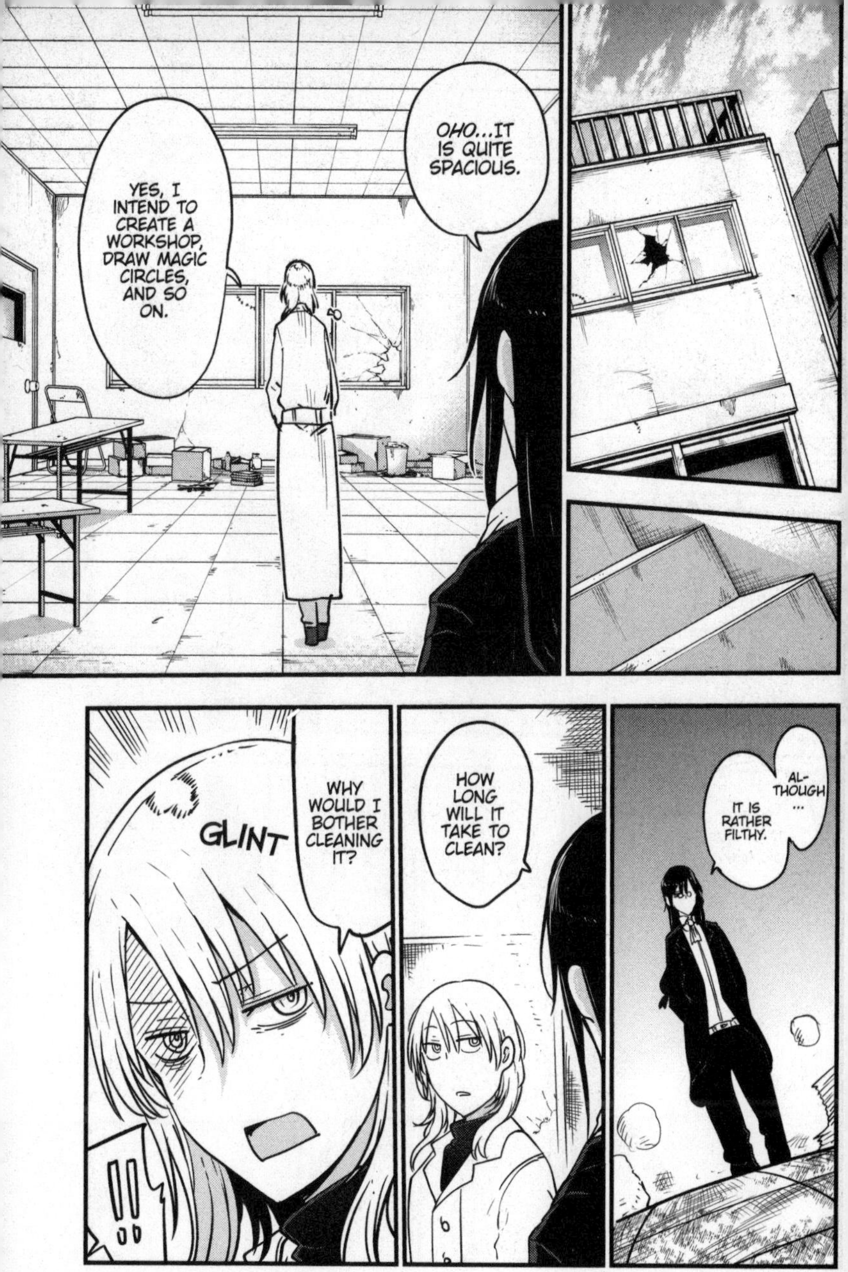
OHO...IT IS QUITE SPACIOUS.
YES, I INTEND TO CREATE A WORKSHOP, DRAW MAGIC CIRCLES, AND SO ON.
ALTHOUGH...
IT IS RATHER FILTHY.
HOW LONG WILL IT TAKE TO CLEAN?
WHY WOULD I BOTHER CLEANING IT?
GLINT
!!

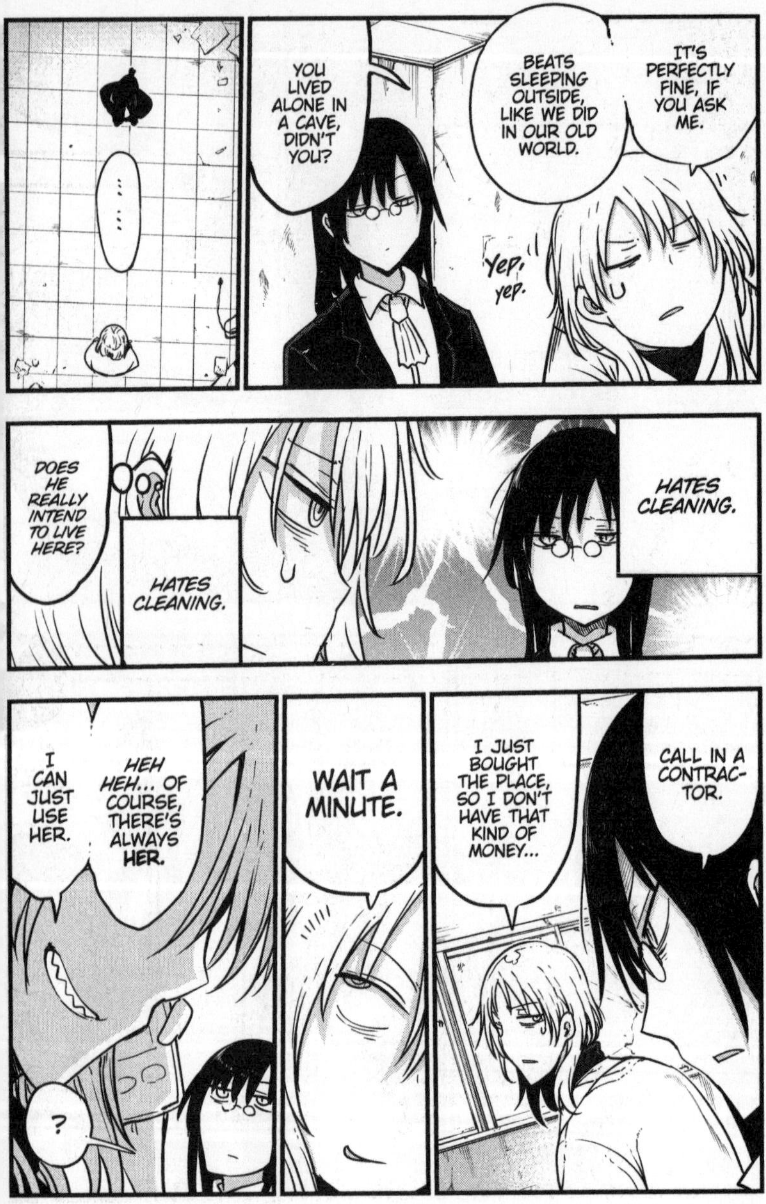
IT'S PERFECTLY FINE, IF YOU ASK ME.
BEATS SLEEPING OUTSIDE, LIKE WE DID IN OUR OLD WORLD.
YOU LIVED ALONE IN A CAVE, DIDN'T YOU?
Yep, yep.
......
HATES CLEANING.
HATES CLEANING.
DOES HE REALLY INTEND TO LIVE HERE?
CALL IN A CONTRAC-TOR.
I JUST BOUGHT THE PLACE, SO I DON'T HAVE THAT KIND OF MONEY...
WAIT A MINUTE.
HEH HEH... OF COURSE, THERE'S ALWAYS HER.
I CAN JUST USE HER.
?

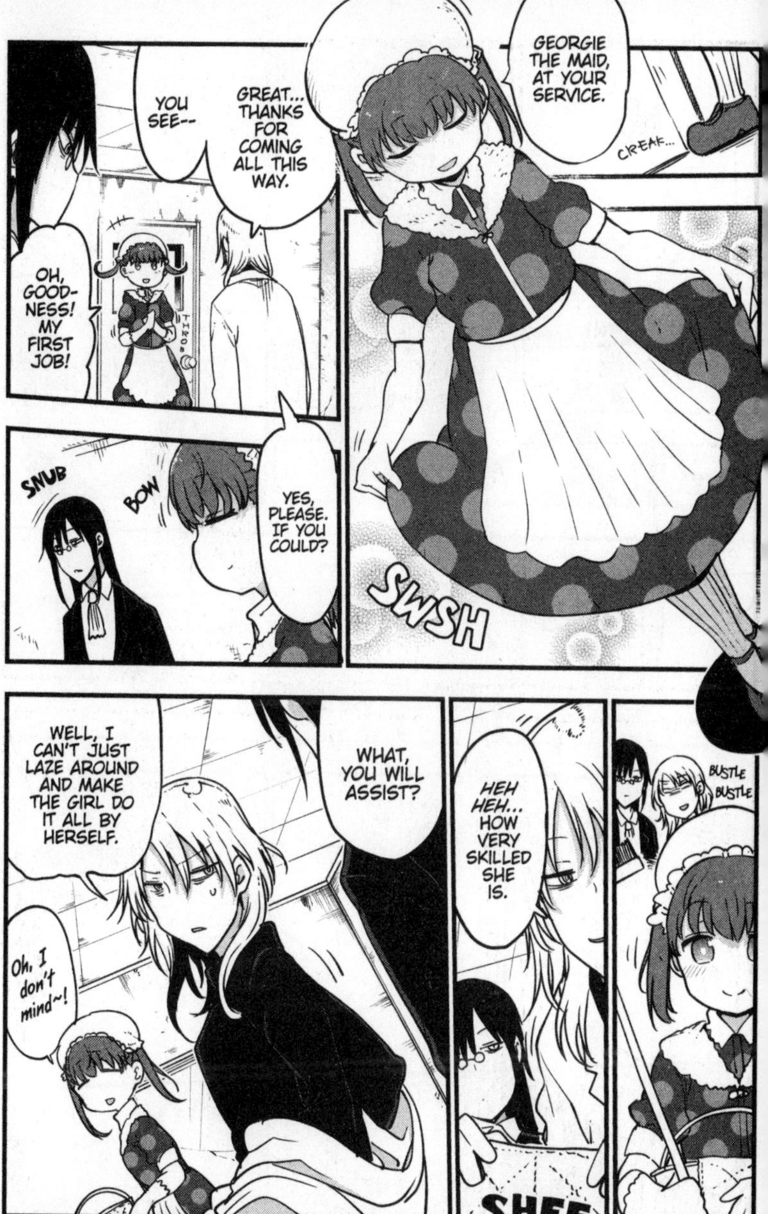
CREAK...
GEORGIE THE MAID, AT YOUR SERVICE.
SWSH
GREAT... THANKS FOR COMING ALL THIS WAY.
YOU SEE--
OH, GOODNESS! MY FIRST JOB!
THROB
YES, PLEASE. IF YOU COULD?
BOW
SNUB
BUSTLE
BUSTLE
HEH HEH... HOW VERY SKILLED SHE IS.
SHFF
WHAT, YOU WILL ASSIST?
WELL, I CAN'T JUST LAZE AROUND AND MAKE THE GIRL DO IT ALL BY HERSELF.
Oh, I don't mind~!

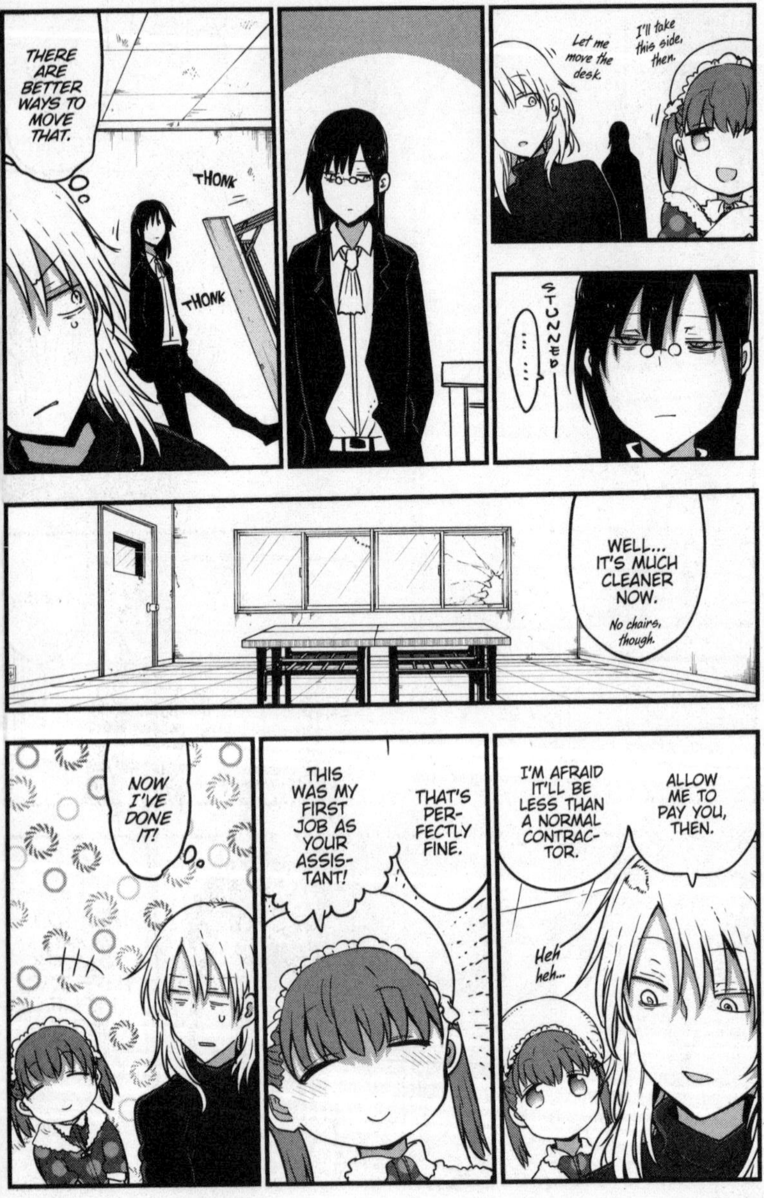
I'll take this side, then.
Let me move the desk.
STUNNED
... ...
THERE ARE BETTER WAYS TO MOVE THAT.
THONK
THONK
WELL... IT'S MUCH CLEANER NOW.
No chairs, though.
ALLOW ME TO PAY YOU, THEN.
I'M AFRAID IT'LL BE LESS THAN A NORMAL CONTRACTOR.
Heh heh...
THAT'S PERFECTLY FINE.
THIS WAS MY FIRST JOB AS YOUR ASSISTANT!
NOW I'VE DONE IT!

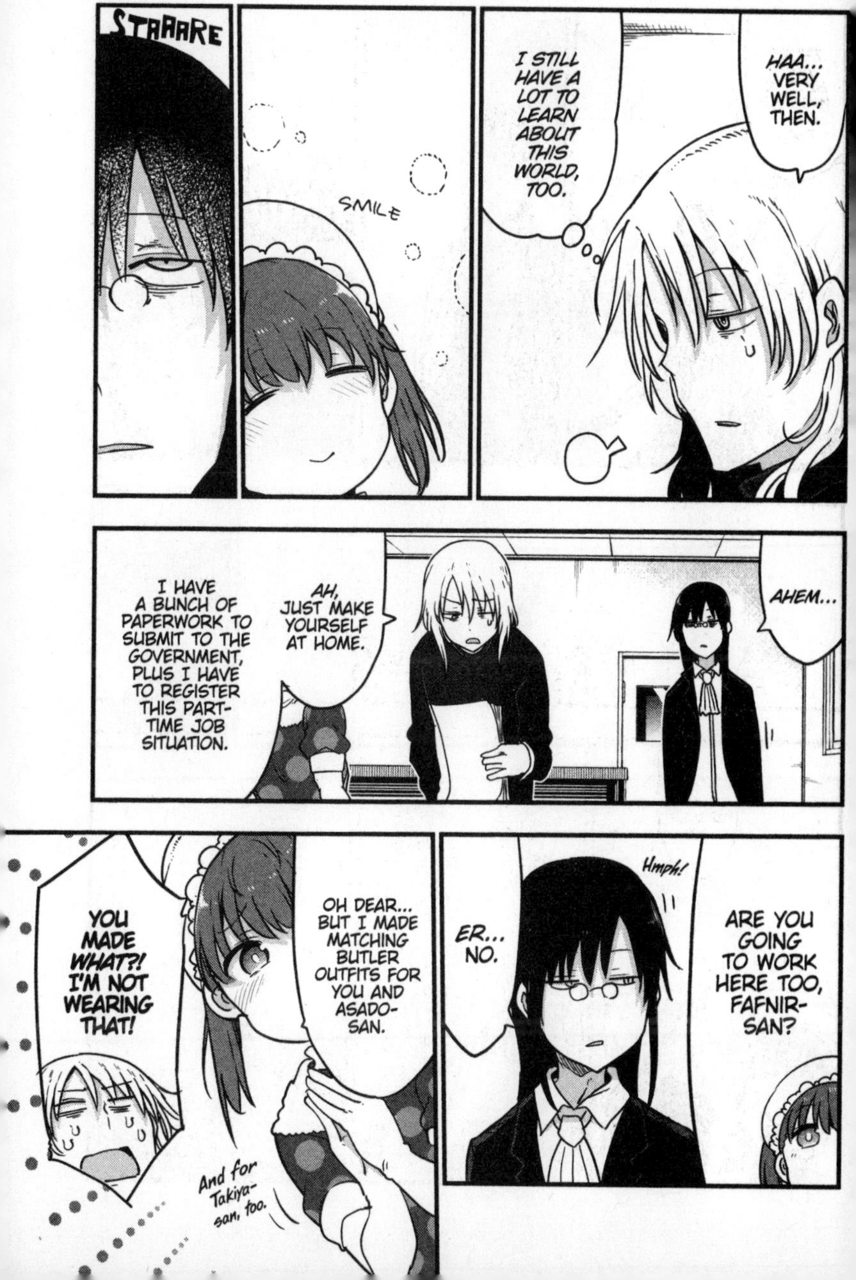

HAA... VERY WELL, THEN.
I STILL HAVE A LOT TO LEARN ABOUT THIS WORLD, TOO.
SMILE
STAAARE
AHEM...
AH, JUST MAKE YOURSELF AT HOME.
I HAVE A BUNCH OF PAPERWORK TO SUBMIT TO THE GOVERNMENT, PLUS I HAVE TO REGISTER THIS PART-TIME JOB SITUATION.
ARE YOU GOING TO WORK HERE TOO, FAFNIR-SAN?
Hmph!
ER... NO.
OH DEAR... BUT I MADE MATCHING BUTLER OUTFITS FOR YOU AND ASADO-SAN.
YOU MADE WHAT?! I'M NOT WEARING THAT!
And for Takiya-san, too.

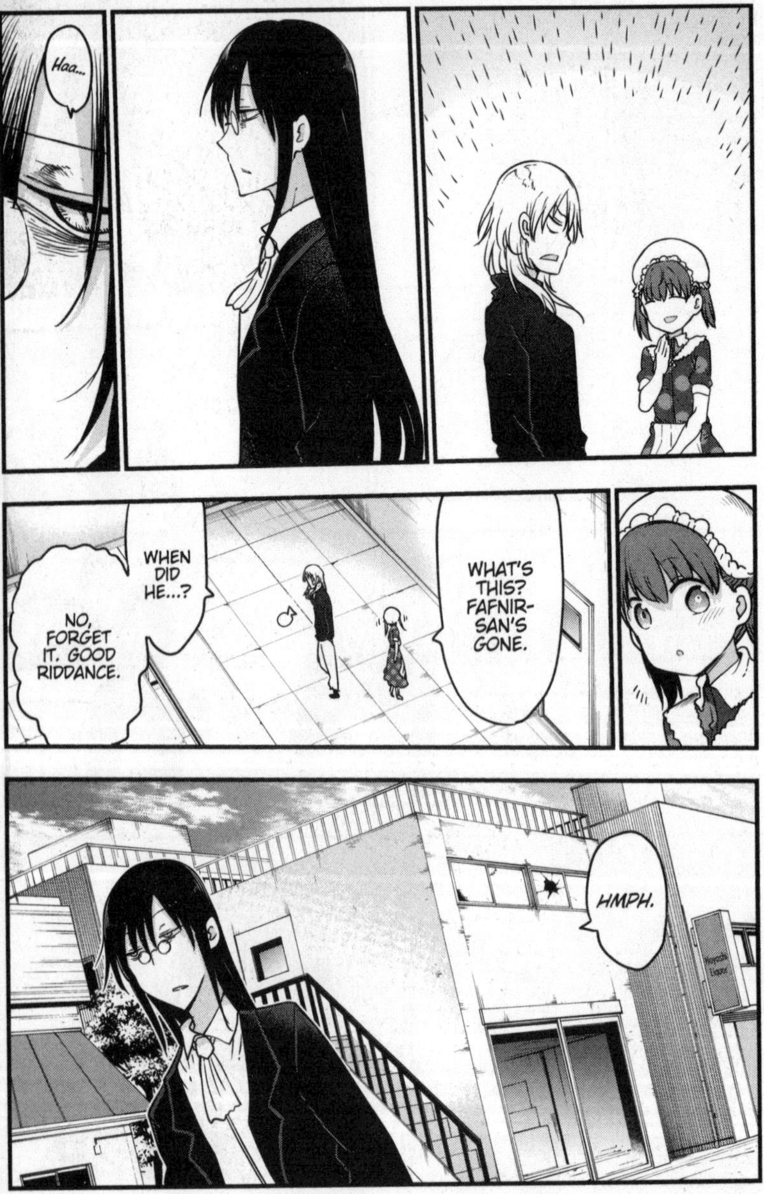
Haa...
WHAT'S THIS? FAFNIR-SAN'S GONE.
WHEN DID HE...?
NO, FORGET IT. GOOD RIDDANCE.
HMPH.

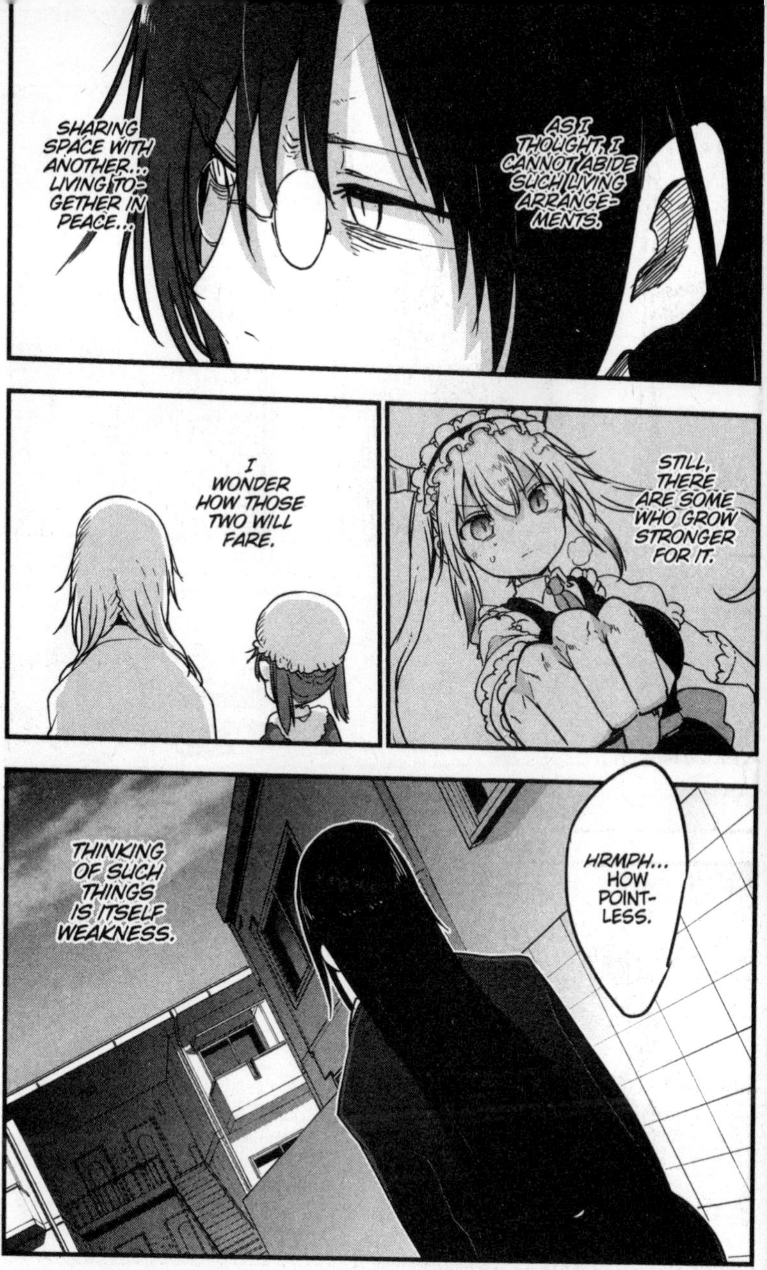
AS I THOUGHT, I CANNOT ABIDE SUCH LIVING ARRANGE-MENTS.
SHARING SPACE WITH ANOTHER... LIVING TO-GETHER IN PEACE...
STILL, THERE ARE SOME WHO GROW STRONGER FOR IT.
I WONDER HOW THOSE TWO WILL FARE.
HRMPH... HOW POINT-LESS.
THINKING OF SUCH THINGS IS ITSELF WEAKNESS.

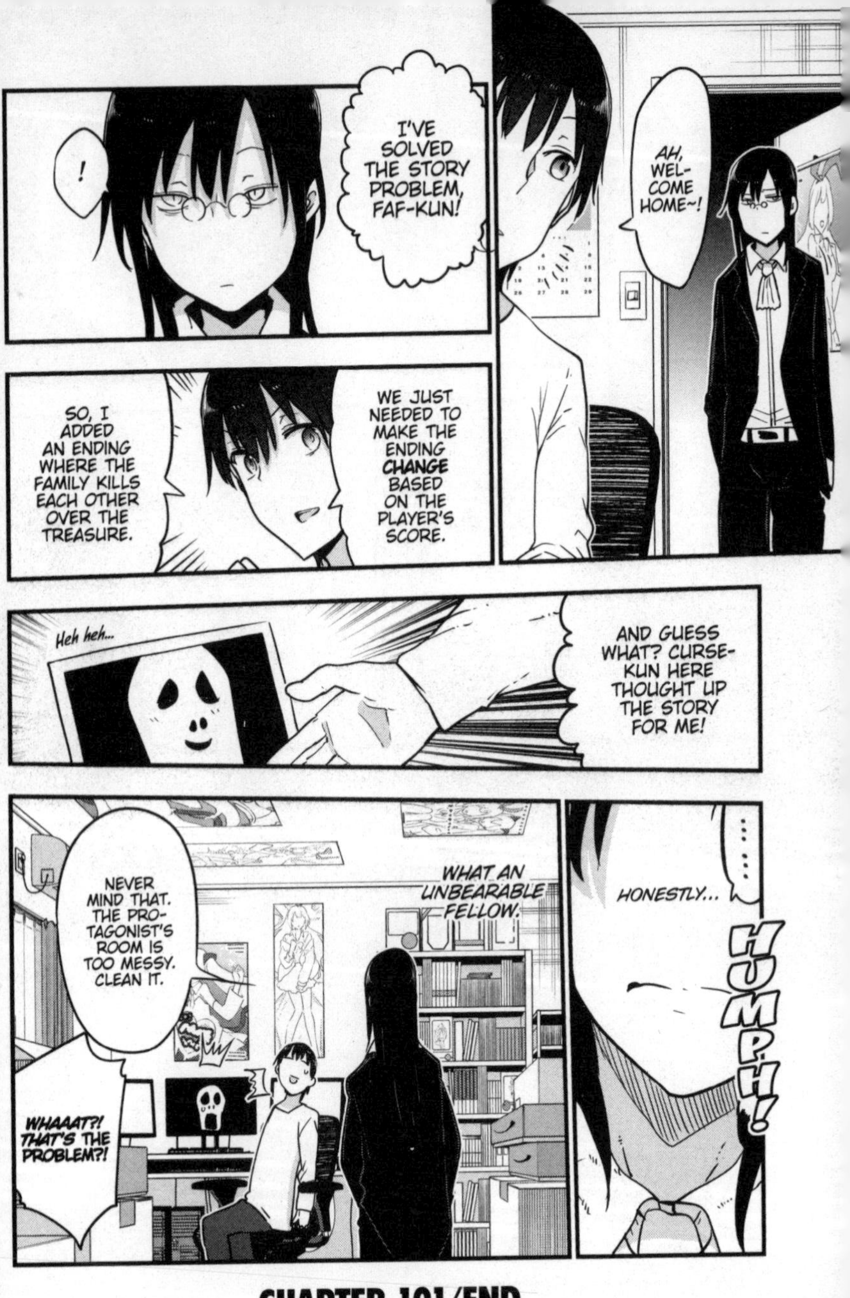
AH, WEL-COME HOME~!
I'VE SOLVED THE STORY PROBLEM, FAF-KUN!
!
WE JUST NEEDED TO MAKE THE ENDING **CHANGE** BASED ON THE PLAYER'S SCORE.
SO, I ADDED AN ENDING WHERE THE FAMILY KILLS EACH OTHER OVER THE TREASURE.
AND GUESS WHAT? CURSE-KUN HERE THOUGHT UP THE STORY FOR ME!
Heh heh...
...
HONESTLY...
HUMPH!
WHAT AN UNBEARABLE FELLOW.
NEVER MIND THAT. THE PRO-TAGONIST'S ROOM IS TOO MESSY. CLEAN IT.
WHAAAT?! THAT'S THE PROBLEM?!

CHAPTER 101/END

THE ASADO DETECTIVE AGENCY IS NOW OPEN.

Miss Kobayashi's
DRAGON MAID

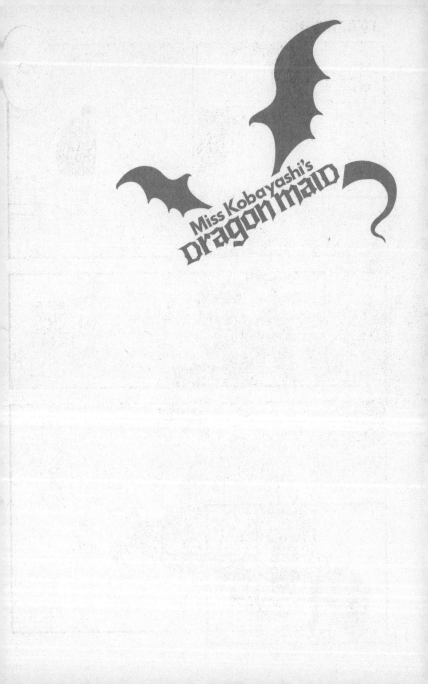

CHAPTER 102

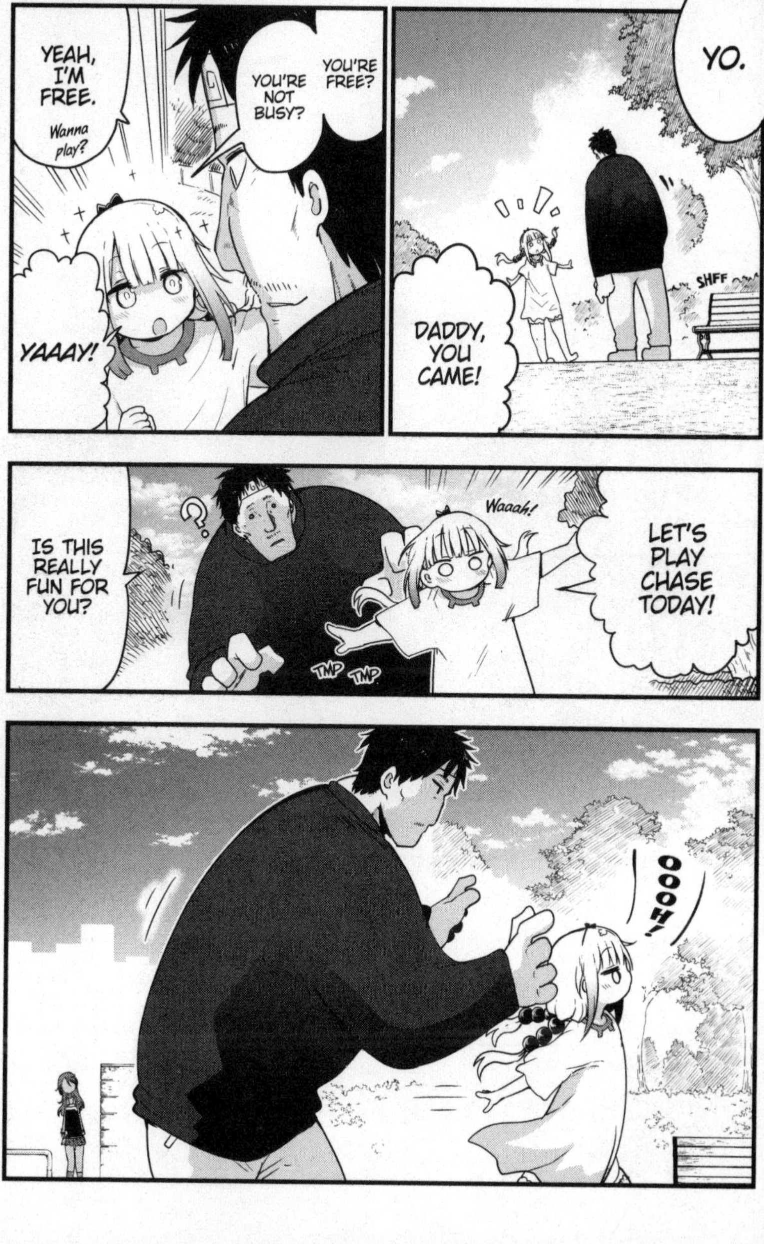

YO.
DADDY, YOU CAME!
SHFF
YOU'RE FREE?
YOU'RE NOT BUSY?
YEAH, I'M FREE.
Wanna play?
YAAAY!
LET'S PLAY CHASE TODAY!
Waaah!
TMP TMP
IS THIS REALLY FUN FOR YOU?
OOOH!

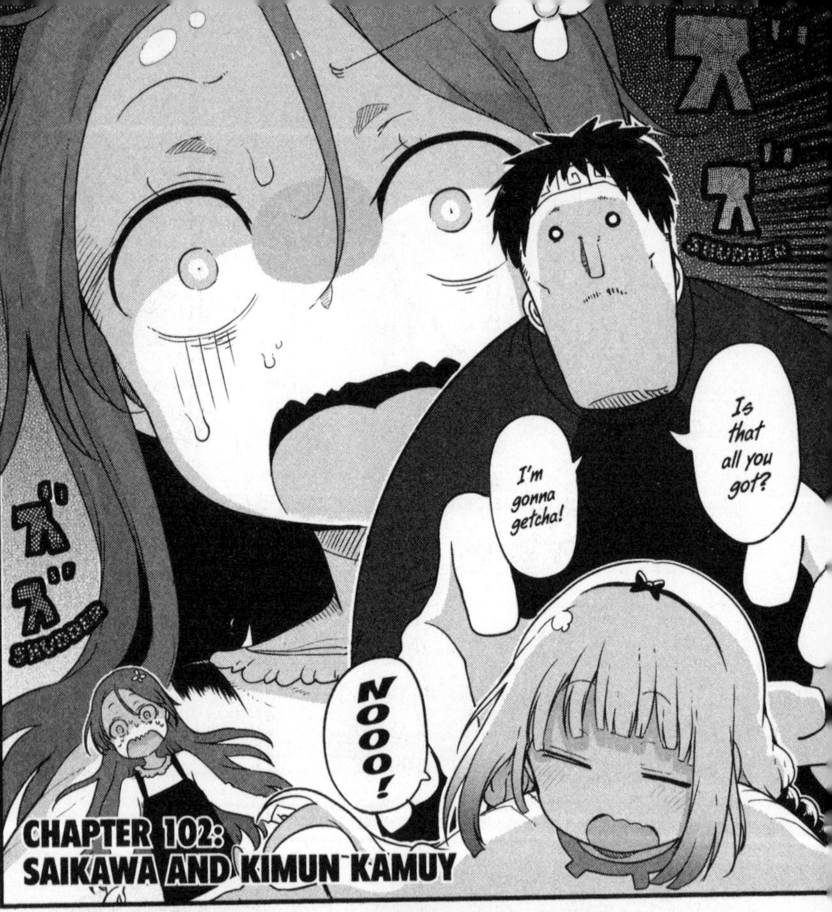
SHUDDER
Is that all you got?
I'm gonna getcha!
NOOO!
SHUDDER

CHAPTER 102: SAIKAWA AND KIMUN KAMUY

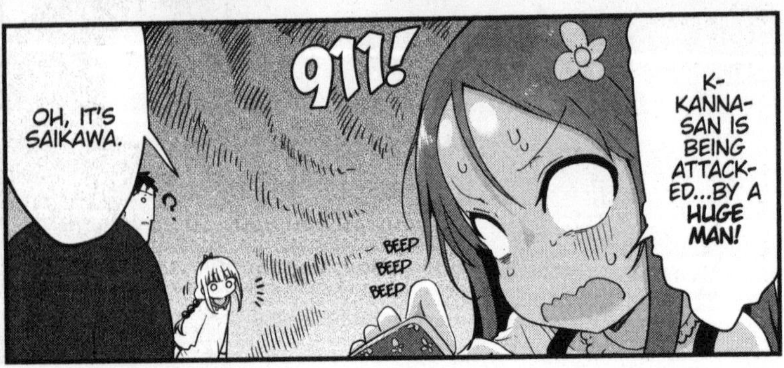
K-KANNA-SAN IS BEING ATTACK-ED...BY A HUGE MAN!
911!
BEEP BEEP BEEP
OH, IT'S SAIKAWA.
?

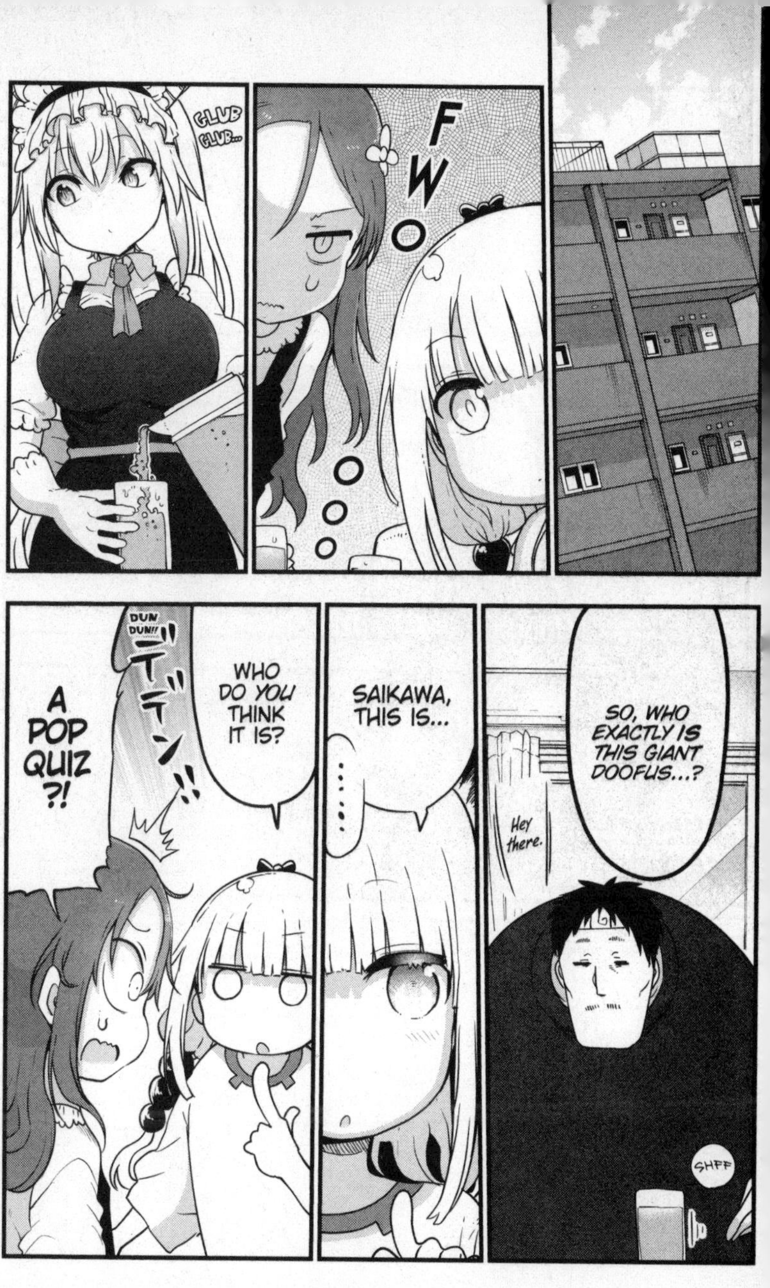
FWOOOOO
GLUB GLUB...
SO, WHO EXACTLY IS THIS GIANT DOOFUS...?
Hey there.
SHFF
SAIKAWA, THIS IS...
......
WHO DO YOU THINK IT IS?
DUN DUN!!
A POP QUIZ?!

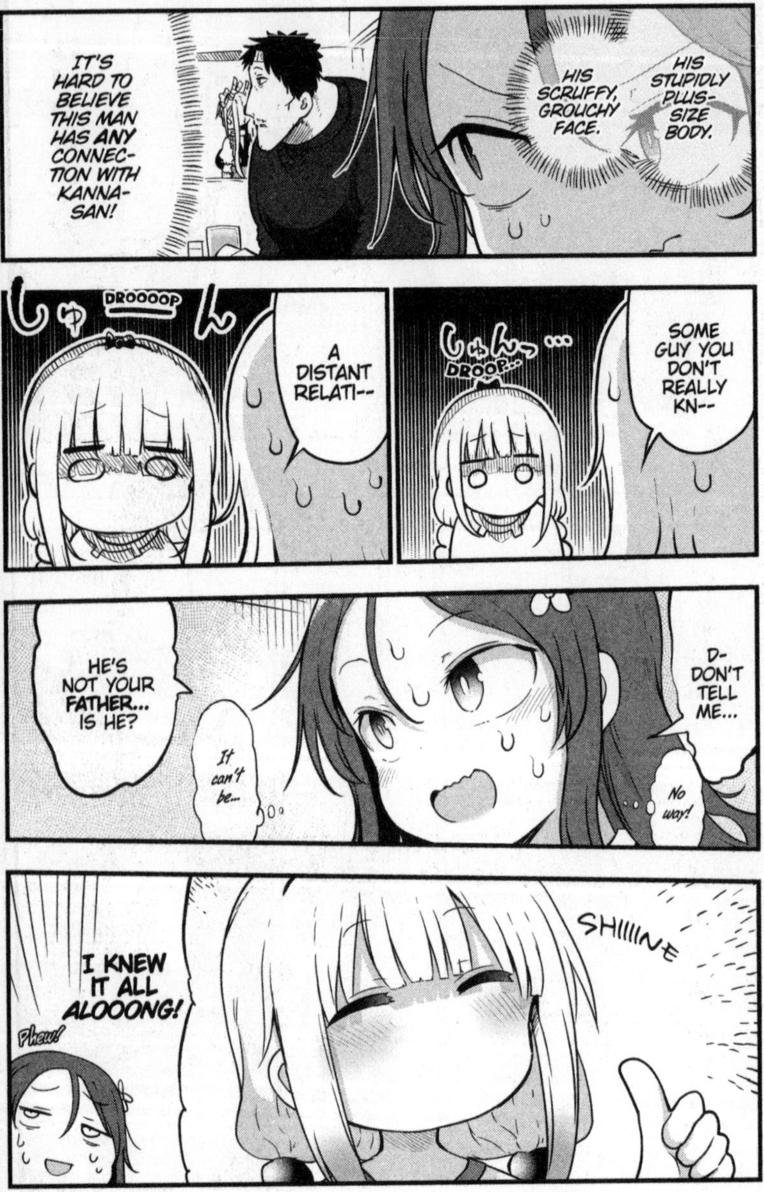
HIS STUPIDLY PLUS-SIZE BODY.
HIS SCRUFFY, GROUCHY FACE.
IT'S HARD TO BELIEVE THIS MAN HAS ANY CONNECTION WITH KANNA-SAN!
しゅんっ…
DROOP...
SOME GUY YOU DON'T REALLY KN--
しゅん
DROOOOP
A DISTANT RELATI--
D-DON'T TELL ME...
No way!
It can't be...
HE'S NOT YOUR FATHER... IS HE?
SHIIIINE
I KNEW IT ALL ALOOONG!
Phew!

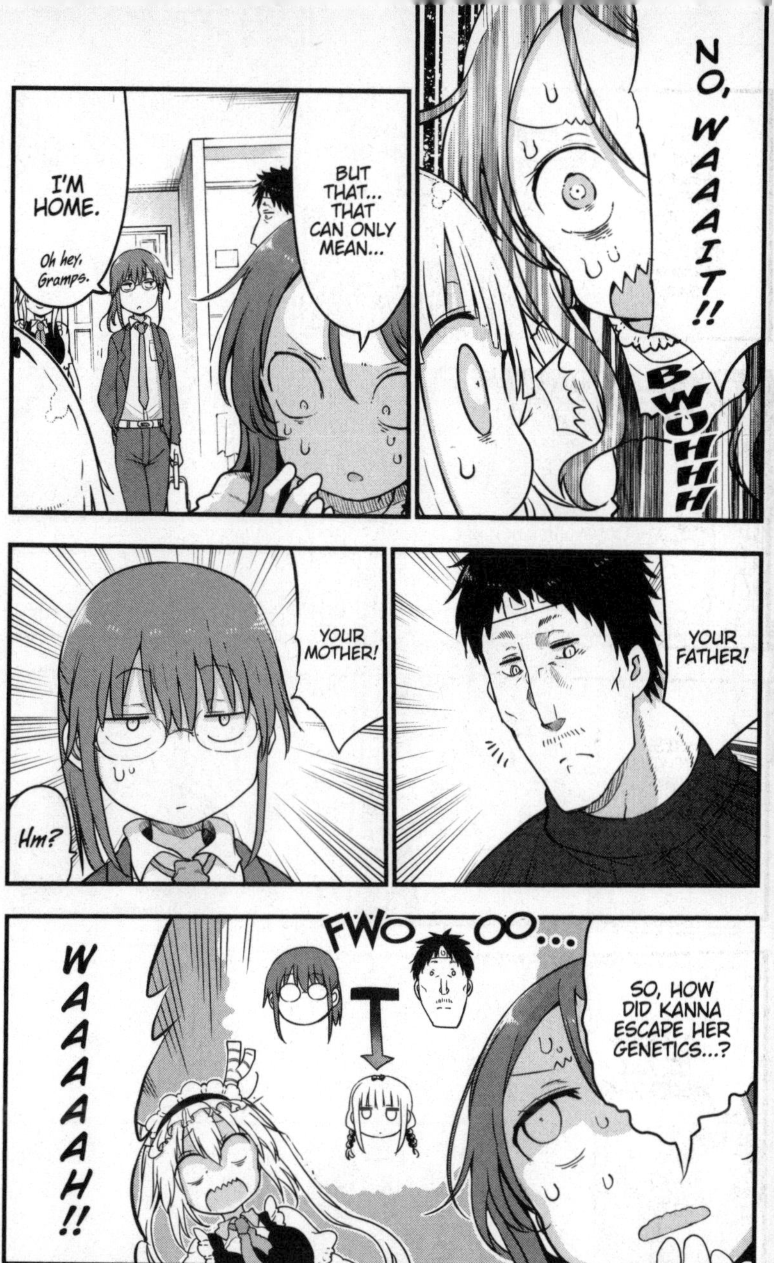
NO, WAAAAIT!!
BWUHHH
BUT THAT... THAT CAN ONLY MEAN...
I'M HOME.
Oh hey, Gramps.
YOUR FATHER!
YOUR MOTHER!
Hm?
SO, HOW DID KANNA ESCAPE HER GENETICS...?
FWO...OO...
WAAAAAAAH!!

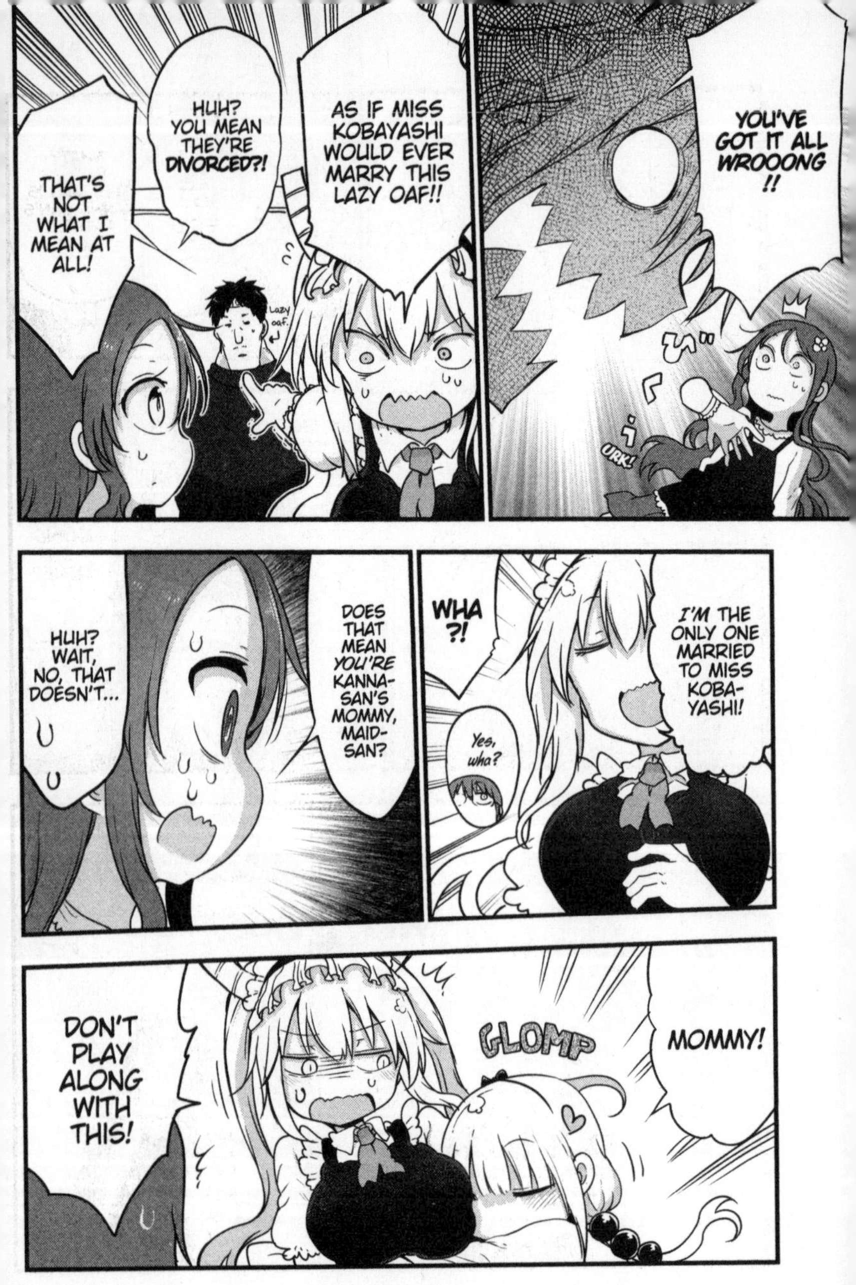
YOU'VE GOT IT ALL WROOONG!!
URK!
AS IF MISS KOBAYASHI WOULD EVER MARRY THIS LAZY OAF!!
HUH? YOU MEAN THEY'RE DIVORCED?!
Lazy oaf.
THAT'S NOT WHAT I MEAN AT ALL!
I'M THE ONLY ONE MARRIED TO MISS KOBAYASHI!
WHA?!
Yes, wha?
DOES THAT MEAN YOU'RE KANNA-SAN'S MOMMY, MAID-SAN?
HUH? WAIT, NO, THAT DOESN'T...
MOMMY!
GLOMP
DON'T PLAY ALONG WITH THIS!

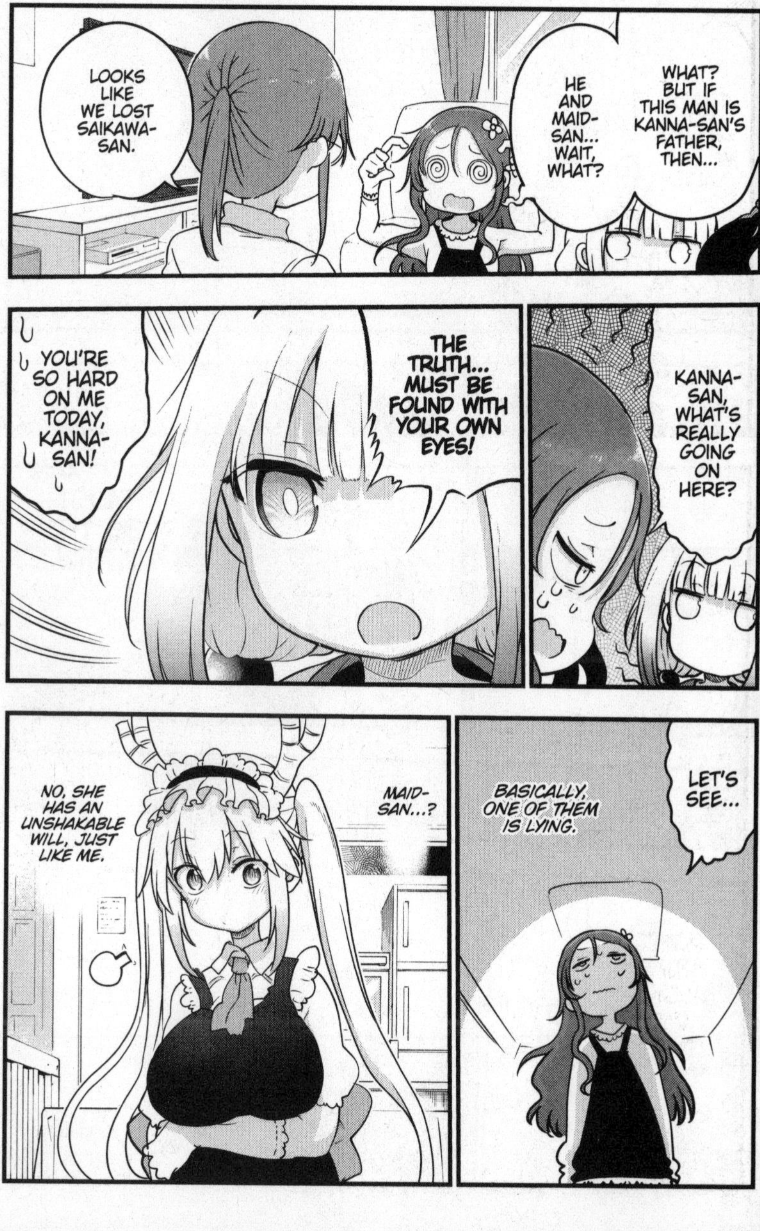
WHAT? BUT IF THIS MAN IS KANNA-SAN'S FATHER, THEN...
HE AND MAID-SAN... WAIT, WHAT?
LOOKS LIKE WE LOST SAIKAWA-SAN.
KANNA-SAN, WHAT'S REALLY GOING ON HERE?
THE TRUTH... MUST BE FOUND WITH YOUR OWN EYES!
YOU'RE SO HARD ON ME TODAY, KANNA-SAN!
LET'S SEE...
BASICALLY, ONE OF THEM IS LYING.
MAID-SAN...?
NO, SHE HAS AN UNSHAKABLE WILL, JUST LIKE ME.

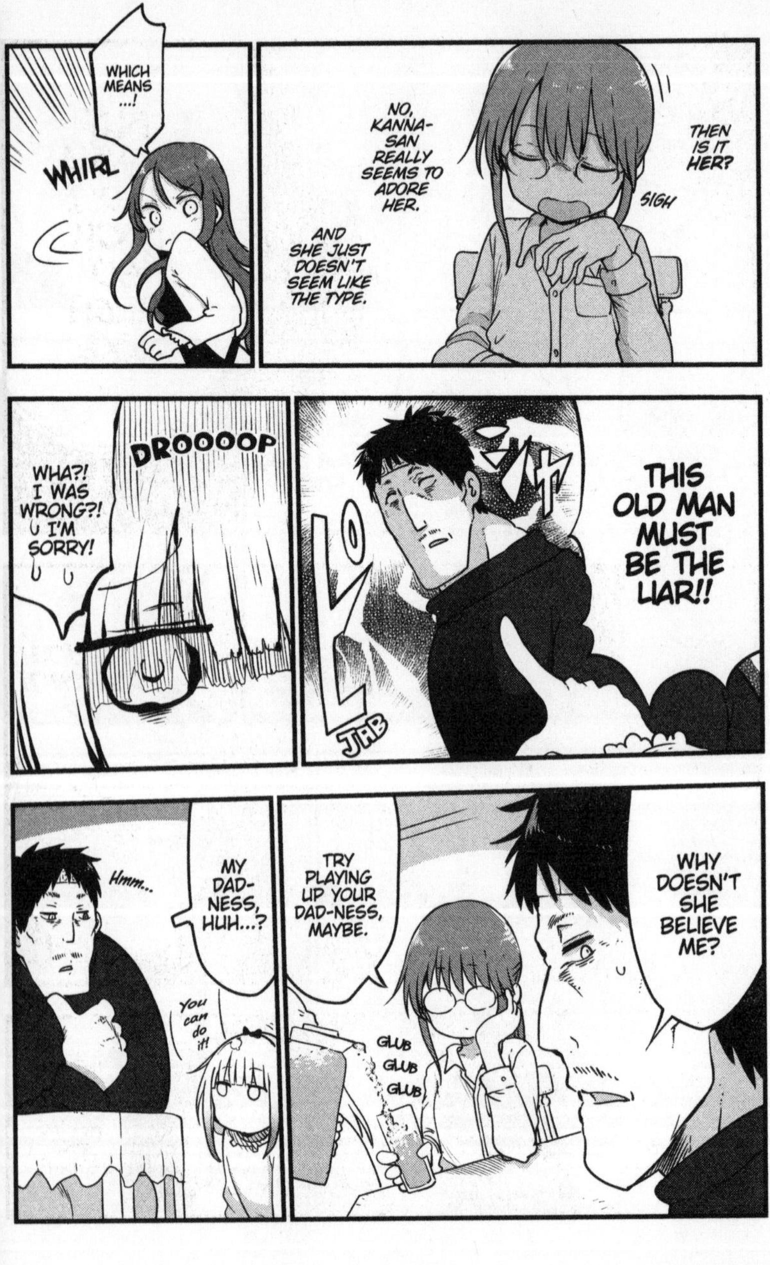
THEN IS IT HER?
SIGH
NO, KANNA-SAN REALLY SEEMS TO ADORE HER.
AND SHE JUST DOESN'T SEEM LIKE THE TYPE.
WHICH MEANS ...!
WHIRL
THIS OLD MAN MUST BE THE LIAR!!
JAB
DROOOOP
WHA?! I WAS WRONG?! I'M SORRY!
WHY DOESN'T SHE BELIEVE ME?
TRY PLAYING UP YOUR DAD-NESS, MAYBE.
GLUB
GLUB
GLUB
MY DAD-NESS, HUH...?
Hmm...
You can do it!

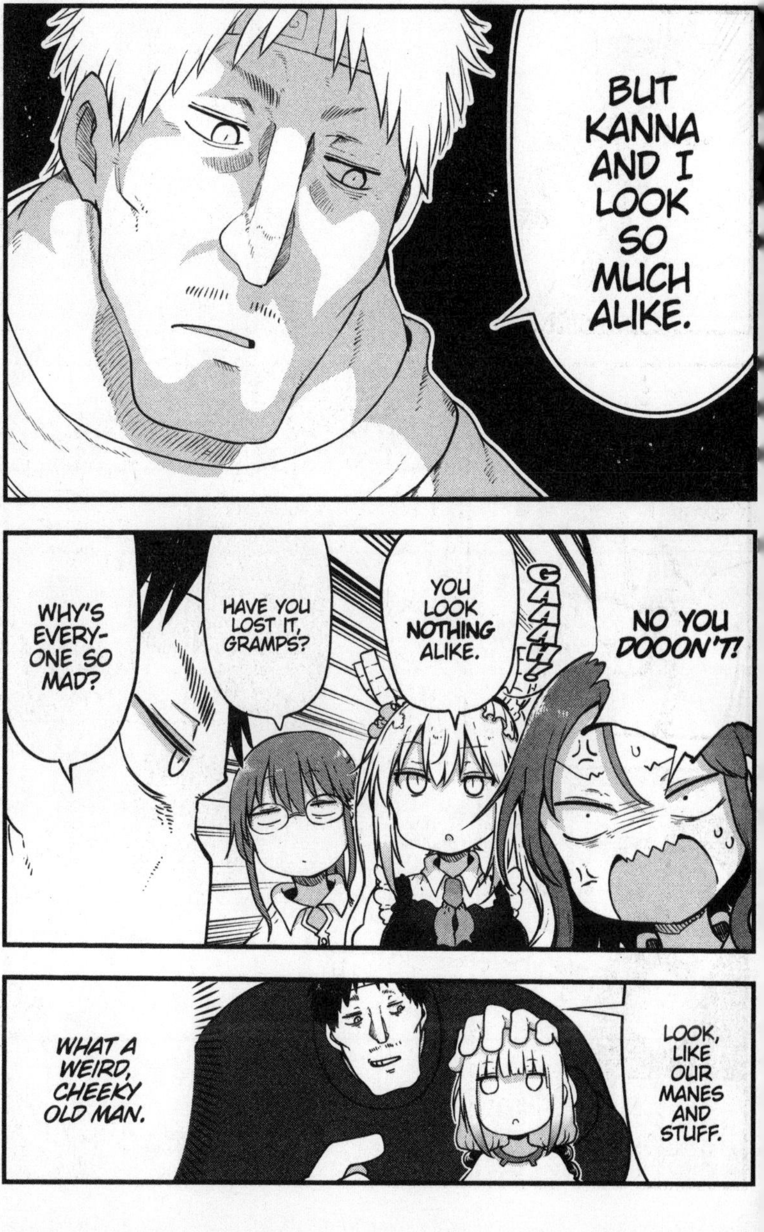
BUT KANNA AND I LOOK SO MUCH ALIKE.
NO YOU DOOON'T!
GAAAAH!
YOU LOOK NOTHING ALIKE.
HAVE YOU LOST IT, GRAMPS?
WHY'S EVERY-ONE SO MAD?
LOOK, LIKE OUR MANES AND STUFF.
WHAT A WEIRD, CHEEKY OLD MAN.

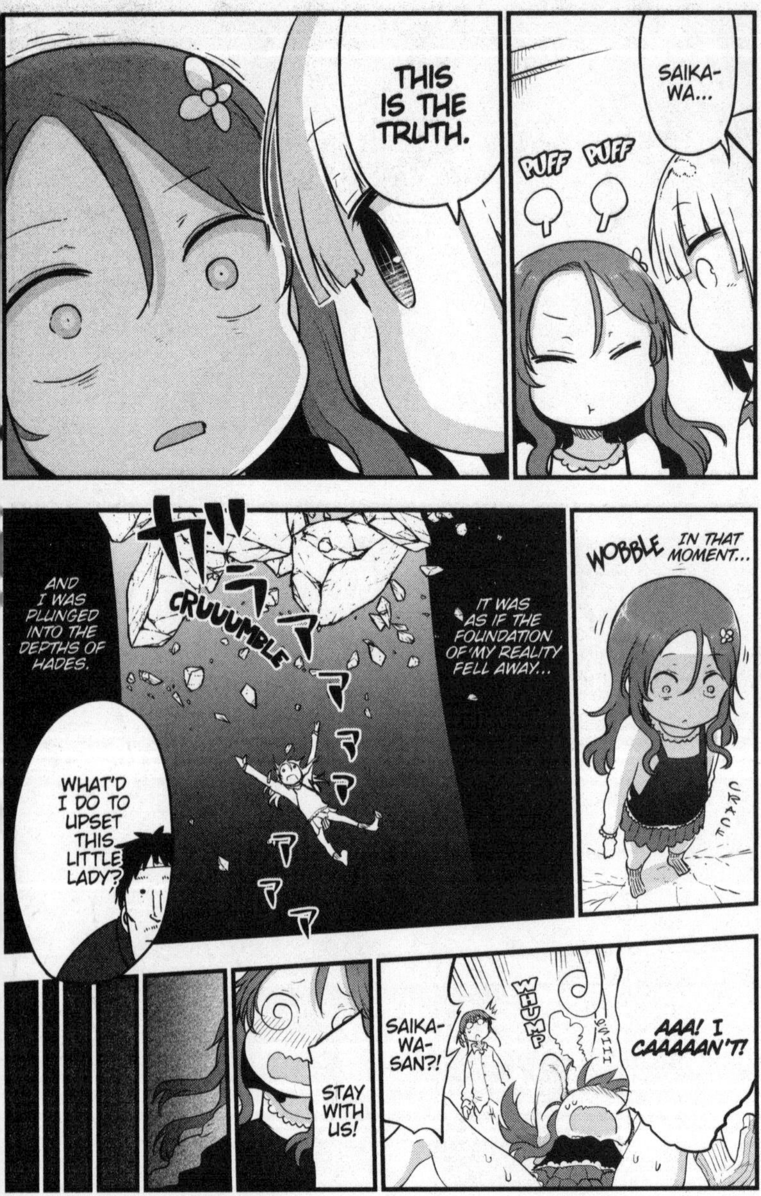
SAIKA-WA...
PUFF PUFF
THIS IS THE TRUTH.
WOBBLE
IN THAT MOMENT...
CRACK
IT WAS AS IF THE FOUNDATION OF MY REALITY FELL AWAY...
CRUUUMBLE
AND I WAS PLUNGED INTO THE DEPTHS OF HADES.
WHAT'D I DO TO UPSET THIS LITTLE LADY?
AAA! I CAAAAAN'T!
WHUMP
SAIKA-WA-SAN?!
STAY WITH US!

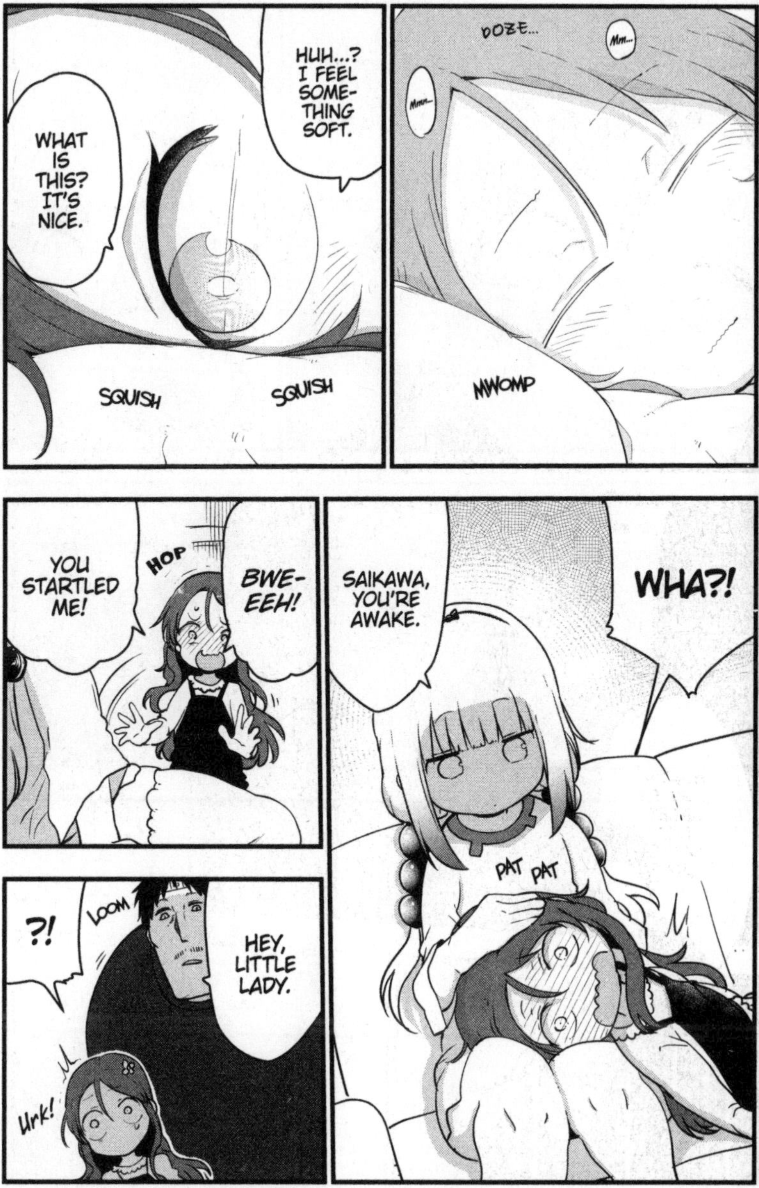
Mm...
DOZE...
Mmm...
MWOMP
HUH...? I FEEL SOME-THING SOFT.
WHAT IS THIS? IT'S NICE.
SQUISH
SQUISH
WHA?!
SAIKAWA, YOU'RE AWAKE.
PAT PAT
BWE-EEH!
HOP
YOU STARTLED ME!
HEY, LITTLE LADY.
LOOM
?!
Urk!

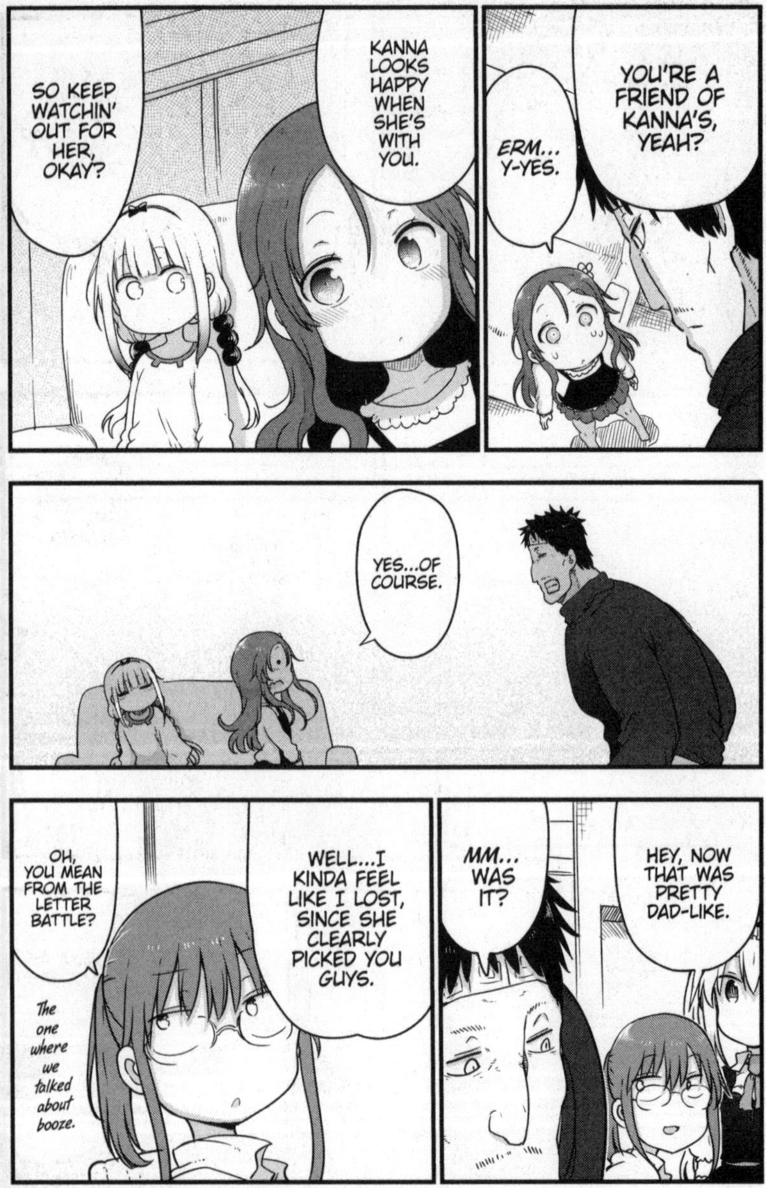
YOU'RE A FRIEND OF KANNA'S, YEAH?
ERM... Y-YES.
KANNA LOOKS HAPPY WHEN SHE'S WITH YOU.
SO KEEP WATCHIN' OUT FOR HER, OKAY?
YES...OF COURSE.
HEY, NOW THAT WAS PRETTY DAD-LIKE.
MM... WAS IT?
WELL...I KINDA FEEL LIKE I LOST, SINCE SHE CLEARLY PICKED YOU GUYS.
OH, YOU MEAN FROM THE LETTER BATTLE?
The one where we talked about booze.

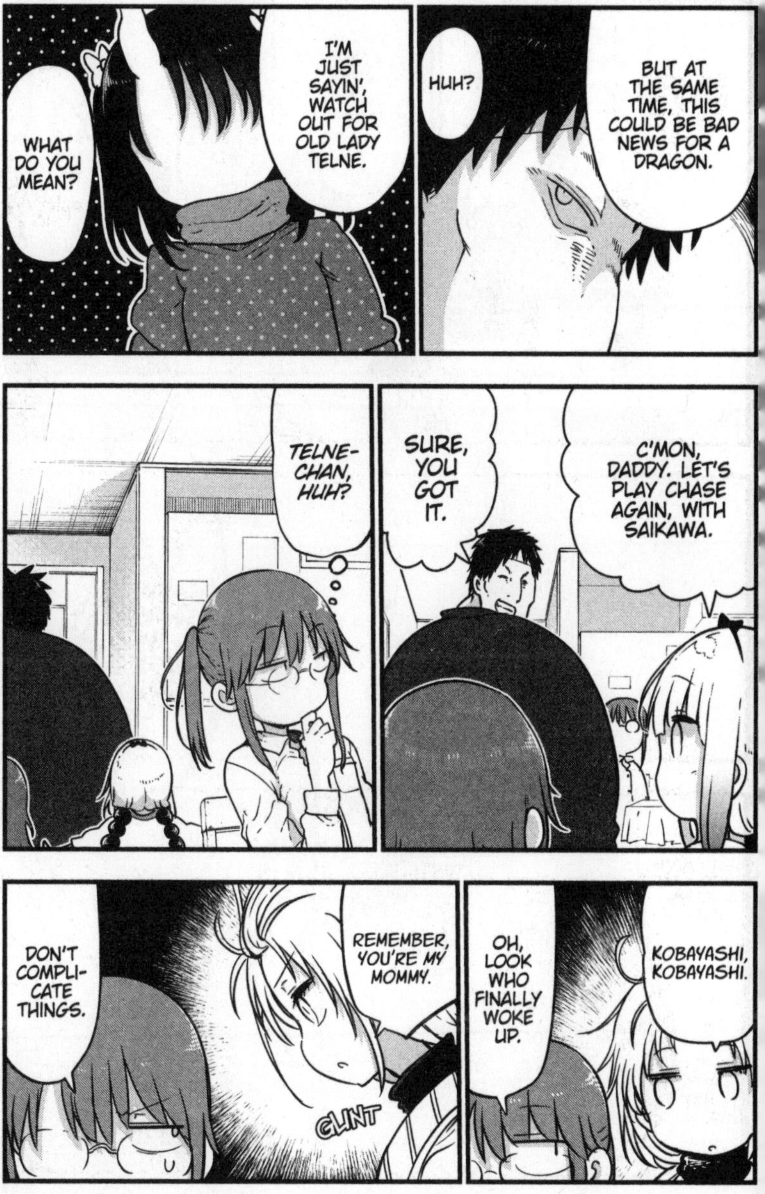
BUT AT THE SAME TIME, THIS COULD BE BAD NEWS FOR A DRAGON.
HUH?
I'M JUST SAYIN', WATCH OUT FOR OLD LADY TELNE.
WHAT DO YOU MEAN?
C'MON, DADDY. LET'S PLAY CHASE AGAIN, WITH SAIKAWA.
SURE, YOU GOT IT.
TELNE-CHAN, HUH?
KOBAYASHI, KOBAYASHI.
OH, LOOK WHO FINALLY WOKE UP.
REMEMBER, YOU'RE MY MOMMY.
GLINT
DON'T COMPLI-CATE THINGS.

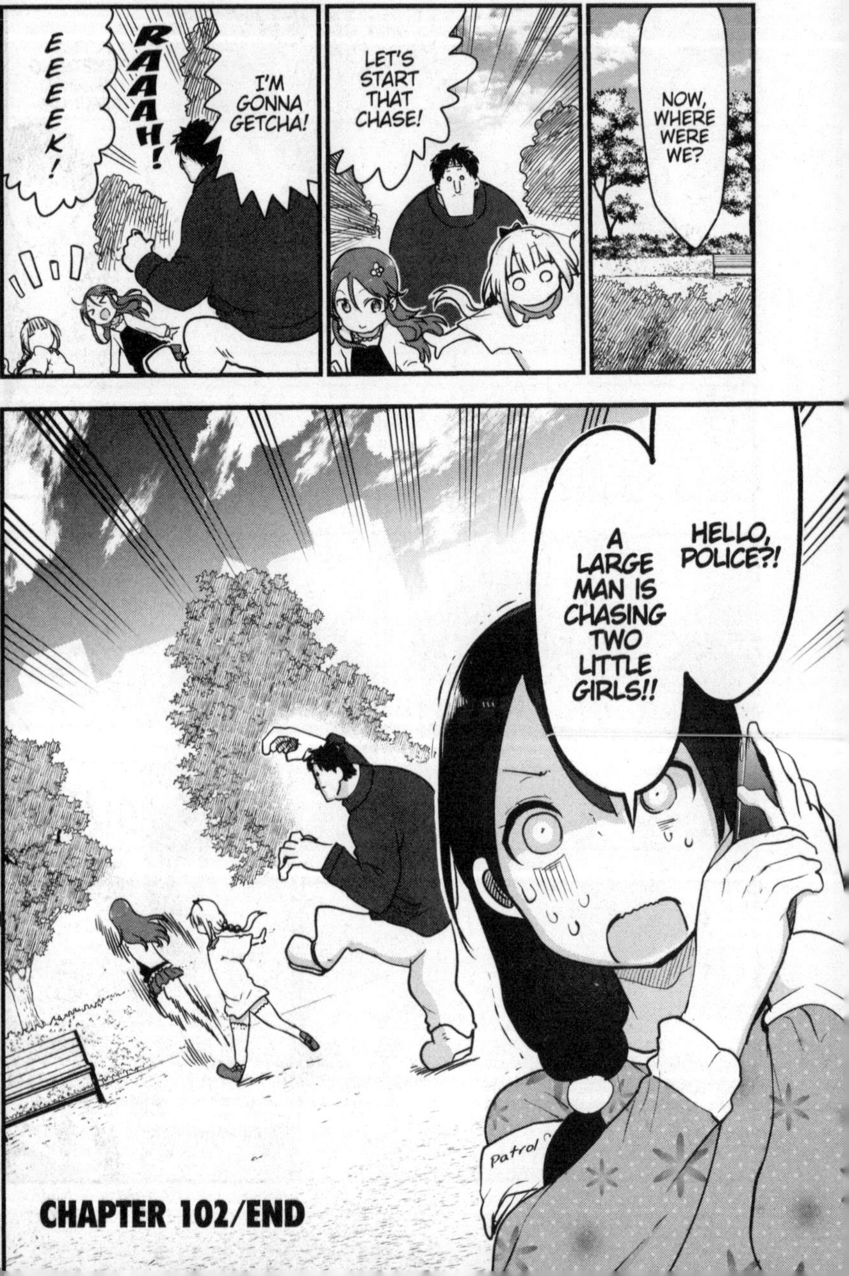
NOW, WHERE WERE WE?
LET'S START THAT CHASE!
I'M GONNA GETCHA!
RAAAAH!
EEEEK!
HELLO, POLICE?!
A LARGE MAN IS CHASING TWO LITTLE GIRLS!!
Patrol

CHAPTER 102/END

CHAPTER 103

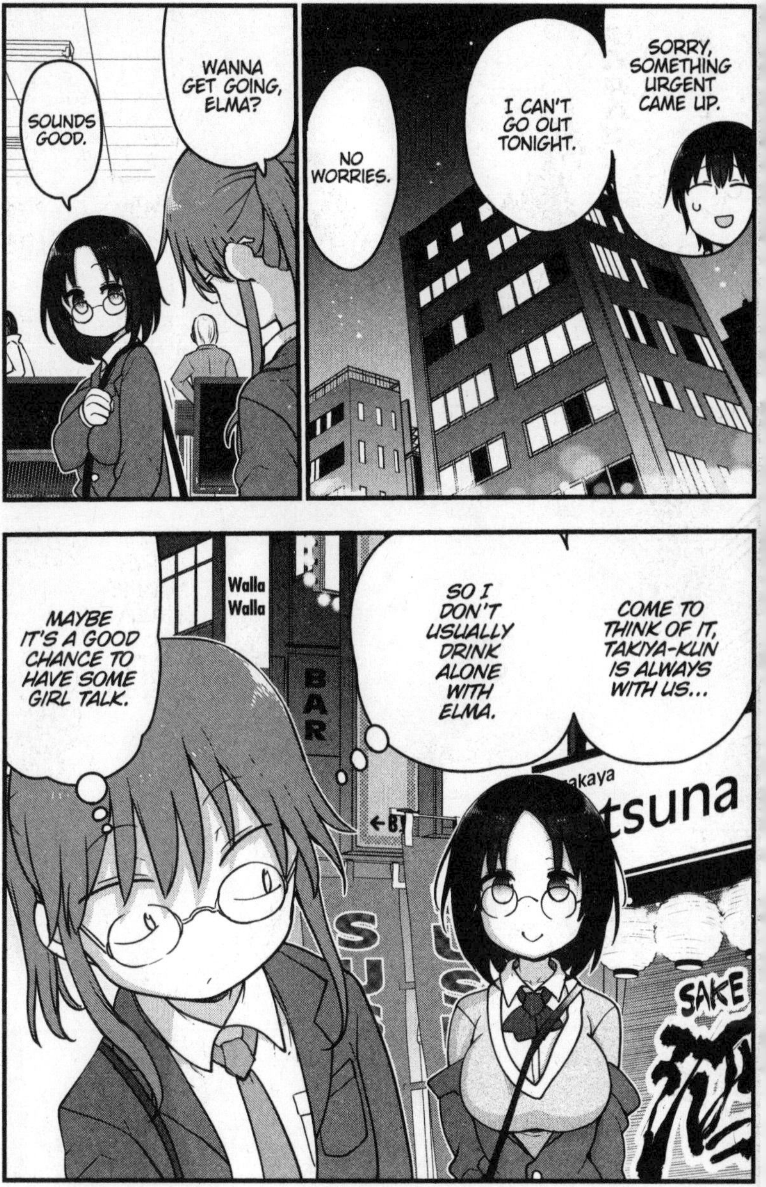
SORRY, SOMETHING URGENT CAME UP.
I CAN'T GO OUT TONIGHT.
NO WORRIES.
WANNA GET GOING, ELMA?
SOUNDS GOOD.
COME TO THINK OF IT, TAKIYA-KUN IS ALWAYS WITH US...
SO I DON'T USUALLY DRINK ALONE WITH ELMA.
SAKE
BAR
Walla Walla
MAYBE IT'S A GOOD CHANCE TO HAVE SOME GIRL TALK.

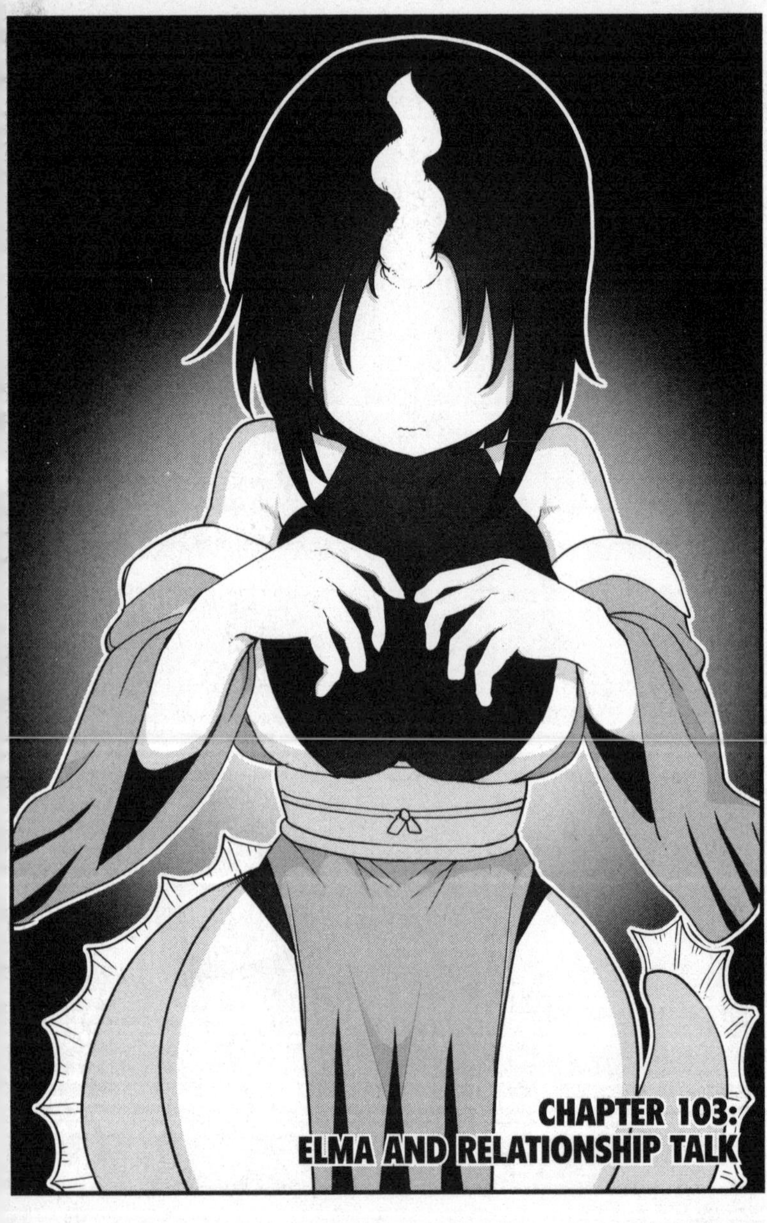
CHAPTER 103:
ELMA AND RELATIONSHIP TALK

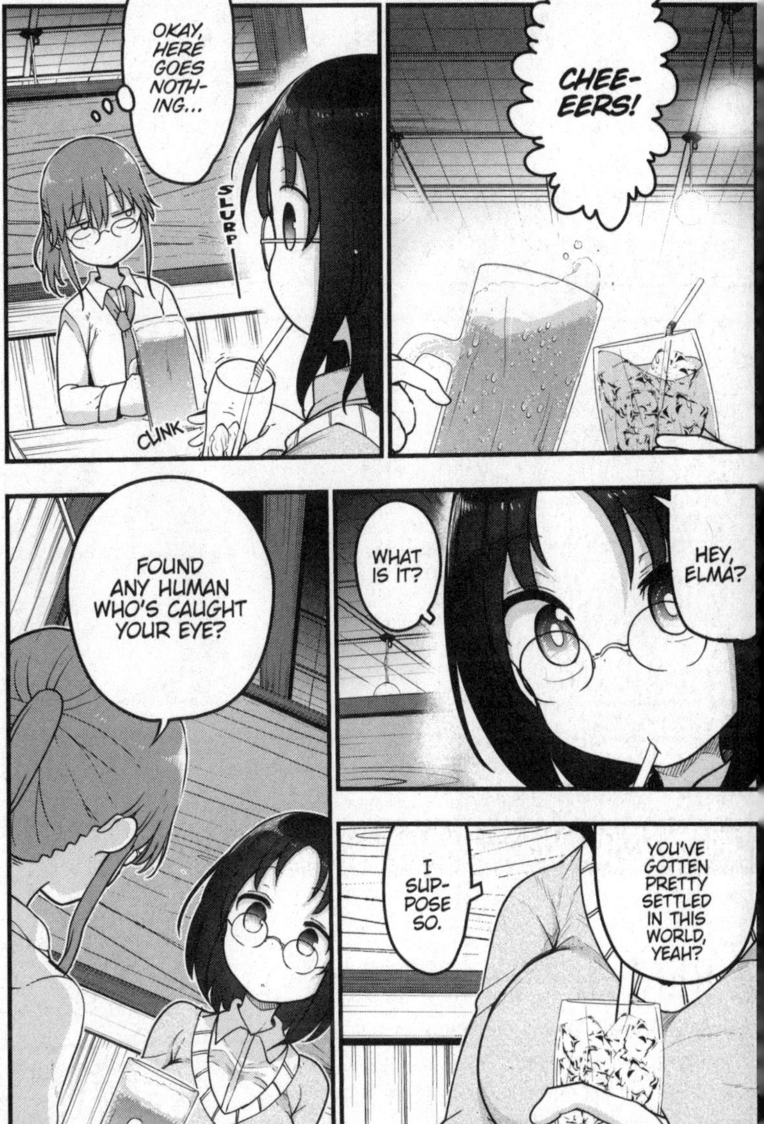
CHEEE-EERS!
OKAY, HERE GOES NOTHING...
SLURP
CUNK
HEY, ELMA?
WHAT IS IT?
YOU'VE GOTTEN PRETTY SETTLED IN THIS WORLD, YEAH?
I SUP-POSE SO.
FOUND ANY HUMAN WHO'S CAUGHT YOUR EYE?

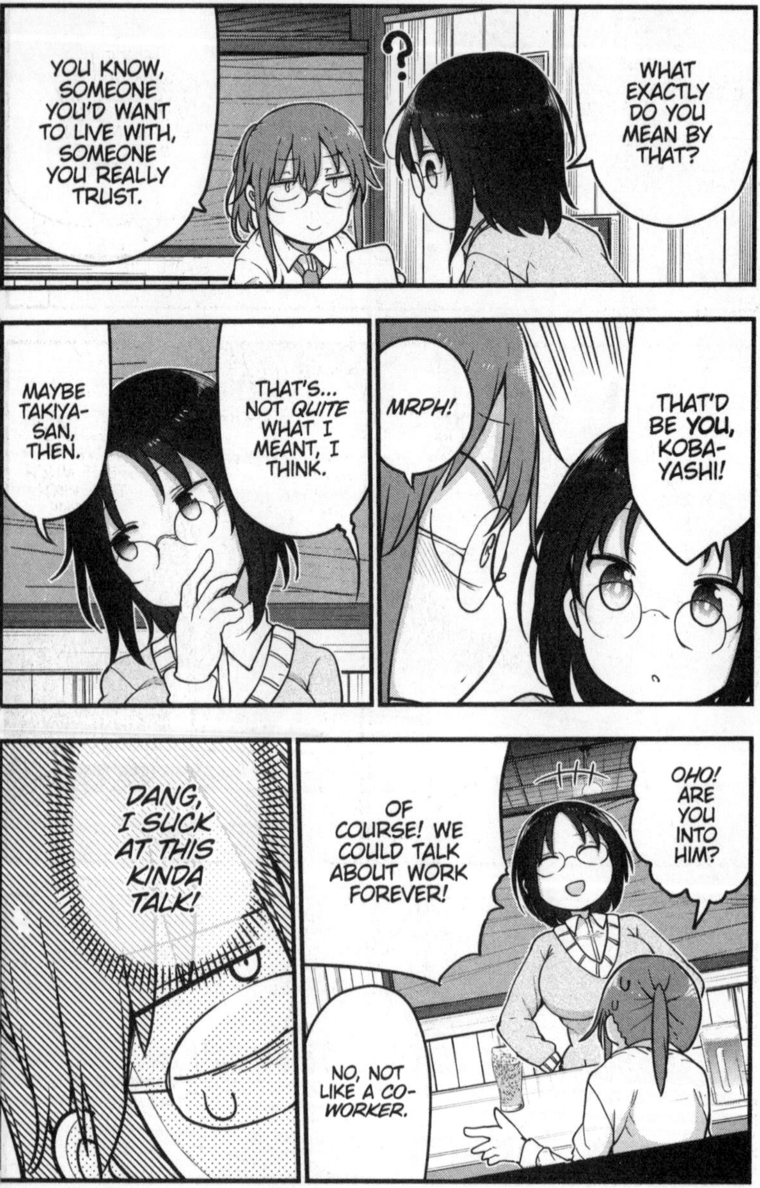
WHAT EXACTLY DO YOU MEAN BY THAT?
?
YOU KNOW, SOMEONE YOU'D WANT TO LIVE WITH, SOMEONE YOU REALLY TRUST.
THAT'D BE YOU, KOBA-YASHI!
MRPH!
THAT'S... NOT *QUITE* WHAT I MEANT, I THINK.
MAYBE TAKIYA-SAN, THEN.
OHO! ARE YOU INTO HIM?
OF COURSE! WE COULD TALK ABOUT WORK FOREVER!
NO, NOT LIKE A CO-WORKER.
DANG, I SUCK AT THIS KINDA TALK!

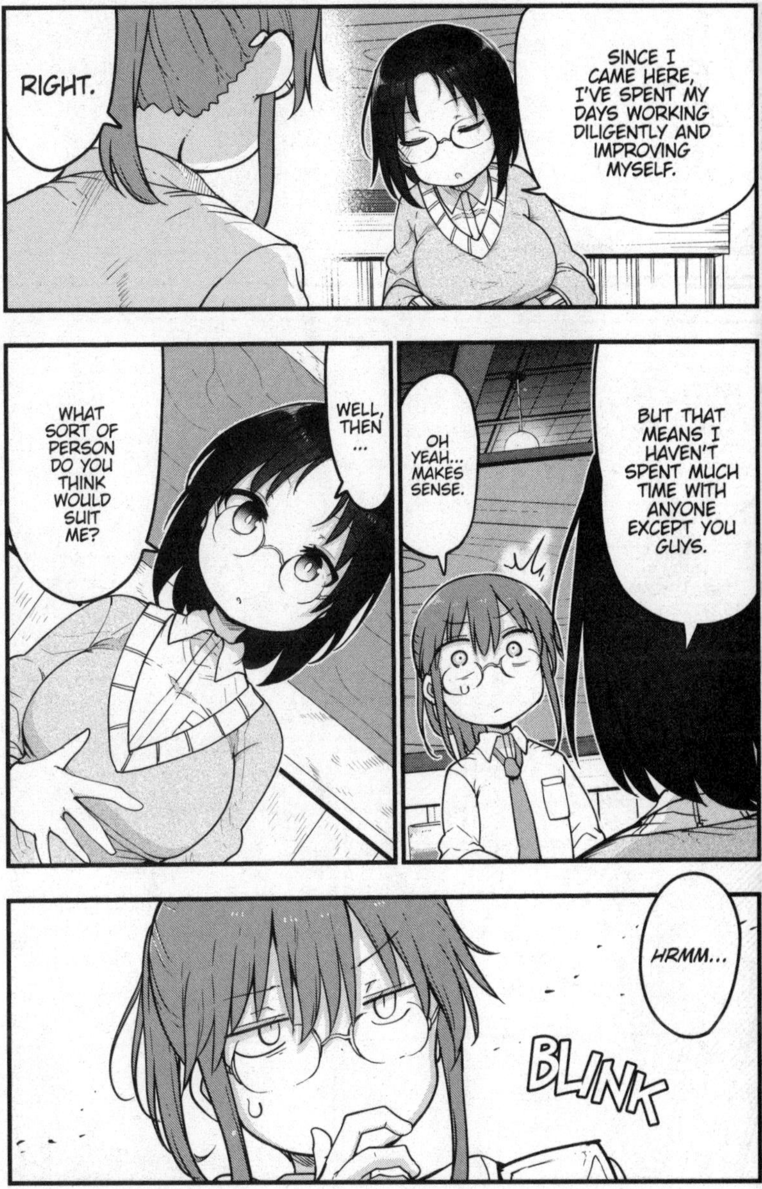
SINCE I CAME HERE, I'VE SPENT MY DAYS WORKING DILIGENTLY AND IMPROVING MYSELF.
RIGHT.
BUT THAT MEANS I HAVEN'T SPENT MUCH TIME WITH ANYONE EXCEPT YOU GUYS.
OH YEAH... MAKES SENSE.
WELL, THEN ...
WHAT SORT OF PERSON DO YOU THINK WOULD SUIT ME?
HRMM...
BLINK

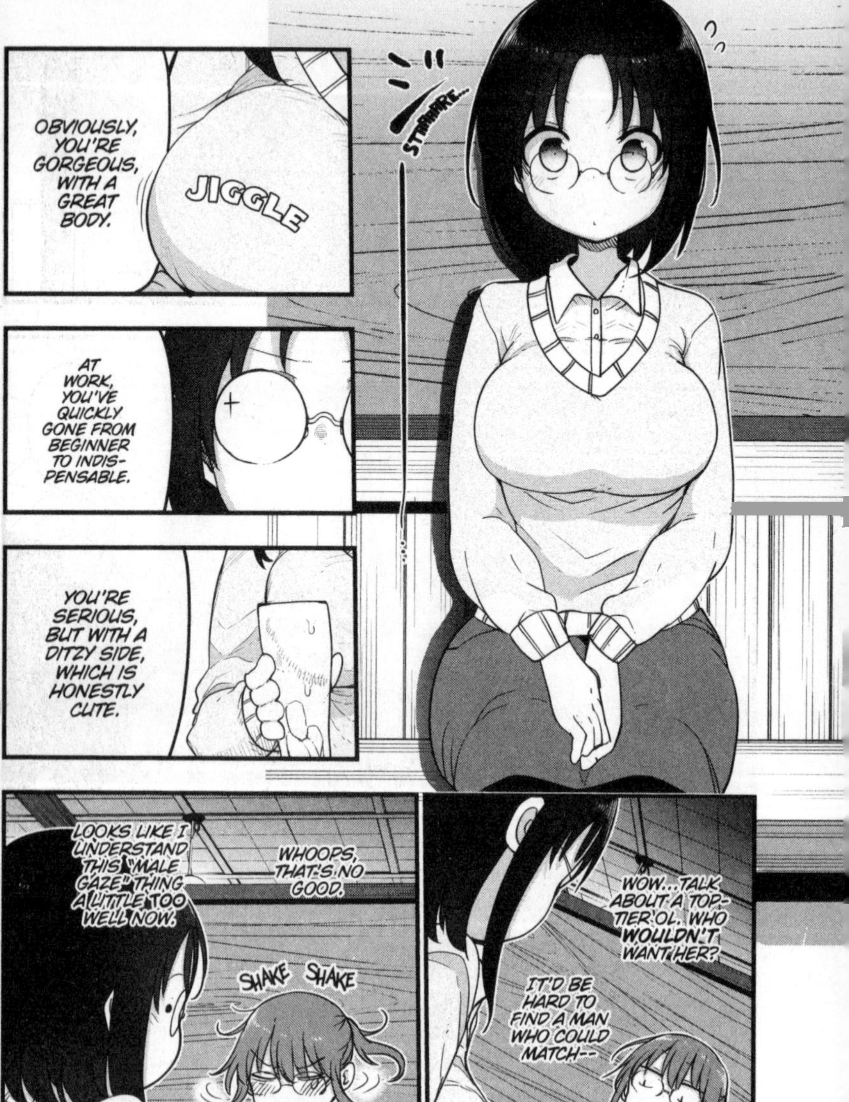
STARRRE...
OBVIOUSLY, YOU'RE GORGEOUS, WITH A GREAT BODY.
JIGGLE
AT WORK, YOU'VE QUICKLY GONE FROM BEGINNER TO INDIS-PENSABLE.
YOU'RE SERIOUS, BUT WITH A DITZY SIDE, WHICH IS HONESTLY CUTE.
WOW... TALK ABOUT A TOP-TIER OL. WHO WOULDN'T WANT HER?
IT'D BE HARD TO FIND A MAN WHO COULD MATCH--
LOOKS LIKE I UNDERSTAND THIS "MALE GAZE" THING A LITTLE TOO WELL NOW.
WHOOPS, THAT'S NO GOOD.
SHAKE SHAKE

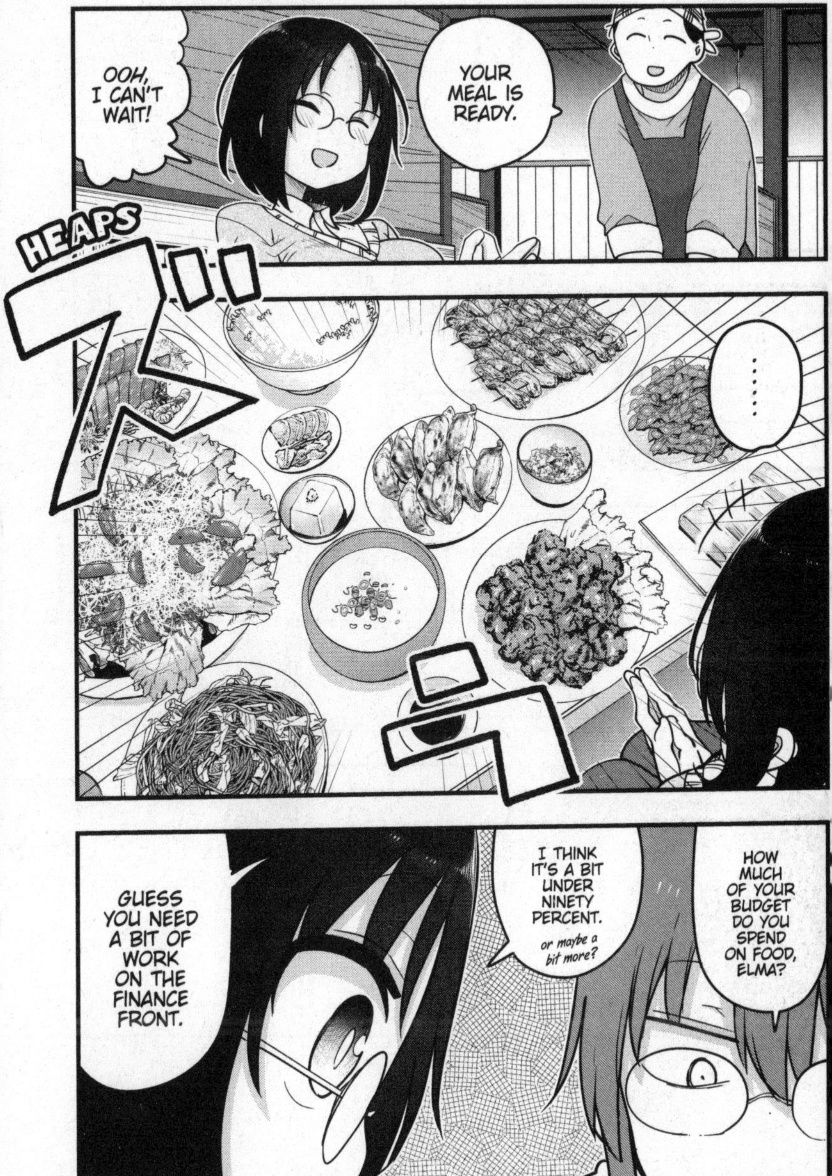
YOUR MEAL IS READY.
OOH, I CAN'T WAIT!
HEAPS
......
HOW MUCH OF YOUR BUDGET DO YOU SPEND ON FOOD, ELMA?
I THINK IT'S A BIT UNDER NINETY PERCENT.
or maybe a bit more?
GUESS YOU NEED A BIT OF WORK ON THE FINANCE FRONT.

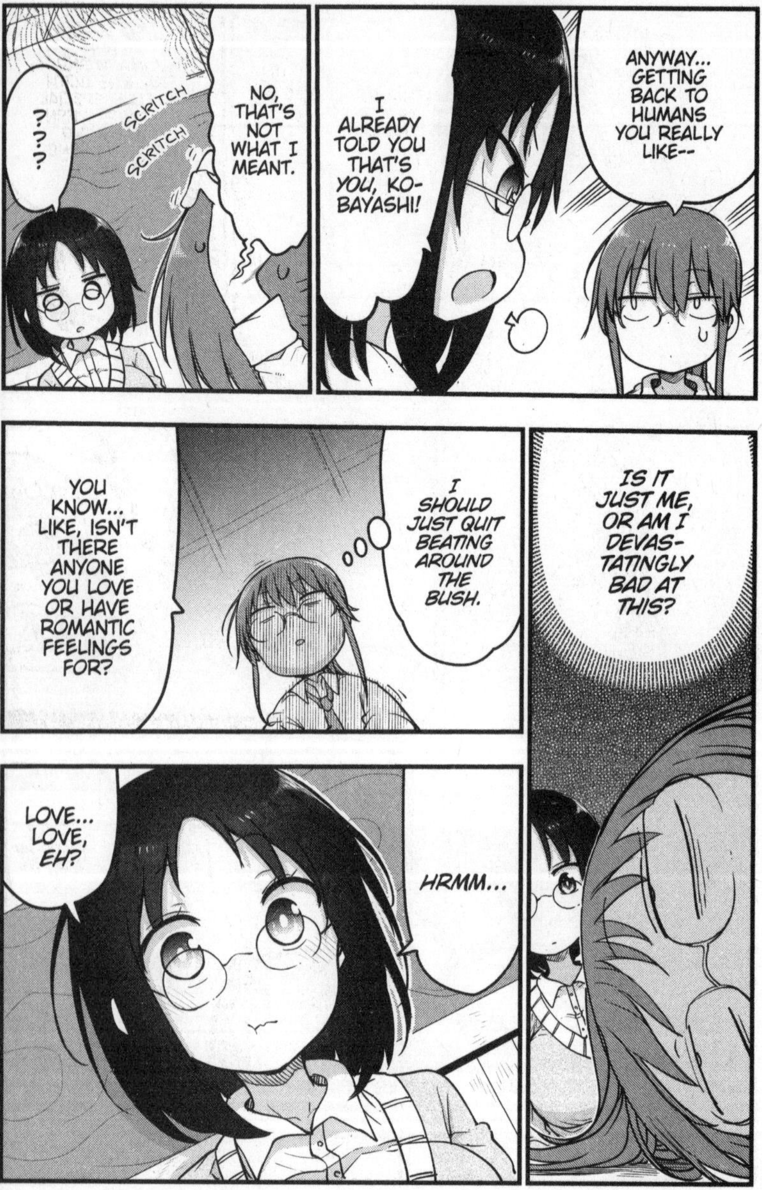
ANYWAY... GETTING BACK TO HUMANS YOU REALLY LIKE--
I ALREADY TOLD YOU THAT'S YOU, KO-BAYASHI!
NO, THAT'S NOT WHAT I MEANT.
SCRITCH
SCRITCH
?.?.?
IS IT JUST ME, OR AM I DEVAS-TATINGLY BAD AT THIS?
I SHOULD JUST QUIT BEATING AROUND THE BUSH.
YOU KNOW... LIKE, ISN'T THERE ANYONE YOU LOVE OR HAVE ROMANTIC FEELINGS FOR?
HRMM...
LOVE... LOVE, EH?

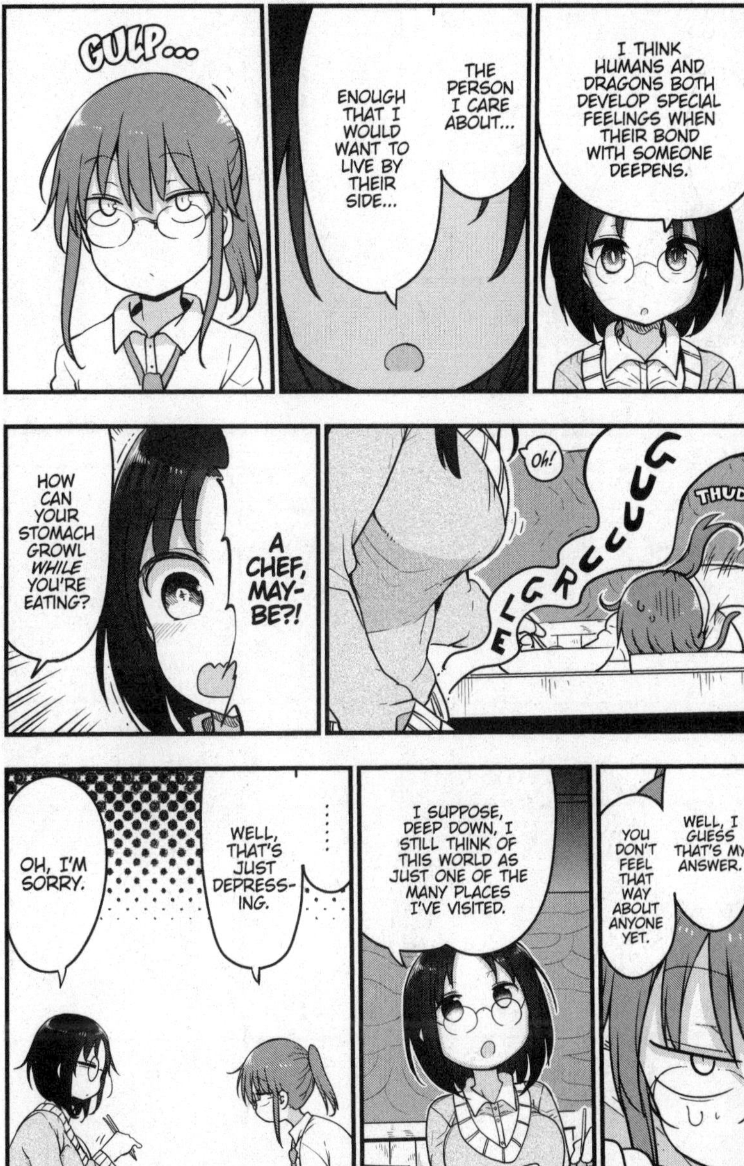
I THINK HUMANS AND DRAGONS BOTH DEVELOP SPECIAL FEELINGS WHEN THEIR BOND WITH SOMEONE DEEPENS.
THE PERSON I CARE ABOUT...
ENOUGH THAT I WOULD WANT TO LIVE BY THEIR SIDE...
GULP...
Oh!
GUUUUURGLE
THUD
A CHEF, MAY-BE?!
HOW CAN YOUR STOMACH GROWL *WHILE* YOU'RE EATING?
WELL, I GUESS THAT'S MY ANSWER.
YOU DON'T FEEL THAT WAY ABOUT ANYONE YET.
I SUPPOSE, DEEP DOWN, I STILL THINK OF THIS WORLD AS JUST ONE OF THE MANY PLACES I'VE VISITED.
......
WELL, THAT'S JUST DEPRESS-ING.
OH, I'M SORRY.

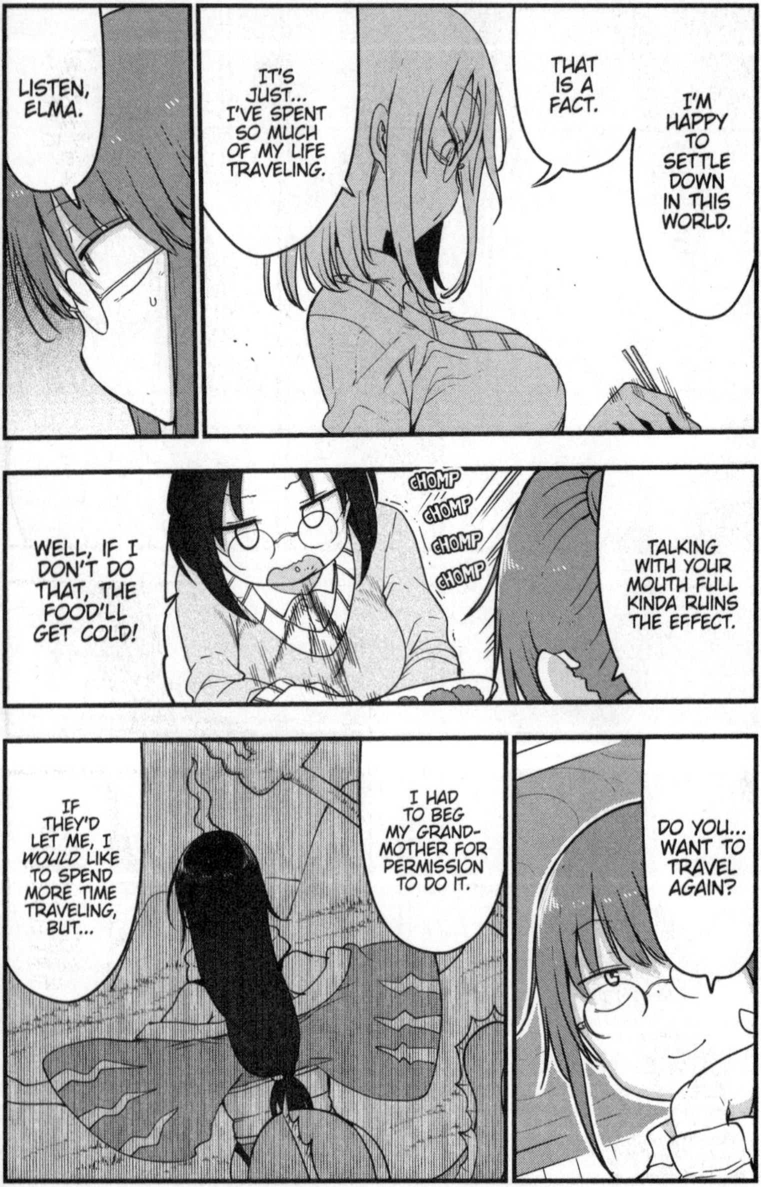
I'M HAPPY TO SETTLE DOWN IN THIS WORLD.
THAT IS A FACT.
IT'S JUST... I'VE SPENT SO MUCH OF MY LIFE TRAVELING.
LISTEN, ELMA.
TALKING WITH YOUR MOUTH FULL KINDA RUINS THE EFFECT.
CHOMP
CHOMP
CHOMP
CHOMP
WELL, IF I DON'T DO THAT, THE FOOD'LL GET COLD!
DO YOU... WANT TO TRAVEL AGAIN?
I HAD TO BEG MY GRAND-MOTHER FOR PERMISSION TO DO IT.
IF THEY'D LET ME, I *WOULD* LIKE TO SPEND MORE TIME TRAVELING, BUT...

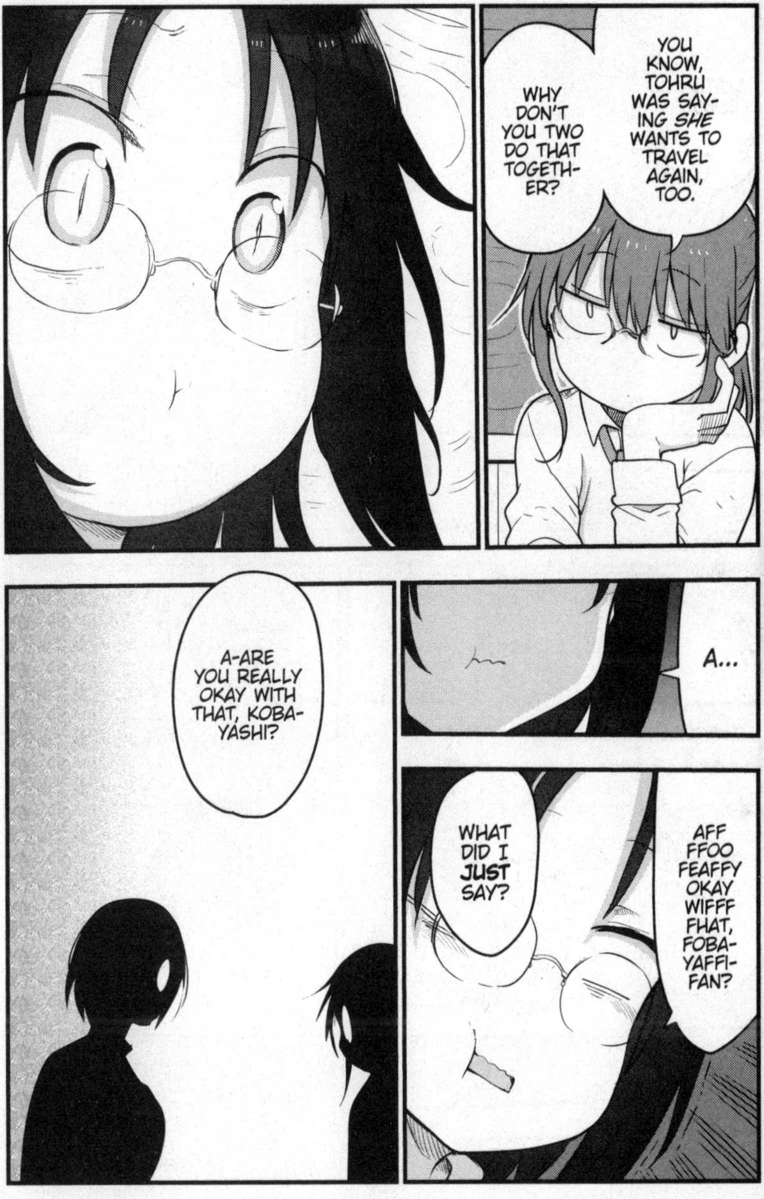
YOU KNOW, TOHRU WAS SAYING *SHE* WANTS TO TRAVEL AGAIN, TOO.
WHY DON'T YOU TWO DO THAT TOGETHER?
A...
AFF FFOO FEAFFY OKAY WIFFF FHAT, FOBA-YAFFI-FAN?
WHAT DID I **JUST** SAY?
A-ARE YOU REALLY OKAY WITH THAT, KOBA-YASHI?

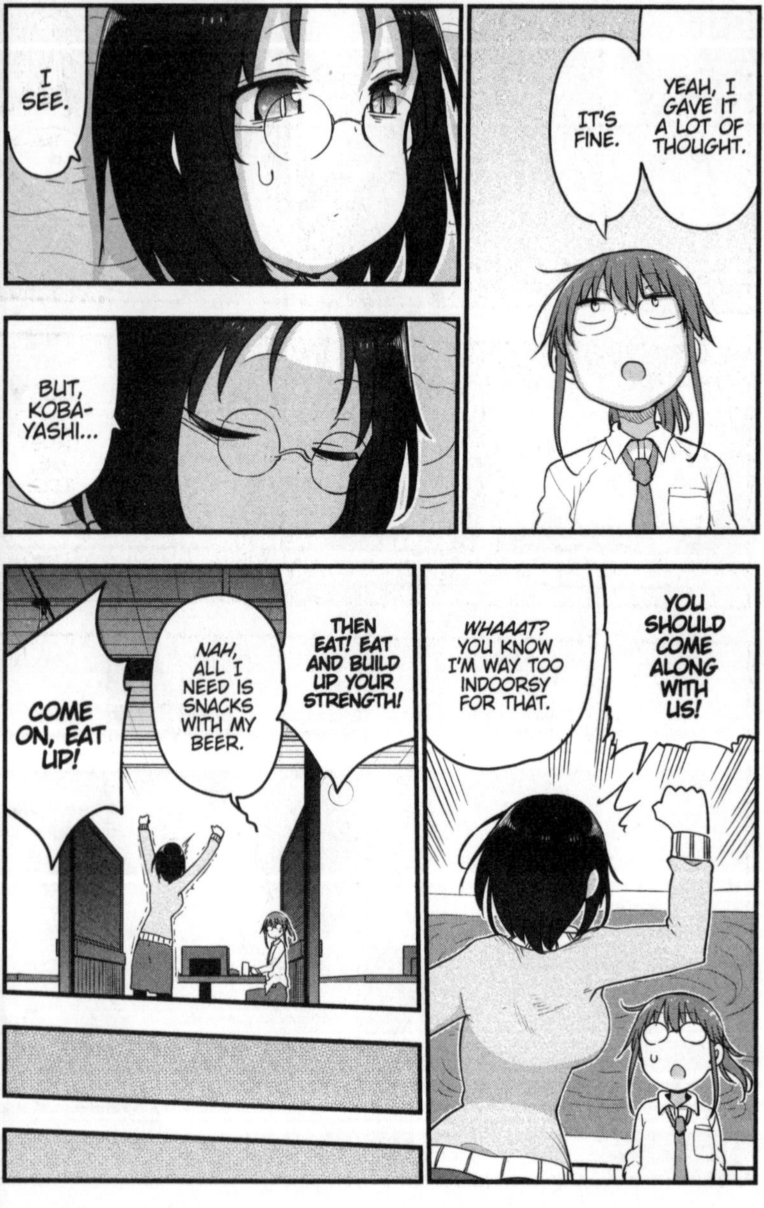
YEAH, I GAVE IT A LOT OF THOUGHT.
IT'S FINE.
I SEE.
BUT, KOBAYASHI...
YOU SHOULD COME ALONG WITH US!
WHAAAT? YOU KNOW I'M WAY TOO INDOORSY FOR THAT.
THEN EAT! EAT AND BUILD UP YOUR STRENGTH!
NAH, ALL I NEED IS SNACKS WITH MY BEER.
COME ON, EAT UP!

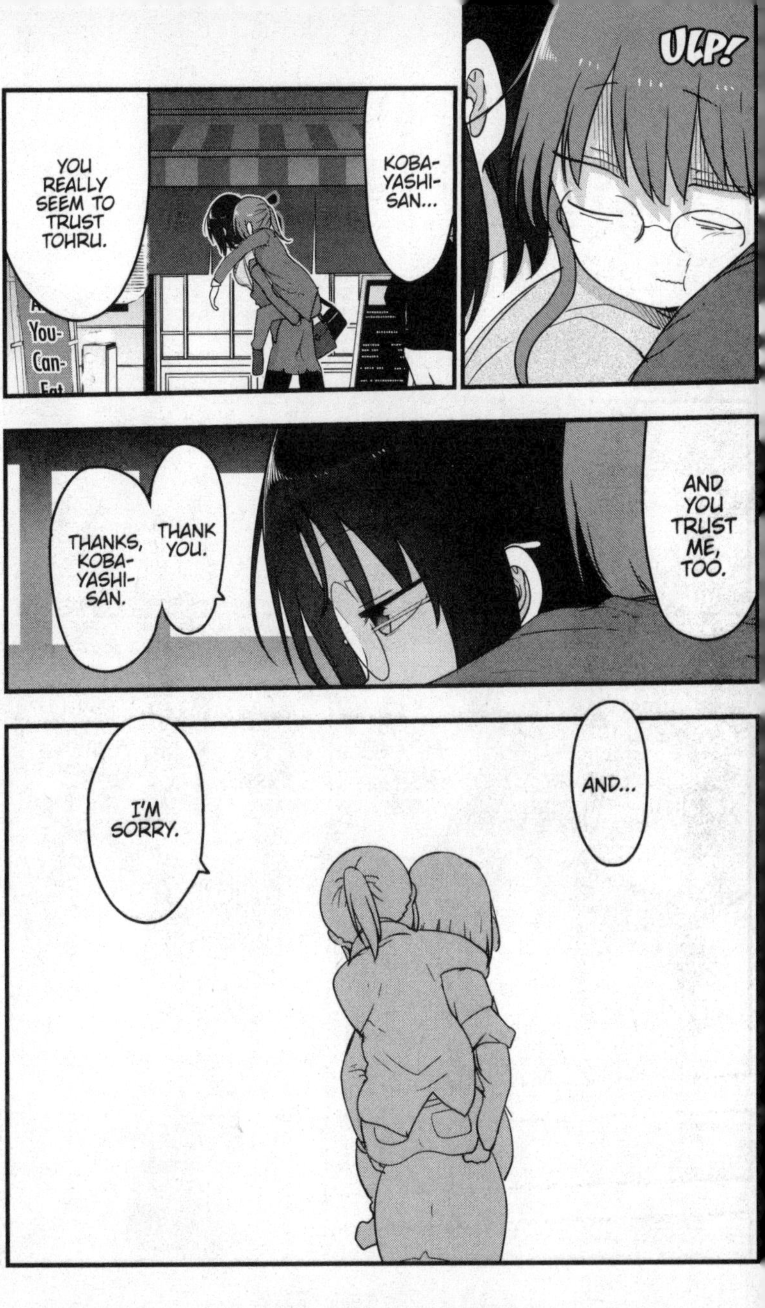
ULP!
KOBA-YASHI-SAN...
YOU REALLY SEEM TO TRUST TOHRU.
You-Can-
AND YOU TRUST ME, TOO.
THANK YOU.
THANKS, KOBA-YASHI-SAN.
AND...
I'M SORRY.

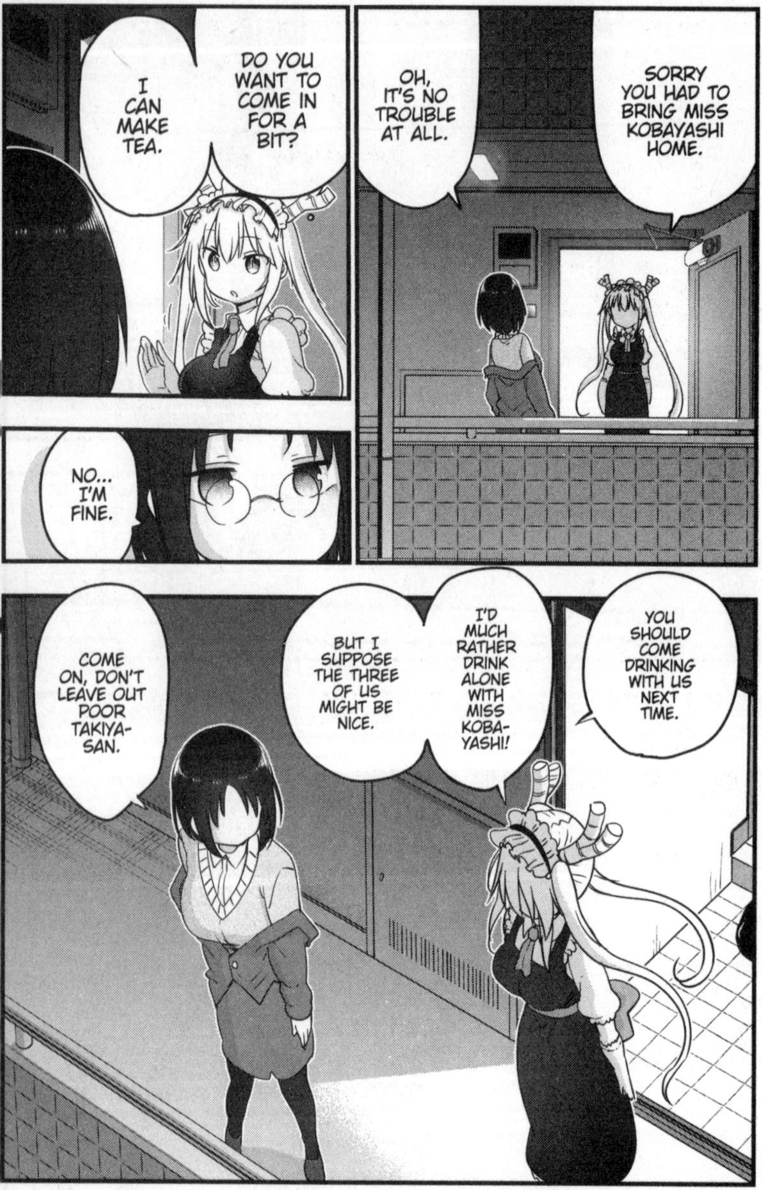
SORRY YOU HAD TO BRING MISS KOBAYASHI HOME.
OH, IT'S NO TROUBLE AT ALL.
DO YOU WANT TO COME IN FOR A BIT?
I CAN MAKE TEA.
NO... I'M FINE.
YOU SHOULD COME DRINKING WITH US NEXT TIME.
I'D MUCH RATHER DRINK ALONE WITH MISS KOBA-YASHI!
BUT I SUPPOSE THE THREE OF US MIGHT BE NICE.
COME ON, DON'T LEAVE OUT POOR TAKIYA-SAN.

CHAPTER 103/END

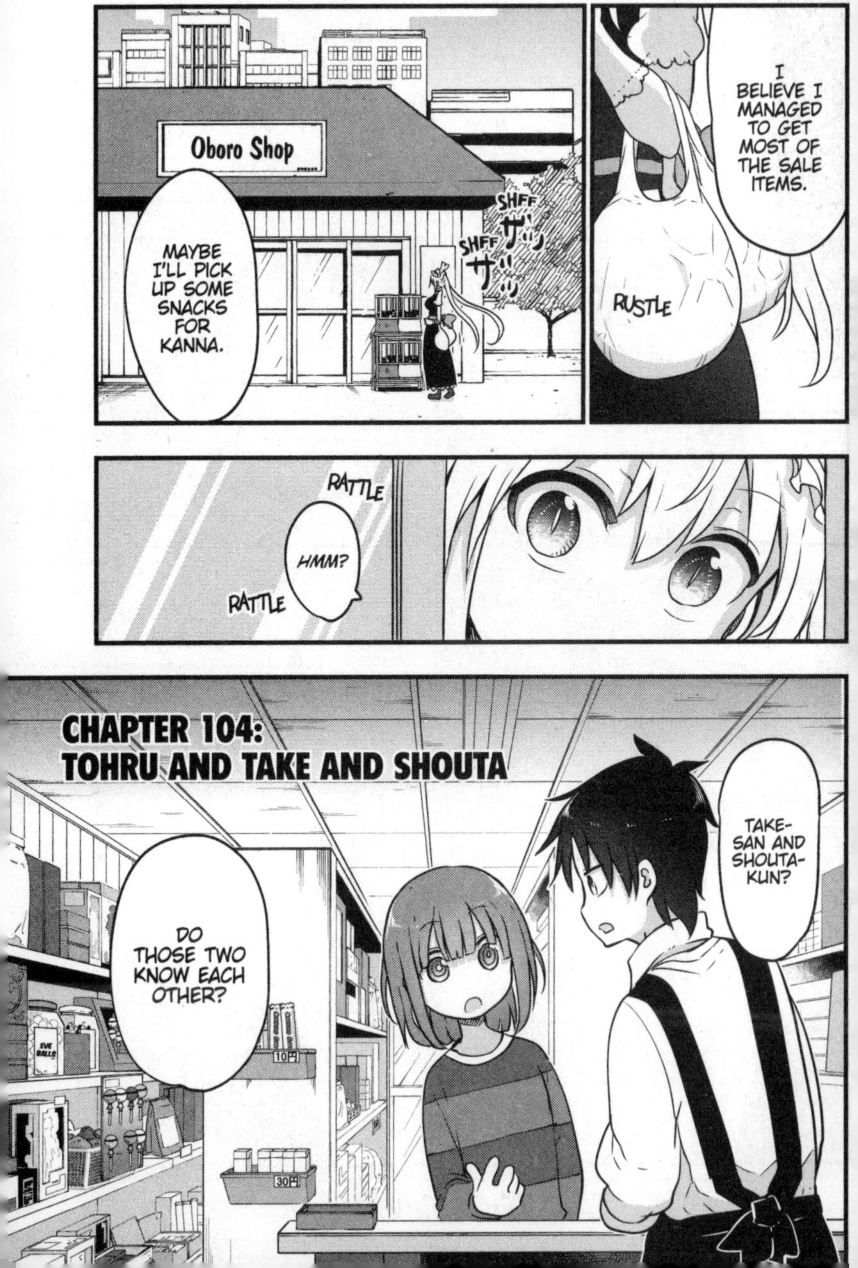
I BELIEVE I MANAGED TO GET MOST OF THE SALE ITEMS.
RUSTLE
Oboro Shop
MAYBE I'LL PICK UP SOME SNACKS FOR KANNA.
SHFF
SHFF
RATTLE
HMM?
RATTLE
CHAPTER 104: TOHRU AND TAKE AND SHOUTA
TAKE-SAN AND SHOUTA-KUN?
DO THOSE TWO KNOW EACH OTHER?
EYE BALLS
10円
30円

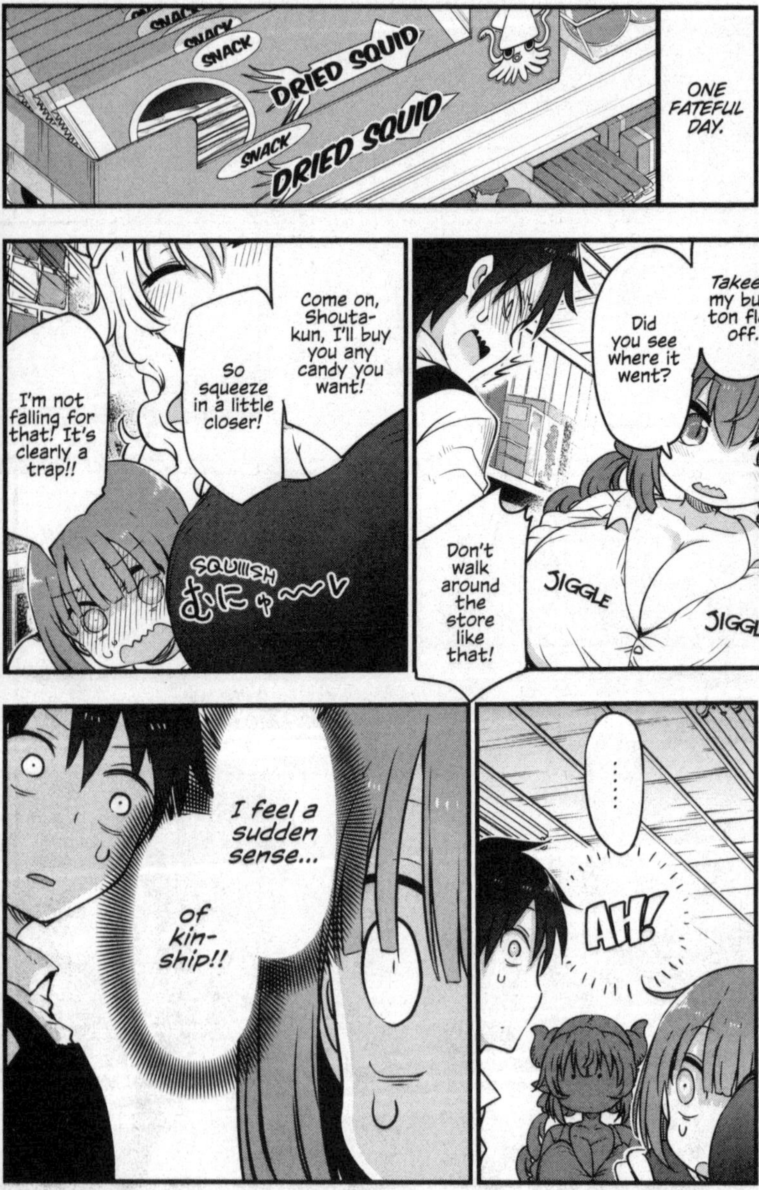
ONE FATEFUL DAY.
SNACK
SNACK
SNACK
DRIED SQUID
DRIED SQUID
SNACK
DRIED SQUID
Takeee, my button flew off.
Did you see where it went?
JIGGLE
JIGGLE
Don't walk around the store like that!
Come on, Shouta-kun, I'll buy you any candy you want!
So squeeze in a little closer!
SQUIIISH
むにゅ〜〜♡
I'm not falling for that! It's clearly a trap!!
......
AH!
I feel a sudden sense...
of kinship!!

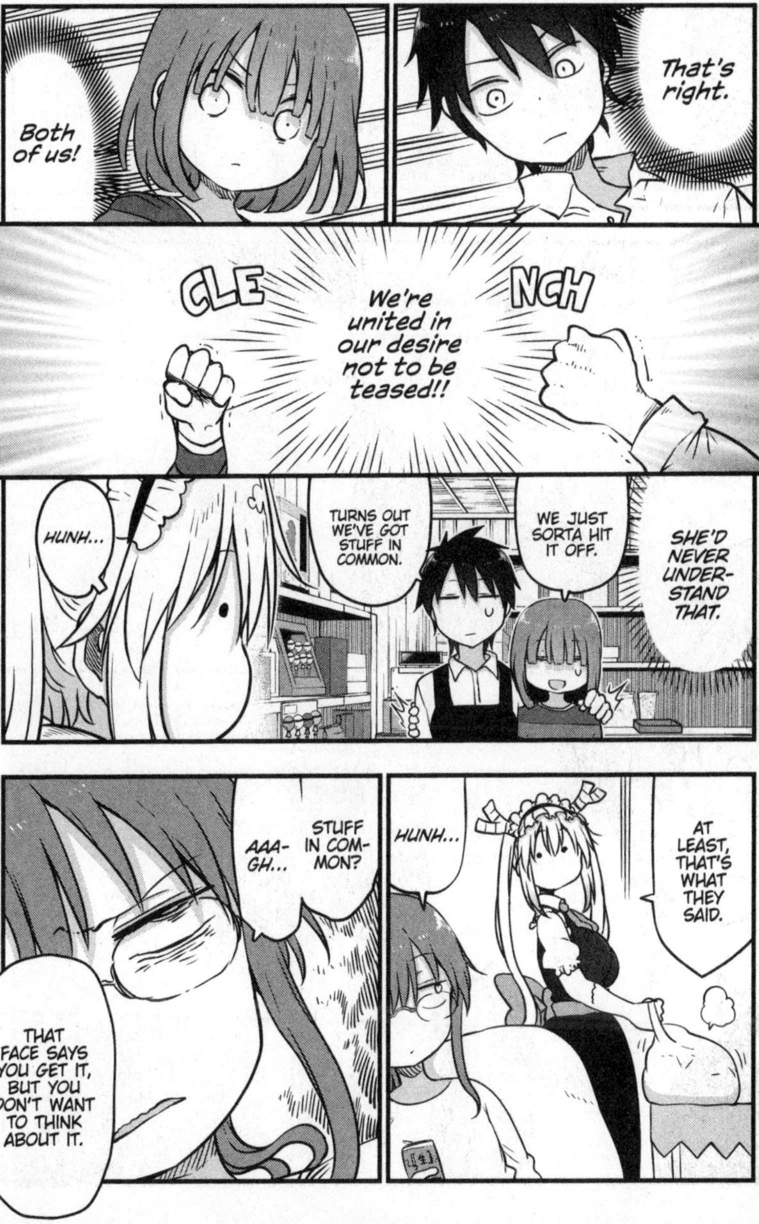
That's right.
Both of us!
CLE NCH
We're united in our desire not to be teased!!
SHE'D NEVER UNDERSTAND THAT.
WE JUST SORTA HIT IT OFF.
TURNS OUT WE'VE GOT STUFF IN COMMON.
HUNH...
AT LEAST, THAT'S WHAT THEY SAID.
HUNH...
STUFF IN COMMON?
AAAGH...
THAT FACE SAYS YOU GET IT, BUT YOU DON'T WANT TO THINK ABOUT IT.

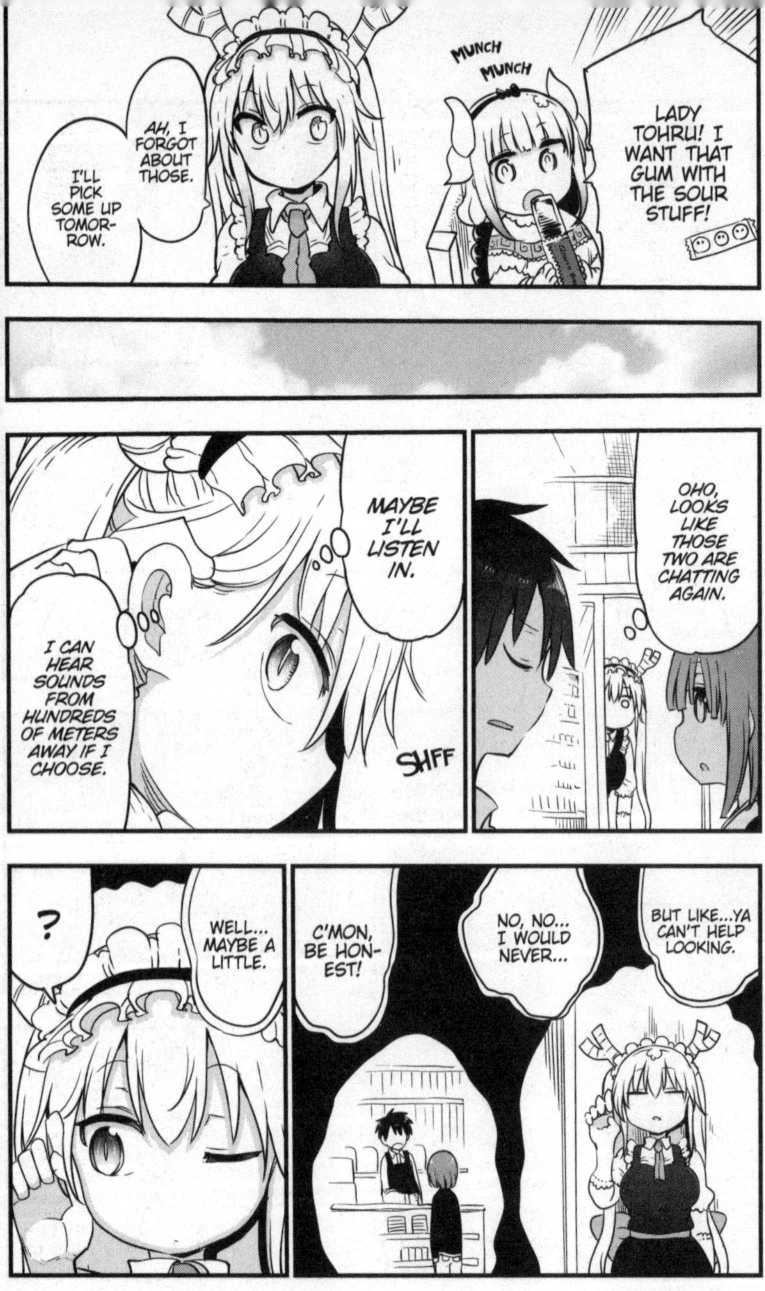
MUNCH MUNCH
LADY TOHRU! I WANT THAT GUM WITH THE SOUR STUFF!
AH, I FORGOT ABOUT THOSE.
I'LL PICK SOME UP TOMOR-ROW.
OHO, LOOKS LIKE THOSE TWO ARE CHATTING AGAIN.
MAYBE I'LL LISTEN IN.
SHFF
I CAN HEAR SOUNDS FROM HUNDREDS OF METERS AWAY IF I CHOOSE.
BUT LIKE...YA CAN'T HELP LOOKING.
NO, NO... I WOULD NEVER...
C'MON, BE HON-EST!
WELL... MAYBE A LITTLE.
?

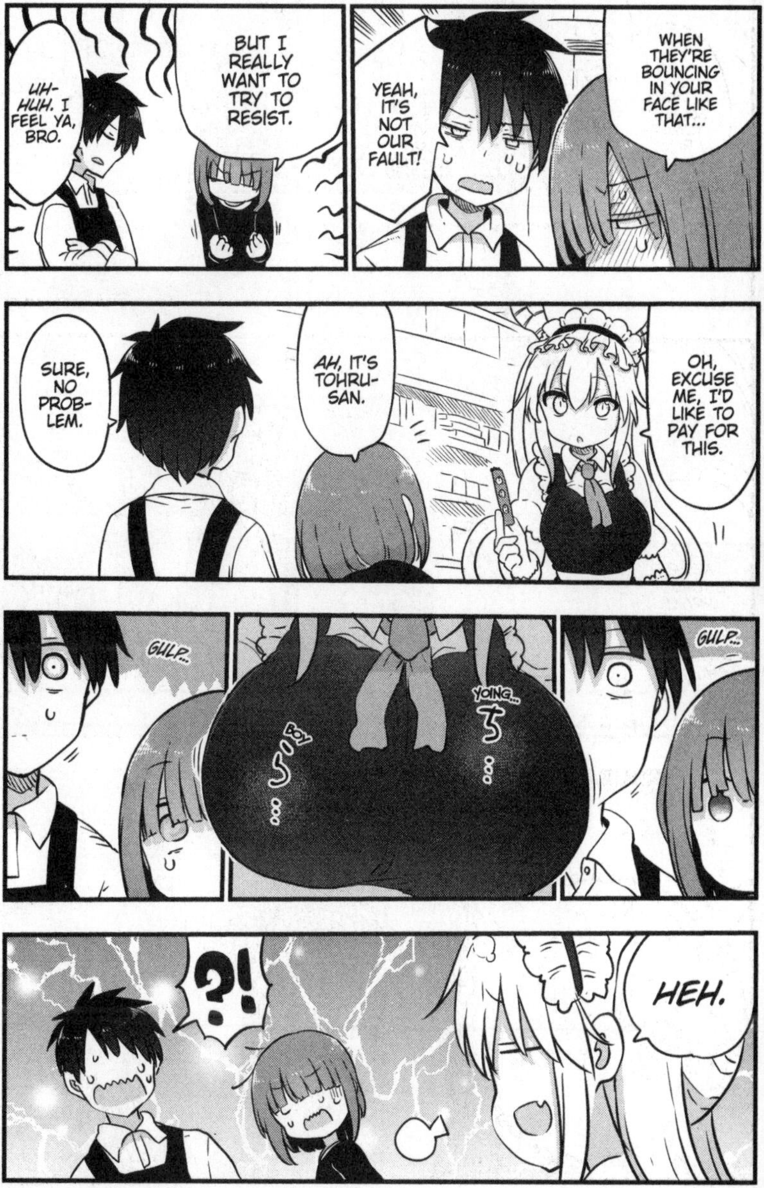
WHEN THEY'RE BOUNCING IN YOUR FACE LIKE THAT...
YEAH, IT'S NOT OUR FAULT!
BUT I REALLY WANT TO TRY TO RESIST.
UH-HUH. I FEEL YA, BRO.
OH, EXCUSE ME, I'D LIKE TO PAY FOR THIS.
AH, IT'S TOHRU-SAN.
SURE, NO PROB-LEM.
GULP...
YOING...
BOY
GULP...
HEH.
?!

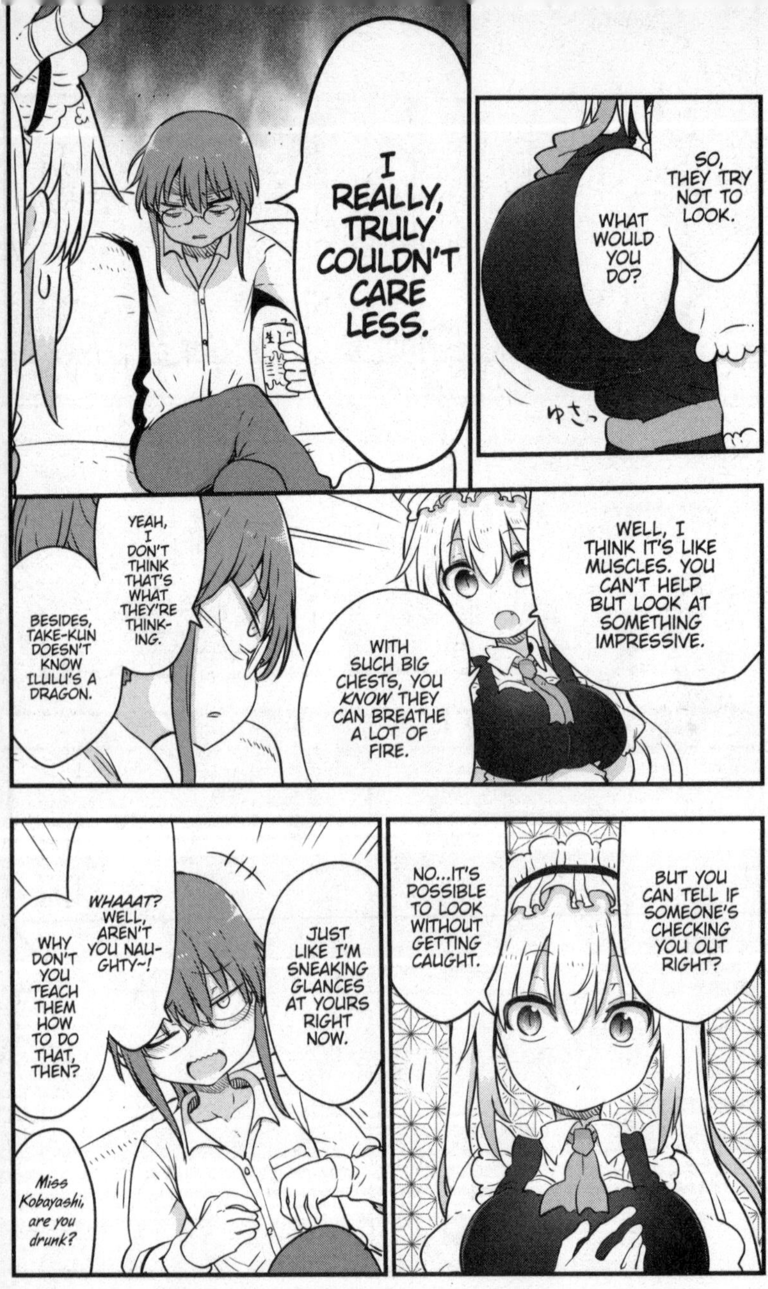
SO, THEY TRY NOT TO LOOK.
WHAT WOULD YOU DO?
ゆさっ
I REALLY, TRULY COULDN'T CARE LESS.
WELL, I THINK IT'S LIKE MUSCLES. YOU CAN'T HELP BUT LOOK AT SOMETHING IMPRESSIVE.
WITH SUCH BIG CHESTS, YOU *KNOW* THEY CAN BREATHE A LOT OF FIRE.
YEAH, I DON'T THINK THAT'S WHAT THEY'RE THINK-ING.
BESIDES, TAKE-KUN DOESN'T KNOW ILULU'S A DRAGON.
BUT YOU CAN TELL IF SOMEONE'S CHECKING YOU OUT RIGHT?
NO...IT'S POSSIBLE TO LOOK WITHOUT GETTING CAUGHT.
JUST LIKE I'M SNEAKING GLANCES AT YOURS RIGHT NOW.
WHAAAT? WELL, AREN'T YOU NAU-GHTY~!
WHY DON'T YOU TEACH THEM HOW TO DO THAT, THEN?
Miss Kobayashi, are you drunk?

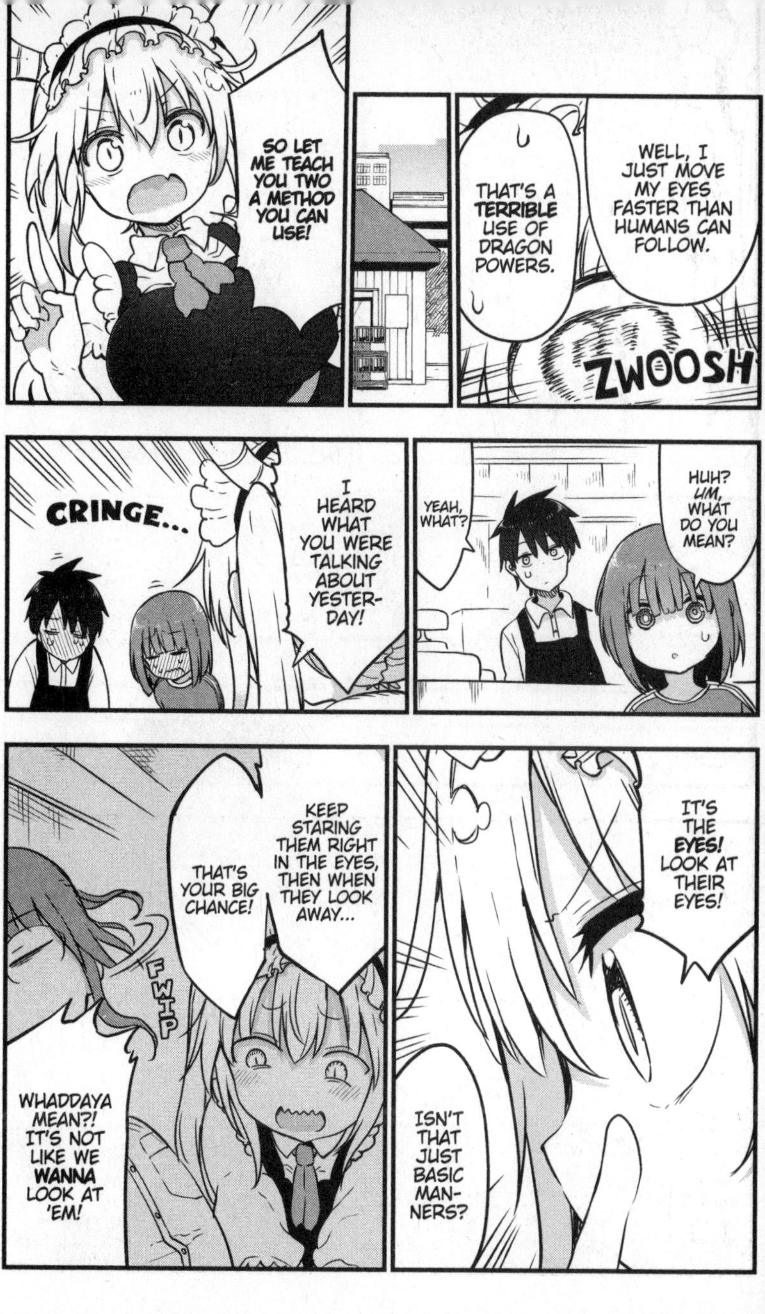
WELL, I JUST MOVE MY EYES FASTER THAN HUMANS CAN FOLLOW.
THAT'S A TERRIBLE USE OF DRAGON POWERS.
ZWOOSH
SO LET ME TEACH YOU TWO A METHOD YOU CAN USE!
HUH? UM, WHAT DO YOU MEAN?
YEAH, WHAT?
I HEARD WHAT YOU WERE TALKING ABOUT YESTER-DAY!
CRINGE...
IT'S THE EYES! LOOK AT THEIR EYES!
ISN'T THAT JUST BASIC MAN-NERS?
KEEP STARING THEM RIGHT IN THE EYES, THEN WHEN THEY LOOK AWAY...
THAT'S YOUR BIG CHANCE!
FWIP
WHADDAYA MEAN?! IT'S NOT LIKE WE WANNA LOOK AT 'EM!

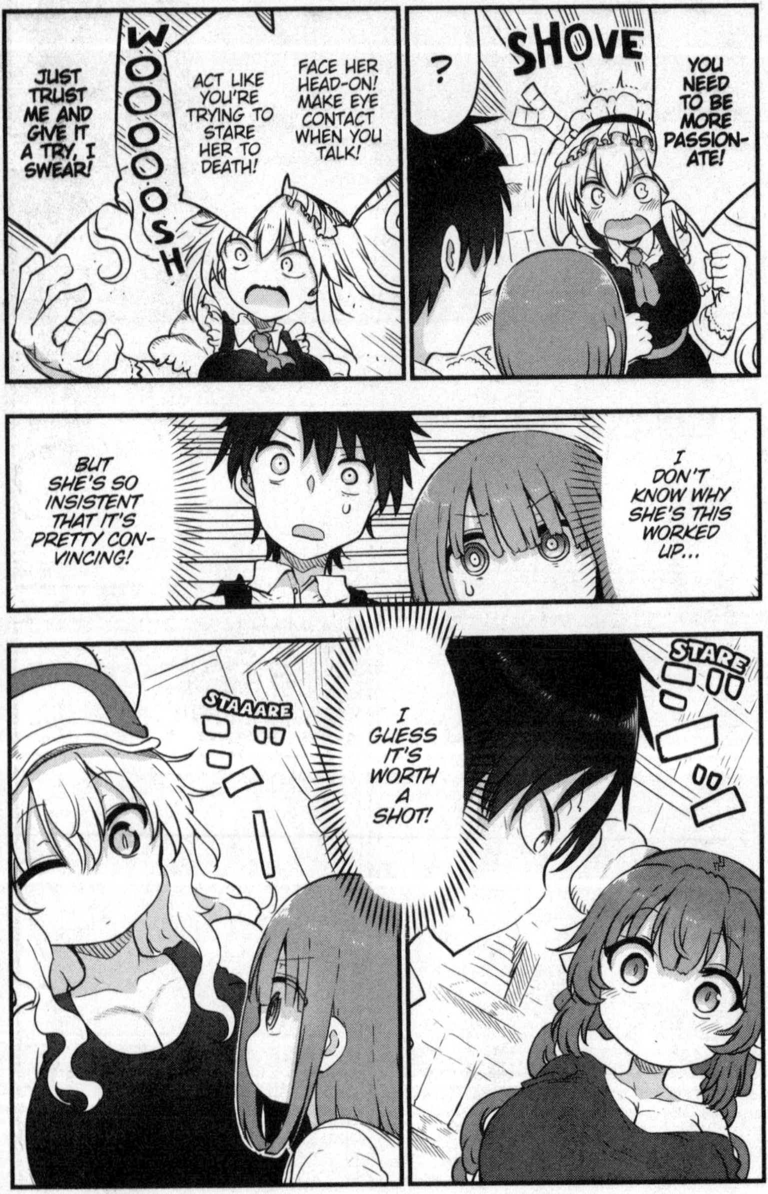
SHOVE
YOU NEED TO BE MORE PASSION-ATE!
?
FACE HER HEAD-ON! MAKE EYE CONTACT WHEN YOU TALK!
ACT LIKE YOU'RE TRYING TO STARE HER TO DEATH!
WOOOOOOSH
JUST TRUST ME AND GIVE IT A TRY, I SWEAR!
I DON'T KNOW WHY SHE'S THIS WORKED UP...
BUT SHE'S SO INSISTENT THAT IT'S PRETTY CON-VINCING!
STARE
I GUESS IT'S WORTH A SHOT!
STAAARE

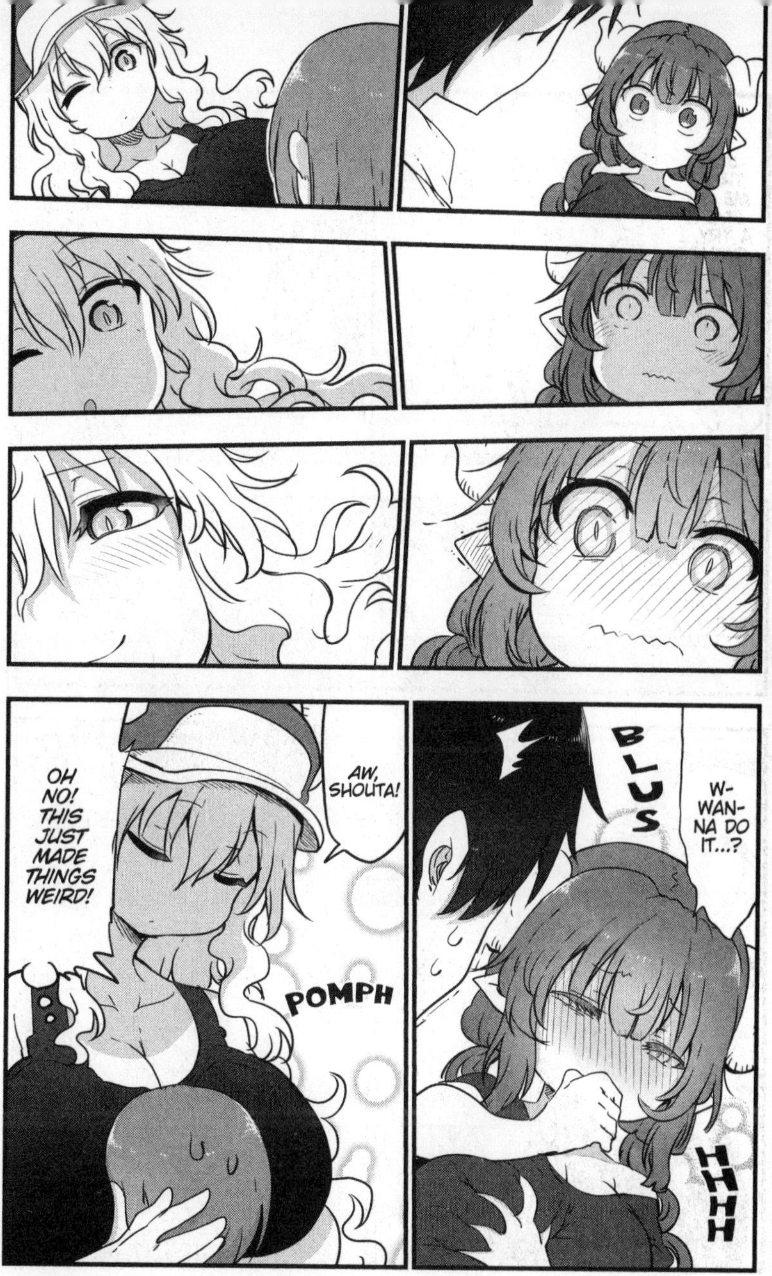
W-WANNA DO IT...?
BLUS
HHHH
AW, SHOUTA!
OH NO! THIS JUST MADE THINGS WEIRD!
POMPH

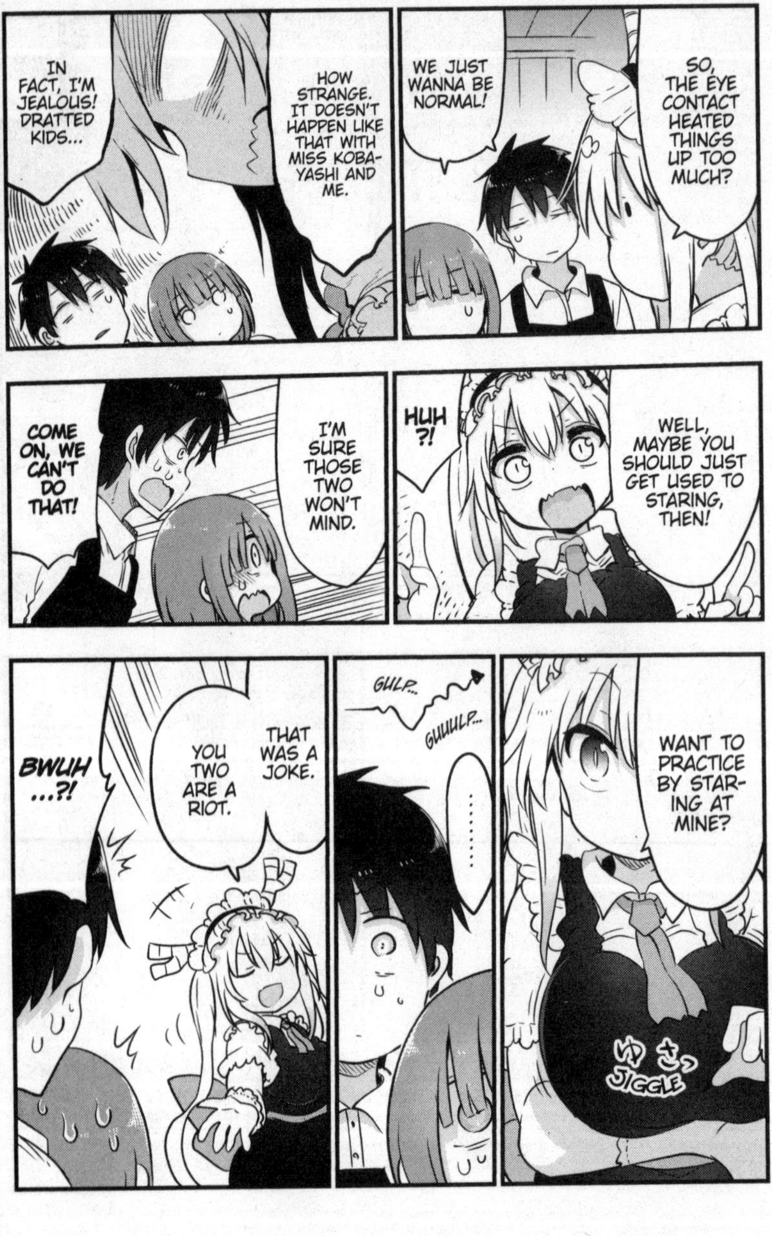
SO, THE EYE CONTACT HEATED THINGS UP TOO MUCH?
WE JUST WANNA BE NORMAL!
HOW STRANGE. IT DOESN'T HAPPEN LIKE THAT WITH MISS KOBA-YASHI AND ME.
IN FACT, I'M JEALOUS! DRATTED KIDS...
WELL, MAYBE YOU SHOULD JUST GET USED TO STARING, THEN!
HUH ?!
I'M SURE THOSE TWO WON'T MIND.
COME ON, WE CAN'T DO THAT!
WANT TO PRACTICE BY STAR-ING AT MINE?
JIGGLE
GULP...
GUUULP...
....
THAT WAS A JOKE.
YOU TWO ARE A RIOT.
BWUH ...?!

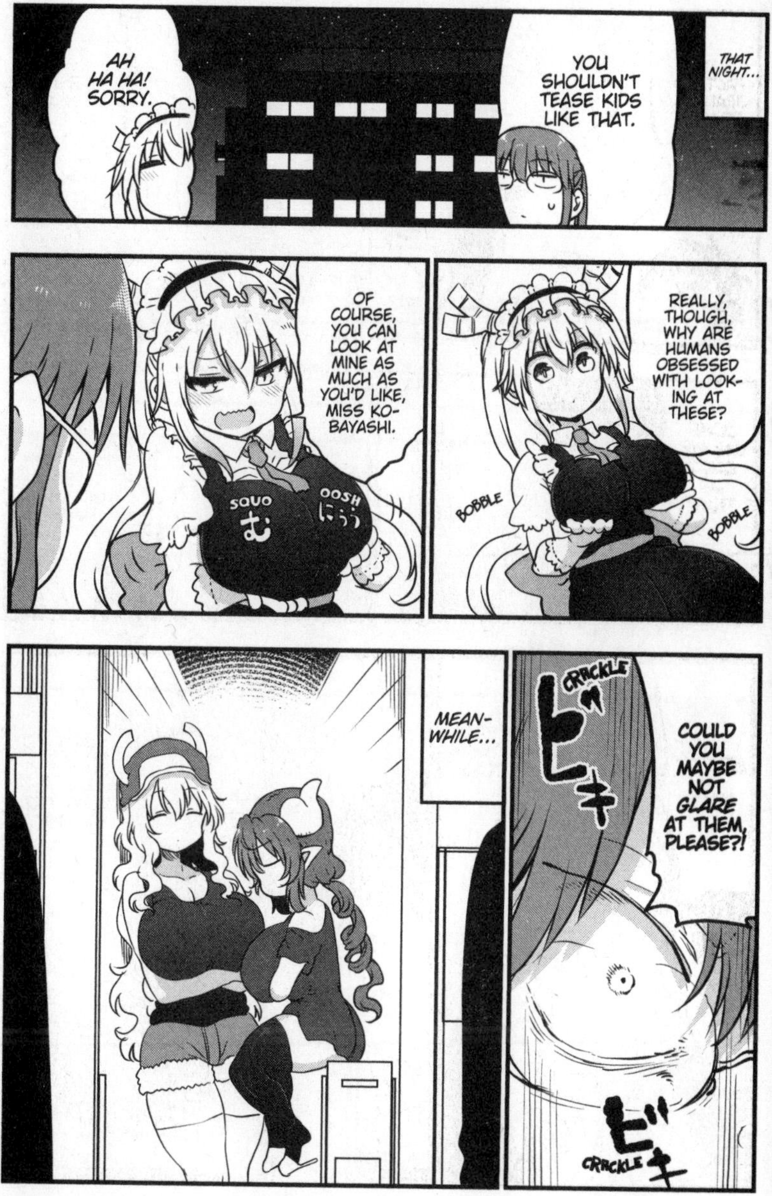
THAT NIGHT...
YOU SHOULDN'T TEASE KIDS LIKE THAT.
AH HA HA! SORRY.
REALLY, THOUGH, WHY ARE HUMANS OBSESSED WITH LOOK-ING AT THESE?
BOBBLE
BOBBLE
OF COURSE, YOU CAN LOOK AT MINE AS MUCH AS YOU'D LIKE, MISS KO-BAYASHI.
SQUO
OOSH
CRACKLE
ビキ
COULD YOU MAYBE NOT GLARE AT THEM, PLEASE?!
CRACKLE
ビキ
MEAN-WHILE...

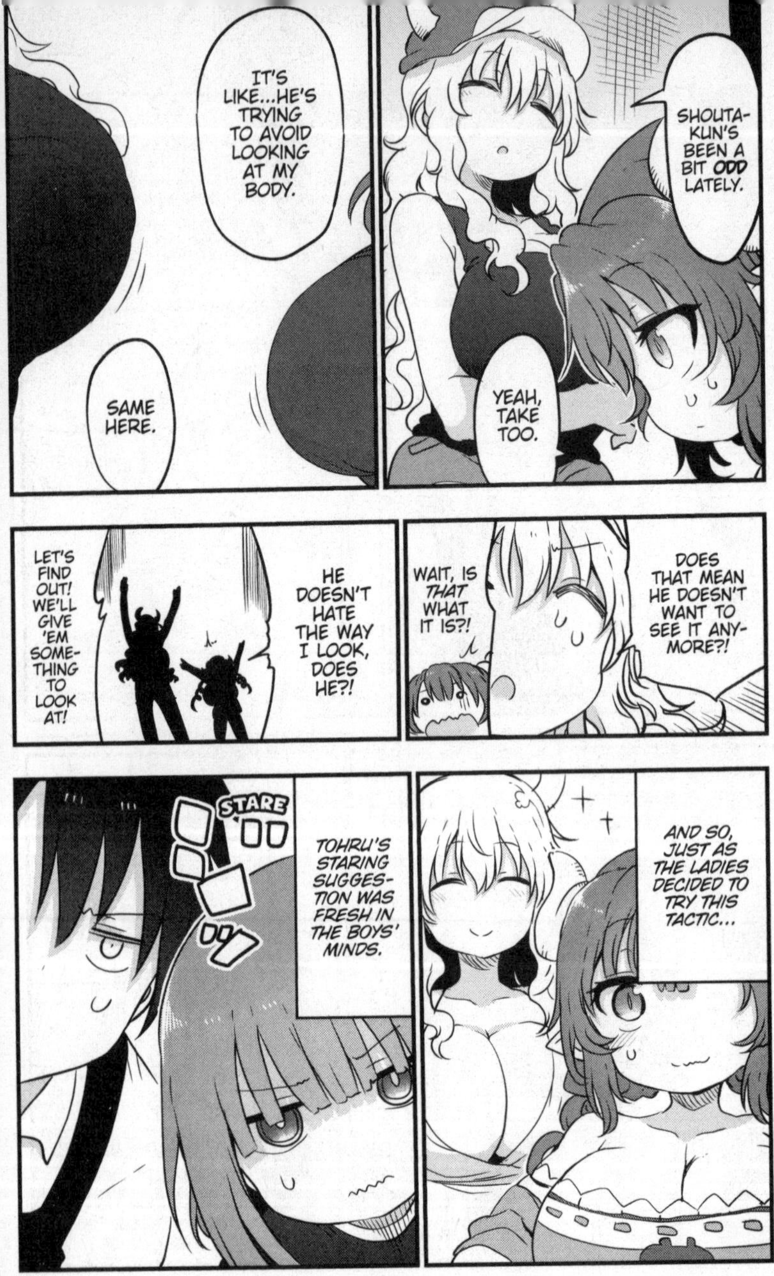
SHOUTA-KUN'S BEEN A BIT **ODD** LATELY.
YEAH, TAKE TOO.
IT'S LIKE...HE'S TRYING TO AVOID LOOKING AT MY BODY.
SAME HERE.
DOES THAT MEAN HE DOESN'T WANT TO SEE IT ANYMORE?!
WAIT, IS *THAT* WHAT IT IS?!
HE DOESN'T HATE THE WAY I LOOK, DOES HE?!
LET'S FIND OUT! WE'LL GIVE 'EM SOMETHING TO LOOK AT!
AND SO, JUST AS THE LADIES DECIDED TO TRY THIS TACTIC...
TOHRU'S STARING SUGGESTION WAS FRESH IN THE BOYS' MINDS.
STARE

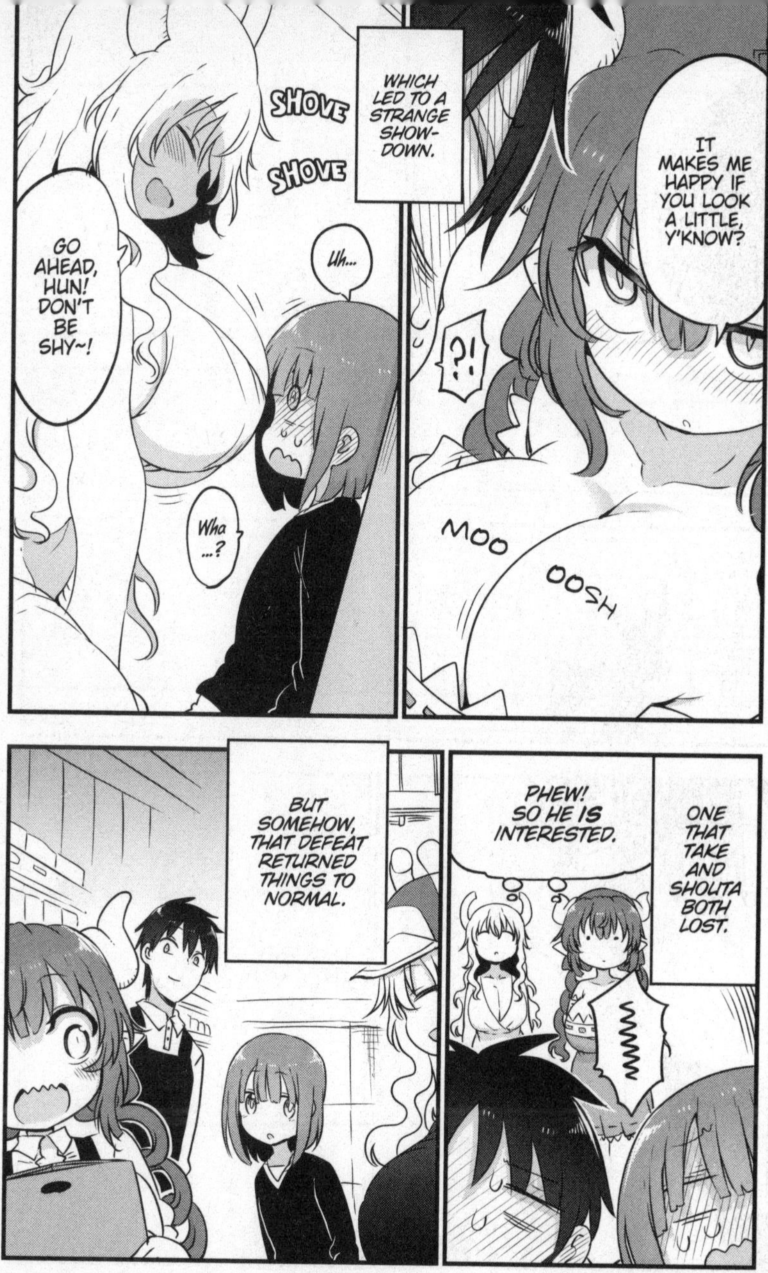
IT MAKES ME HAPPY IF YOU LOOK A LITTLE, Y'KNOW?
?!
MOO OOSH
WHICH LED TO A STRANGE SHOW-DOWN.
SHOVE
SHOVE
GO AHEAD, HUN! DON'T BE SHY~!
Uh...
Wha ...?
ONE THAT TAKE AND SHOUTA BOTH LOST.
PHEW! SO HE IS INTERESTED.
BUT SOMEHOW, THAT DEFEAT RETURNED THINGS TO NORMAL.

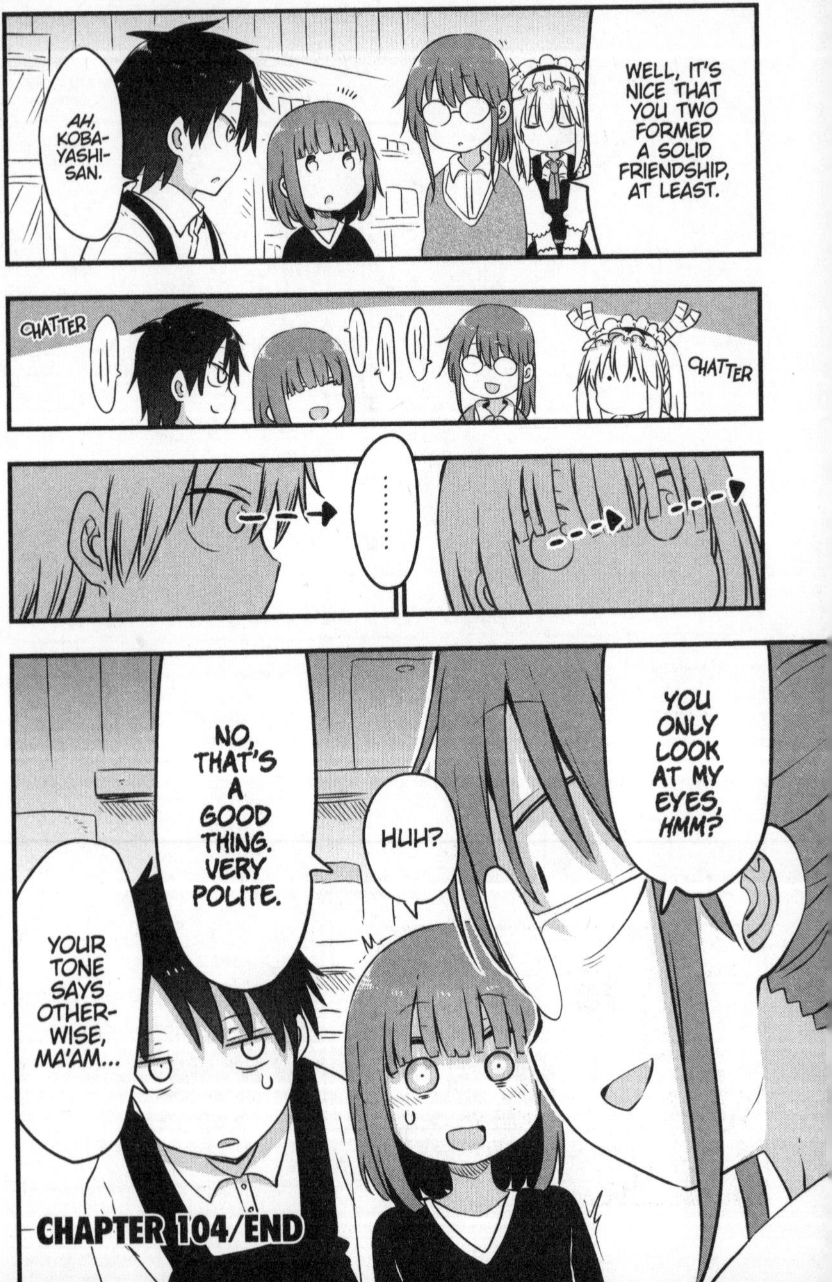
WELL, IT'S NICE THAT YOU TWO FORMED A SOLID FRIENDSHIP, AT LEAST.
AH, KOBA-YASHI-SAN.
CHATTER
CHATTER
......
YOU ONLY LOOK AT MY EYES, HMM?
HUH?
NO, THAT'S A GOOD THING. VERY POLITE.
YOUR TONE SAYS OTHER-WISE, MA'AM...
CHAPTER 104/END

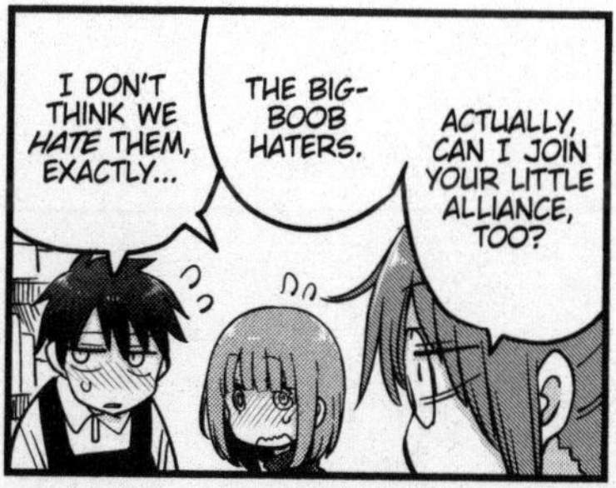
ACTUALLY, CAN I JOIN YOUR LITTLE ALLIANCE, TOO?
THE BIG-BOOB HATERS.
I DON'T THINK WE *HATE* THEM, EXACTLY...

Miss Kobayashi's
Dragon Maid

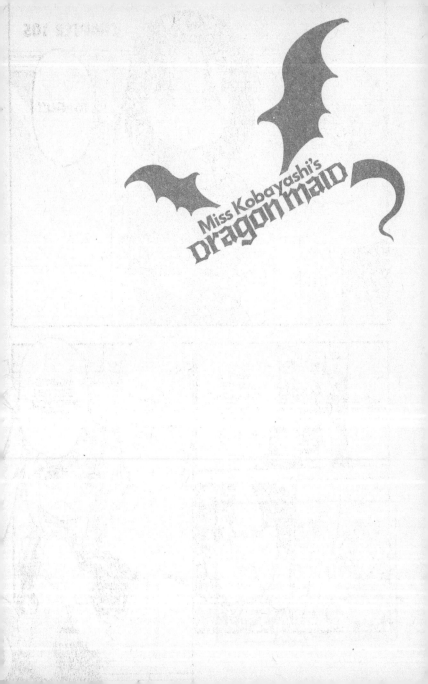

CHAPTER 105

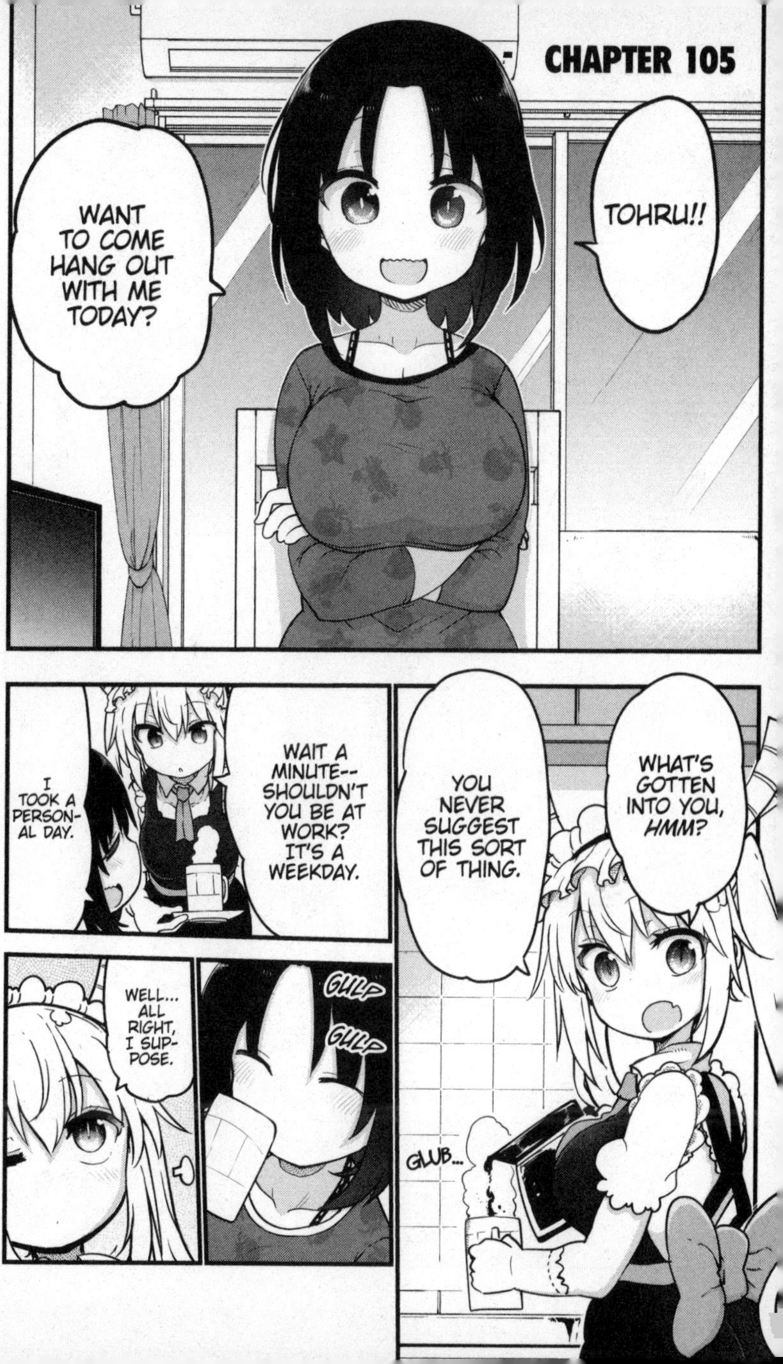
TOHRU!!
WANT TO COME HANG OUT WITH ME TODAY?
WHAT'S GOTTEN INTO YOU, HMM?
YOU NEVER SUGGEST THIS SORT OF THING.
GLUB...
WAIT A MINUTE-- SHOULDN'T YOU BE AT WORK? IT'S A WEEKDAY.
I TOOK A PERSON-AL DAY.
GULP
GULP
WELL... ALL RIGHT, I SUP-POSE.

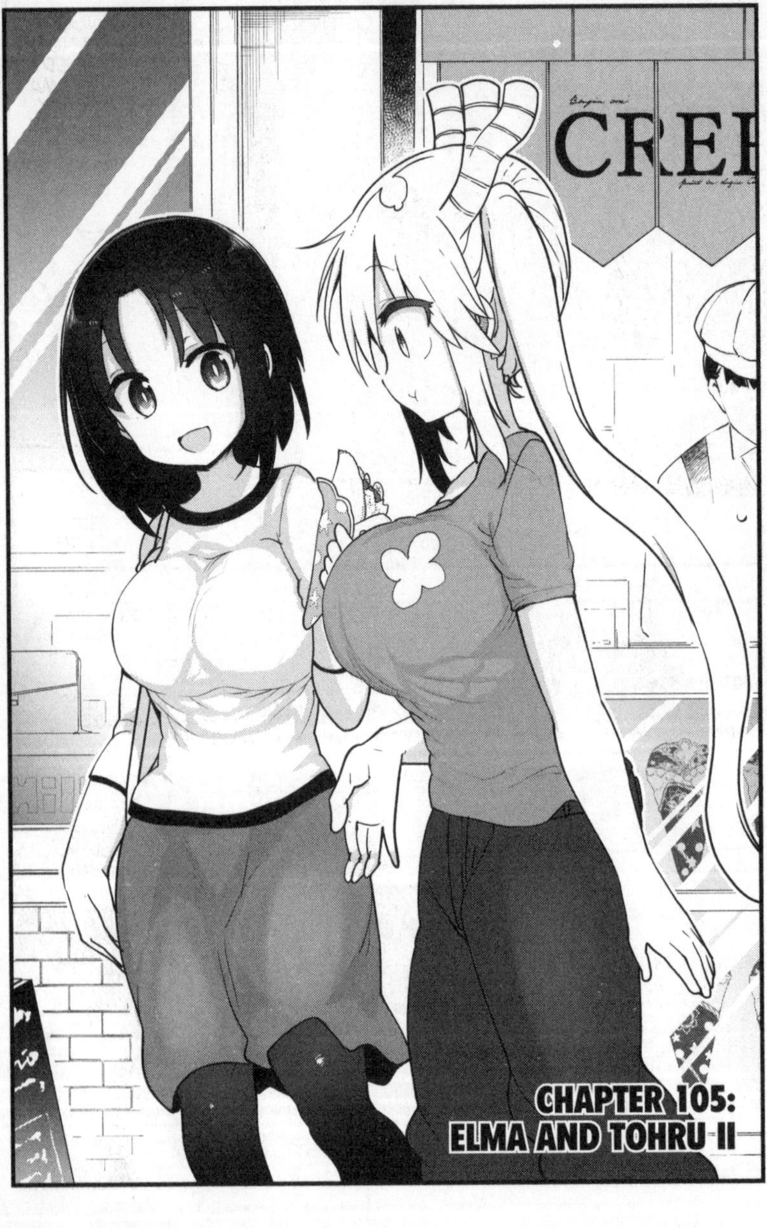
CREP
CHAPTER 105:
ELMA AND TOHRU II

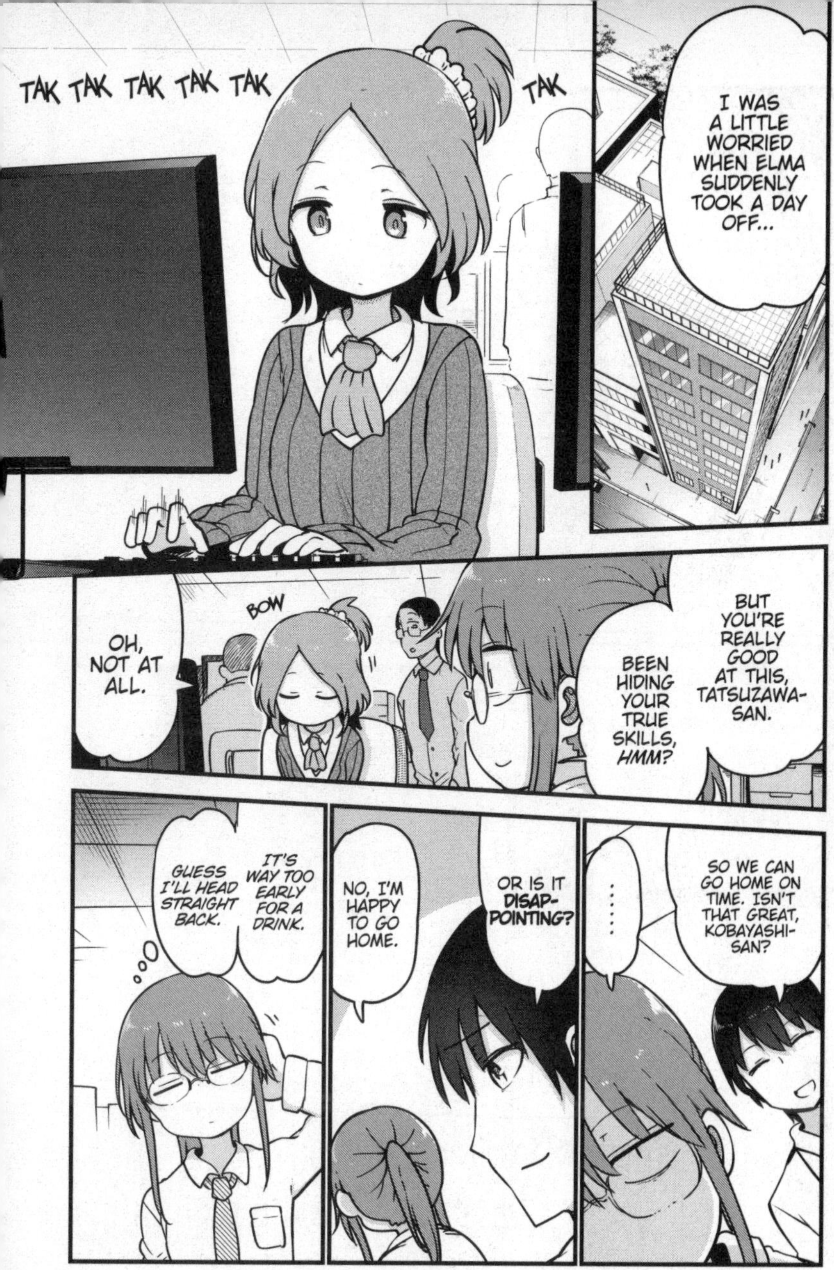
I WAS A LITTLE WORRIED WHEN ELMA SUDDENLY TOOK A DAY OFF...
TAK
TAK TAK TAK TAK TAK
BUT YOU'RE REALLY GOOD AT THIS, TATSUZAWA-SAN.
BEEN HIDING YOUR TRUE SKILLS, *HMM?*
BOW
OH, NOT AT ALL.
SO WE CAN GO HOME ON TIME. ISN'T THAT GREAT, KOBAYASHI-SAN?
......
OR IS IT **DISAPPOINTING?**
NO, I'M HAPPY TO GO HOME.
IT'S WAY TOO EARLY FOR A DRINK.
GUESS I'LL HEAD STRAIGHT BACK.

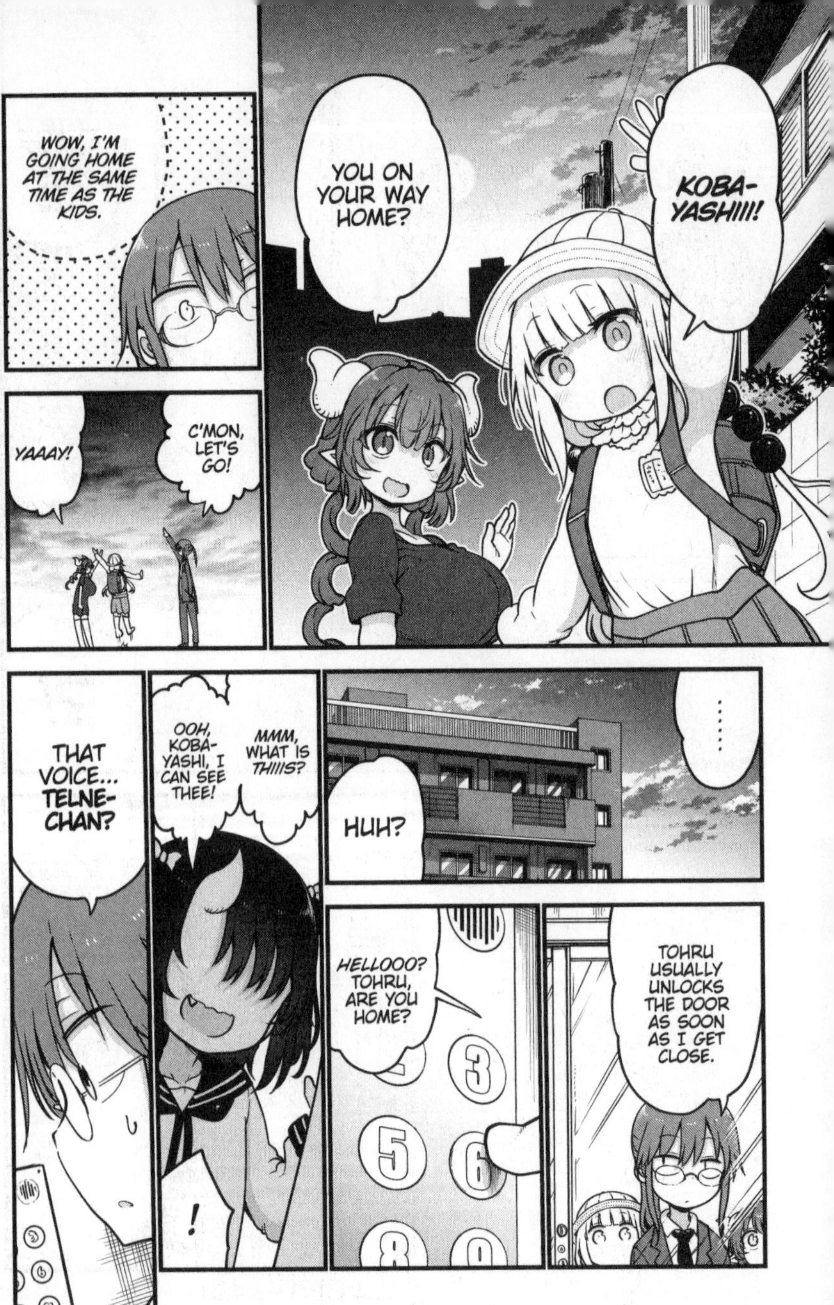
KOBA-YASHIIII!
YOU ON YOUR WAY HOME?
WOW, I'M GOING HOME AT THE SAME TIME AS THE KIDS.
C'MON, LET'S GO!
YAAAY!
......
HUH?
TOHRU USUALLY UNLOCKS THE DOOR AS SOON AS I GET CLOSE.
HELLOOO? TOHRU, ARE YOU HOME?
3
5
6
MMM, WHAT IS THIIIS?
OOH, KOBA-YASHI, I CAN SEE THEE!
!
THAT VOICE... TELNE-CHAN?

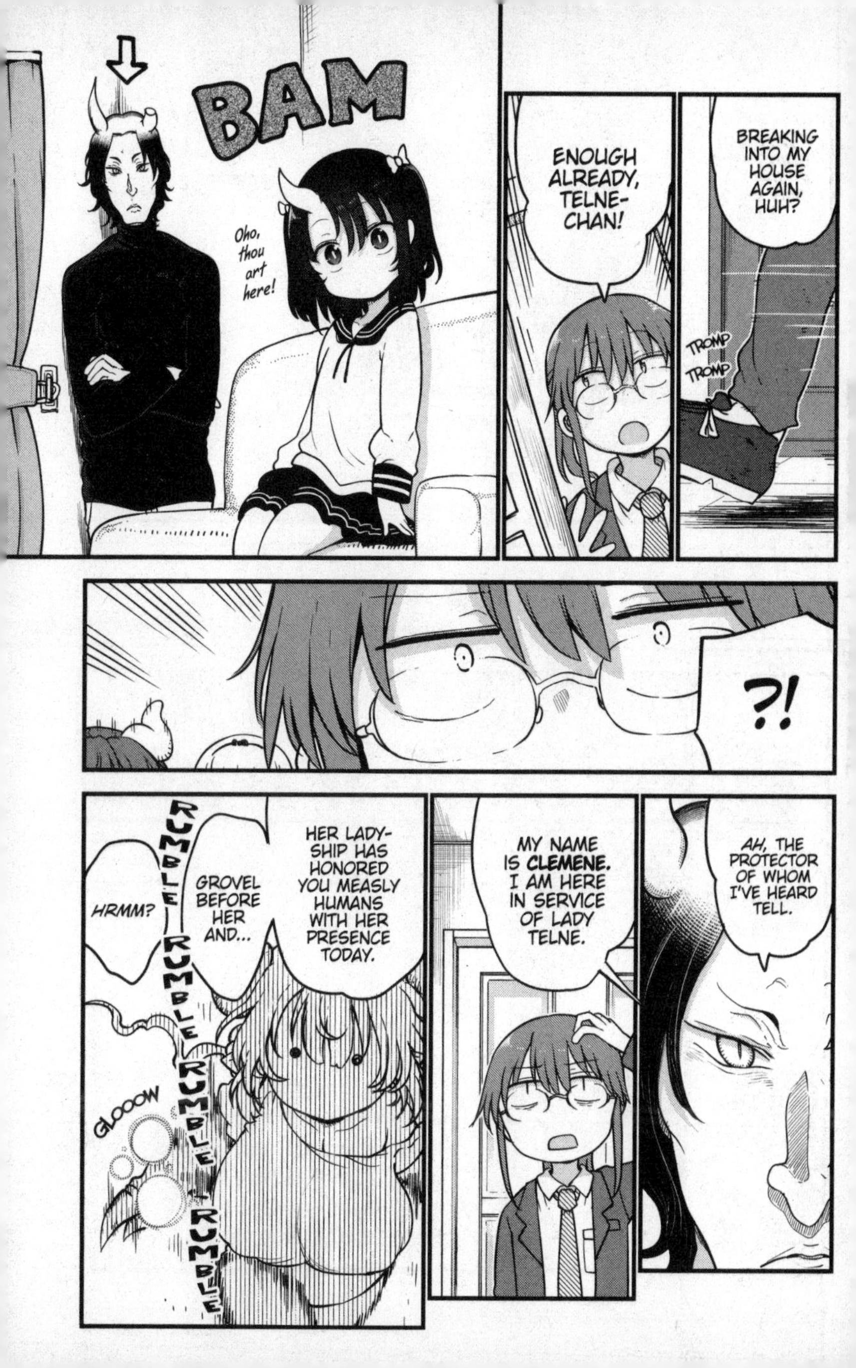
BREAKING INTO MY HOUSE AGAIN, HUH?
TROMP TROMP
ENOUGH ALREADY, TELNE-CHAN!
BAM
Oho, thou art here!
?!
AH, THE PROTECTOR OF WHOM I'VE HEARD TELL.
MY NAME IS CLEMENE. I AM HERE IN SERVICE OF LADY TELNE.
HER LADYSHIP HAS HONORED YOU MEASLY HUMANS WITH HER PRESENCE TODAY.
GROVEL BEFORE HER AND...
HRMM?
RUMBLE RUMBLE RUMBLE RUMBLE
GLOOOW

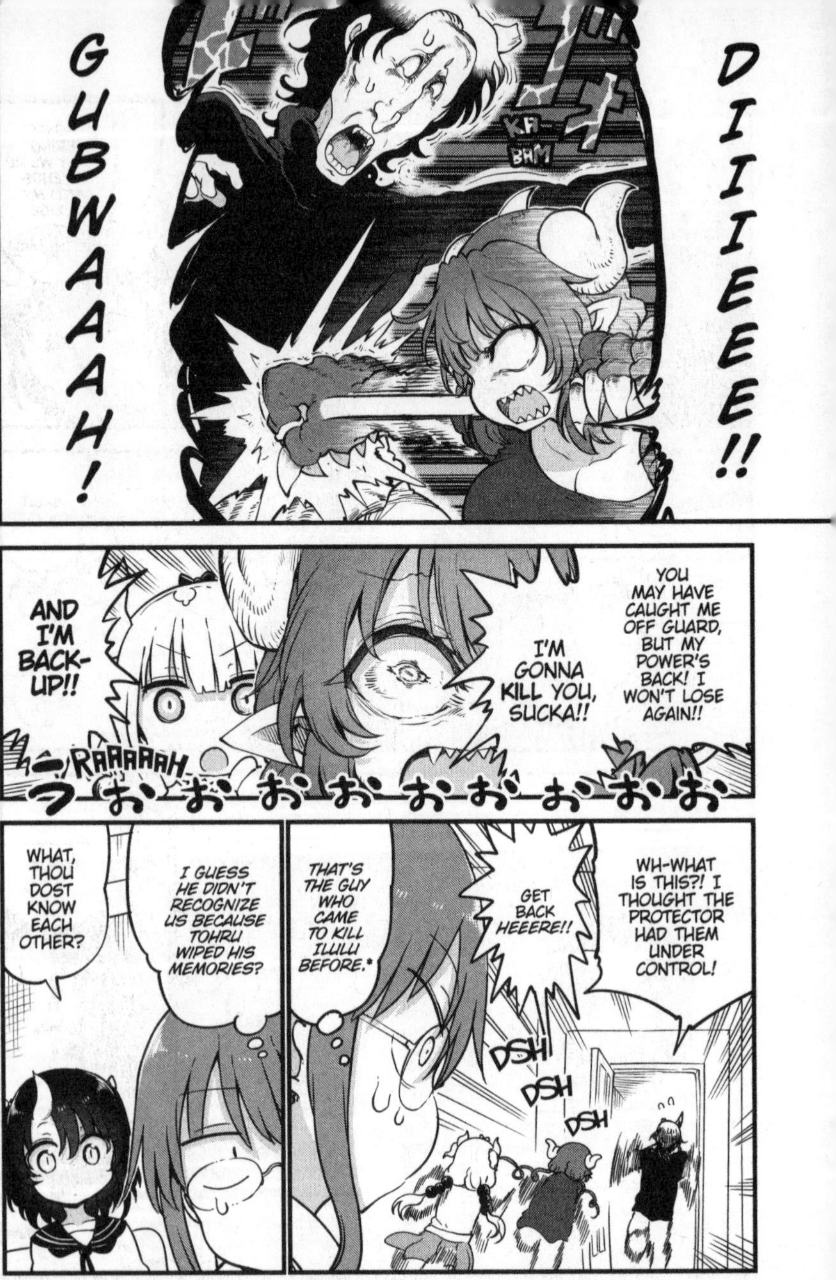
DIIIEEE!!
KA-BAM
GUBWAAAAH!
YOU MAY HAVE CAUGHT ME OFF GUARD, BUT MY POWER'S BACK! I WON'T LOSE AGAIN!!
I'M GONNA KILL YOU, SUCKA!!
AND I'M BACK-UP!!
RAAAAAH
WH-WHAT IS THIS?! I THOUGHT THE PROTECTOR HAD THEM UNDER CONTROL!
GET BACK HEEEERE!!
DSH
DSH
DSH
THAT'S THE GUY WHO CAME TO KILL ILULU BEFORE.*
I GUESS HE DIDN'T RECOGNIZE US BECAUSE TOHRU WIPED HIS MEMORIES?
WHAT, THOU DOST KNOW EACH OTHER?

* See Chapter 33.

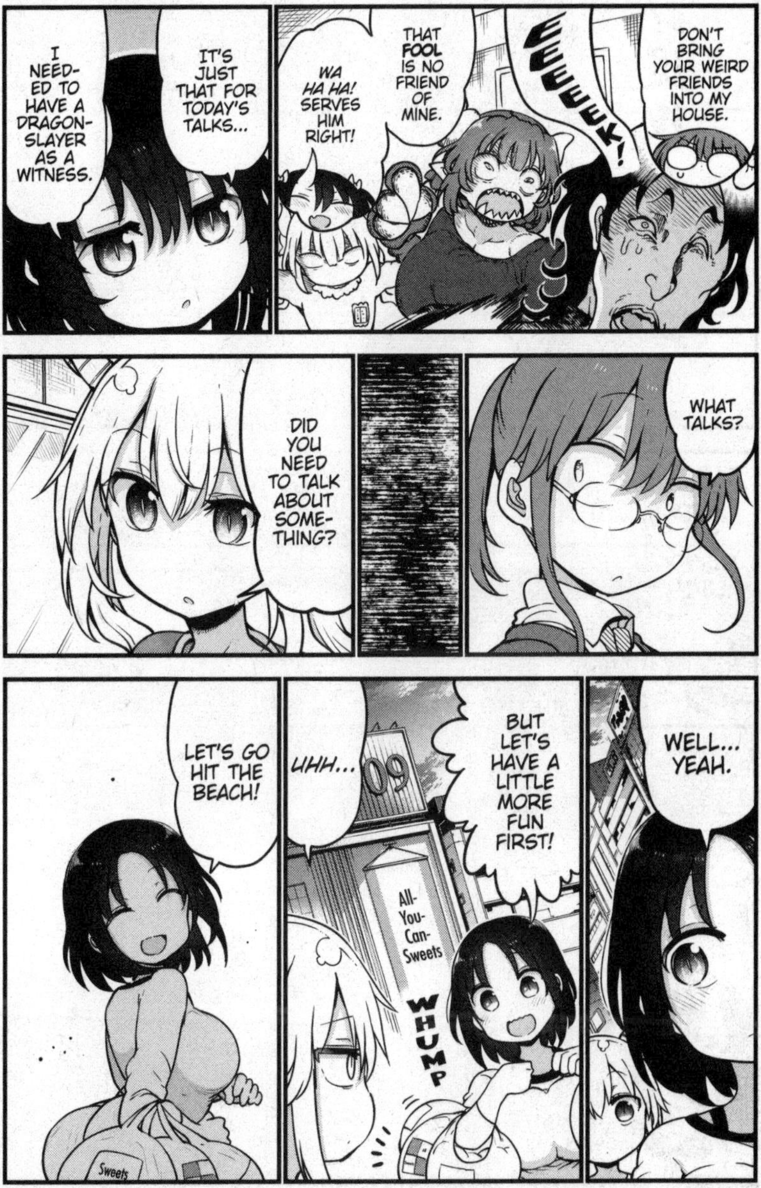
DON'T BRING YOUR WEIRD FRIENDS INTO MY HOUSE.
EEEEEEK!
THAT **FOOL** IS NO FRIEND OF MINE.
WA HA HA! SERVES HIM RIGHT!
IT'S JUST THAT FOR TODAY'S TALKS...
I NEEDED TO HAVE A DRAGON-SLAYER AS A WITNESS.
WHAT TALKS?
DID YOU NEED TO TALK ABOUT SOMETHING?
WELL... YEAH.
BUT LET'S HAVE A LITTLE MORE FUN FIRST!
UHH...
09
All-You-Can-Sweets
WHUMP
LET'S GO HIT THE BEACH!
Sweets

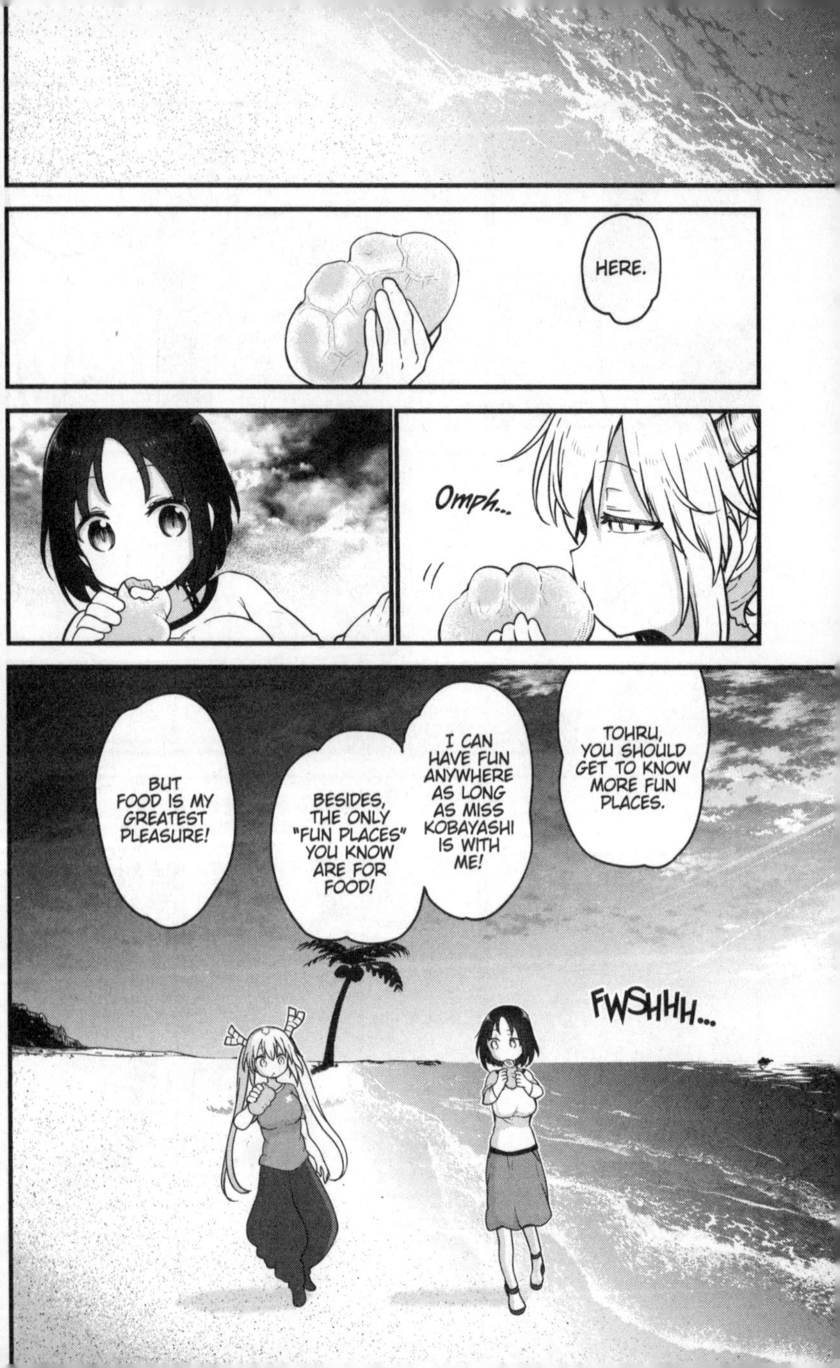
HERE.
Omph...
TOHRU, YOU SHOULD GET TO KNOW MORE FUN PLACES.
I CAN HAVE FUN ANYWHERE AS LONG AS MISS KOBAYASHI IS WITH ME!
BESIDES, THE ONLY "FUN PLACES" YOU KNOW ARE FOR FOOD!
BUT FOOD IS MY GREATEST PLEASURE!
FWSHHH...

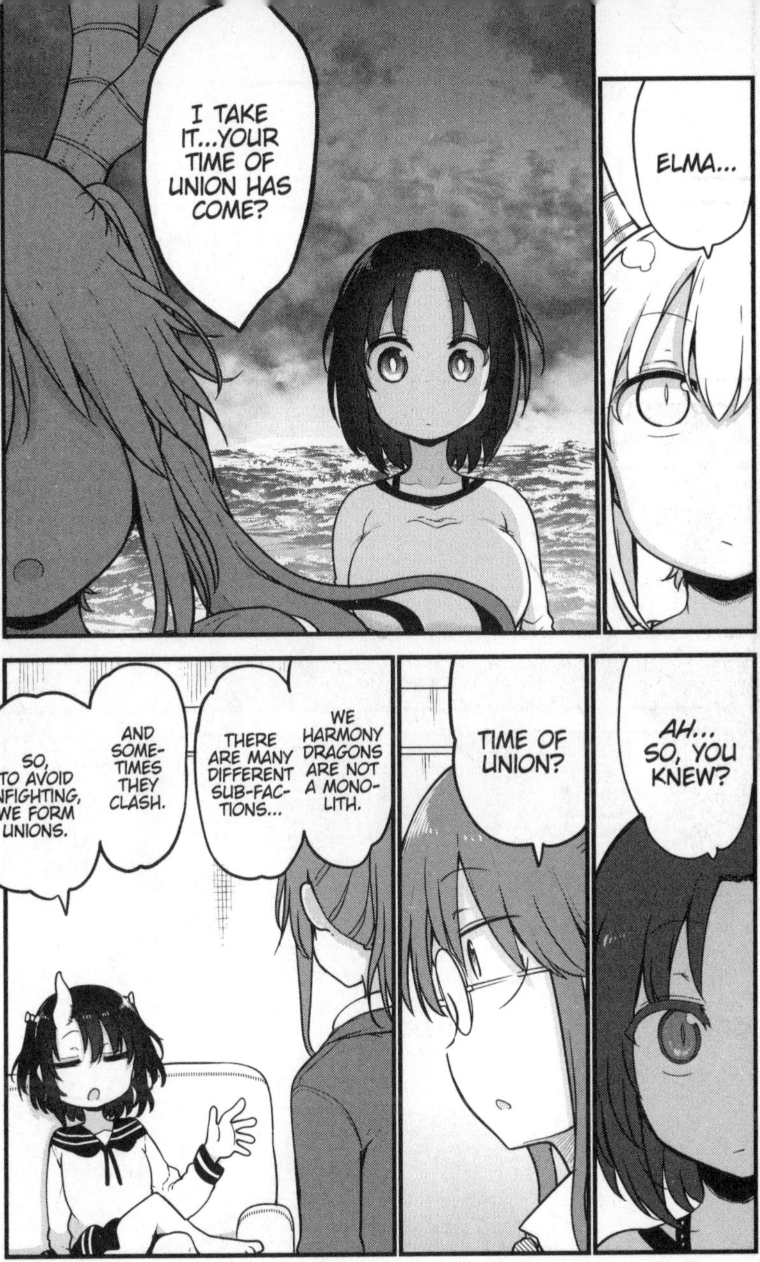
ELMA...
I TAKE IT...YOUR TIME OF UNION HAS COME?
AH... SO, YOU KNEW?
TIME OF UNION?
WE HARMONY DRAGONS ARE NOT A MONO-LITH.
THERE ARE MANY DIFFERENT SUB-FAC-TIONS...
AND SOME-TIMES THEY CLASH.
SO, TO AVOID INFIGHTING, WE FORM UNIONS.

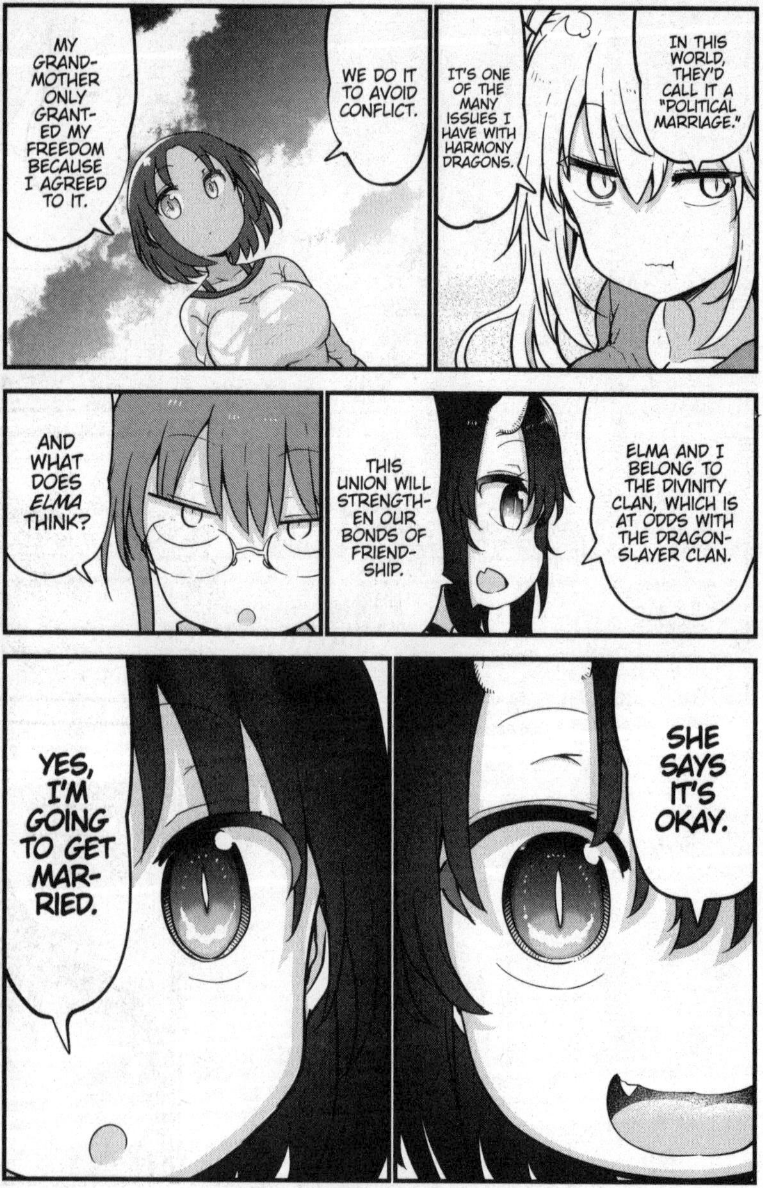
IN THIS WORLD, THEY'D CALL IT A "POLITICAL MARRIAGE."
IT'S ONE OF THE MANY ISSUES I HAVE WITH HARMONY DRAGONS.
WE DO IT TO AVOID CONFLICT.
MY GRANDMOTHER ONLY GRANTED MY FREEDOM BECAUSE I AGREED TO IT.
ELMA AND I BELONG TO THE DIVINITY CLAN, WHICH IS AT ODDS WITH THE DRAGON-SLAYER CLAN.
THIS UNION WILL STRENGTHEN OUR BONDS OF FRIENDSHIP.
AND WHAT DOES *ELMA* THINK?
SHE SAYS IT'S OKAY.
YES, I'M GOING TO GET MARRIED.

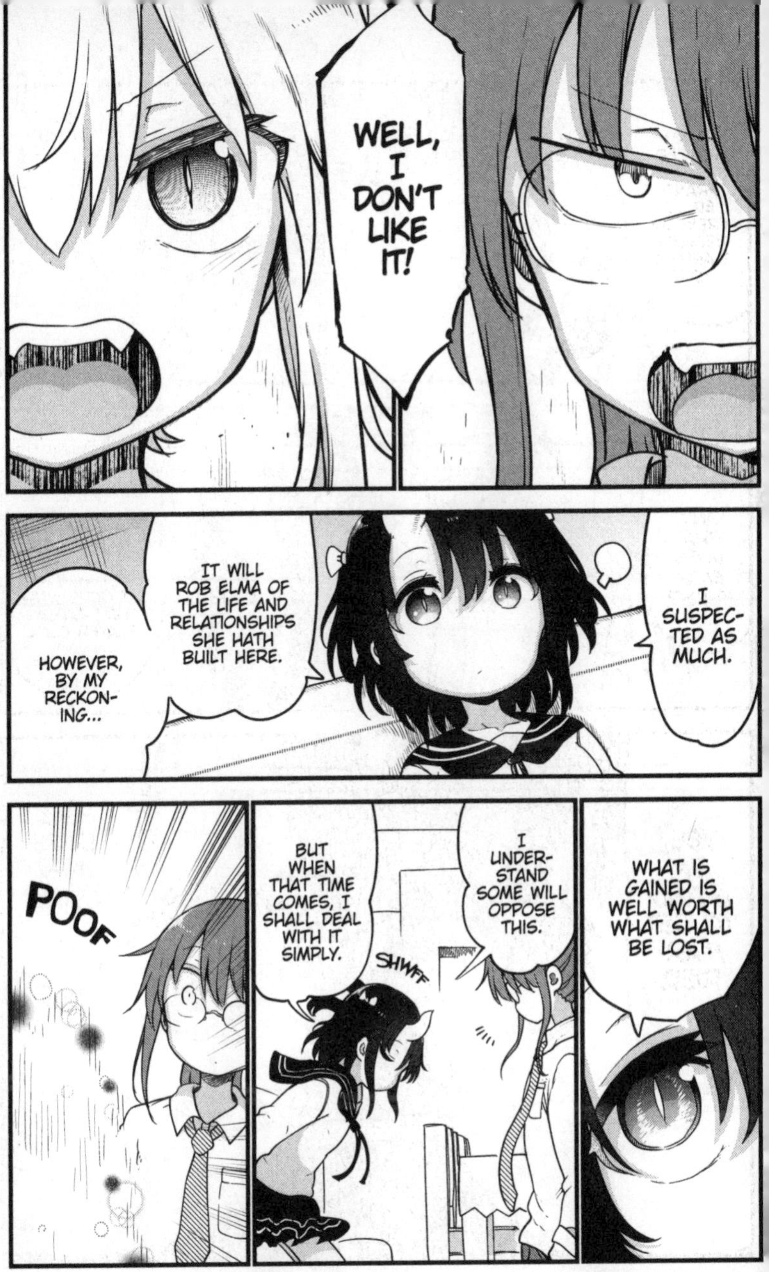
WELL, I DON'T LIKE IT!
I SUSPECTED AS MUCH.
IT WILL ROB ELMA OF THE LIFE AND RELATIONSHIPS SHE HATH BUILT HERE.
HOWEVER, BY MY RECKONING...
WHAT IS GAINED IS WELL WORTH WHAT SHALL BE LOST.
I UNDERSTAND SOME WILL OPPOSE THIS.
BUT WHEN THAT TIME COMES, I SHALL DEAL WITH IT SIMPLY.
SHWFF
POOF

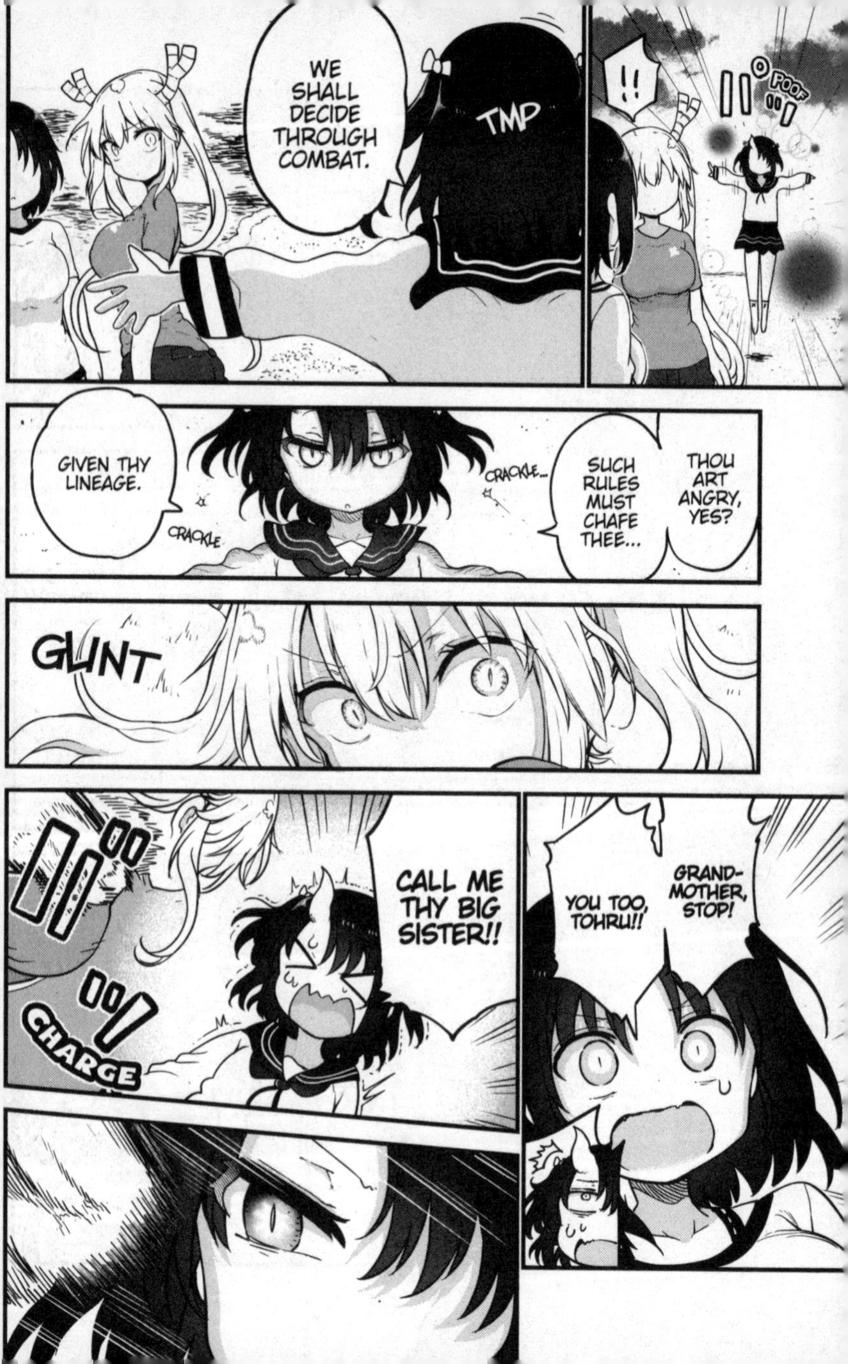
!!
POOF
WE SHALL DECIDE THROUGH COMBAT.
TMP
THOU ART ANGRY, YES?
SUCH RULES MUST CHAFE THEE...
CRACKLE...
GIVEN THY LINEAGE.
CRACKLE
GLINT
GRAND-MOTHER, STOP!
YOU TOO, TOHRU!!
CALL ME THY BIG SISTER!!
CHARGE

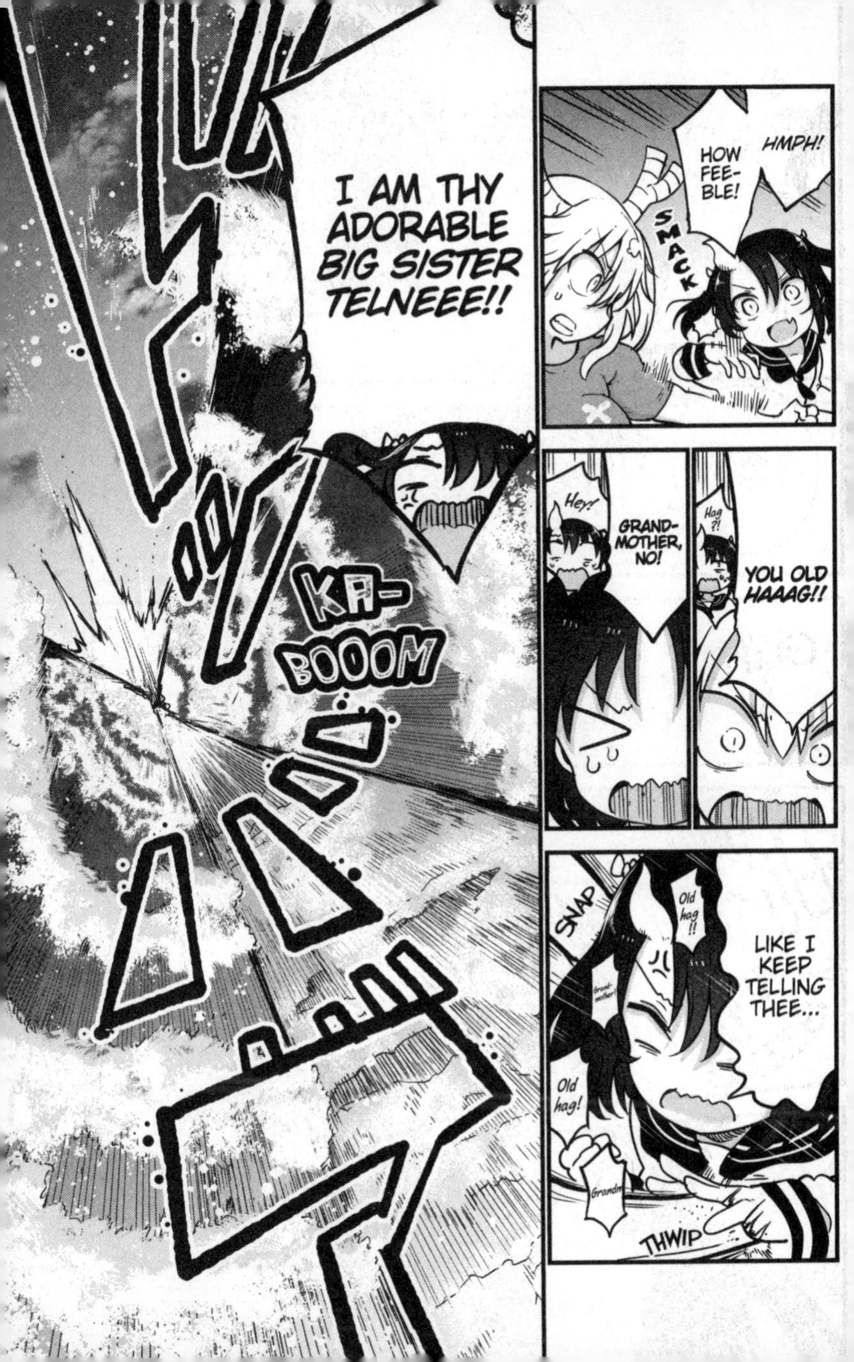
HMPH!
HOW FEE-BLE!
SMACK
Hag?!
YOU OLD HAAAG!!
Hey!
GRAND-MOTHER, NO!
LIKE I KEEP TELLING THEE...
Old hag!!
SNAP
Grand-mother!
Old hag!
Grandm
THWIP
I AM THY ADORABLE BIG SISTER TELNEEE!!
KA-BOOOM

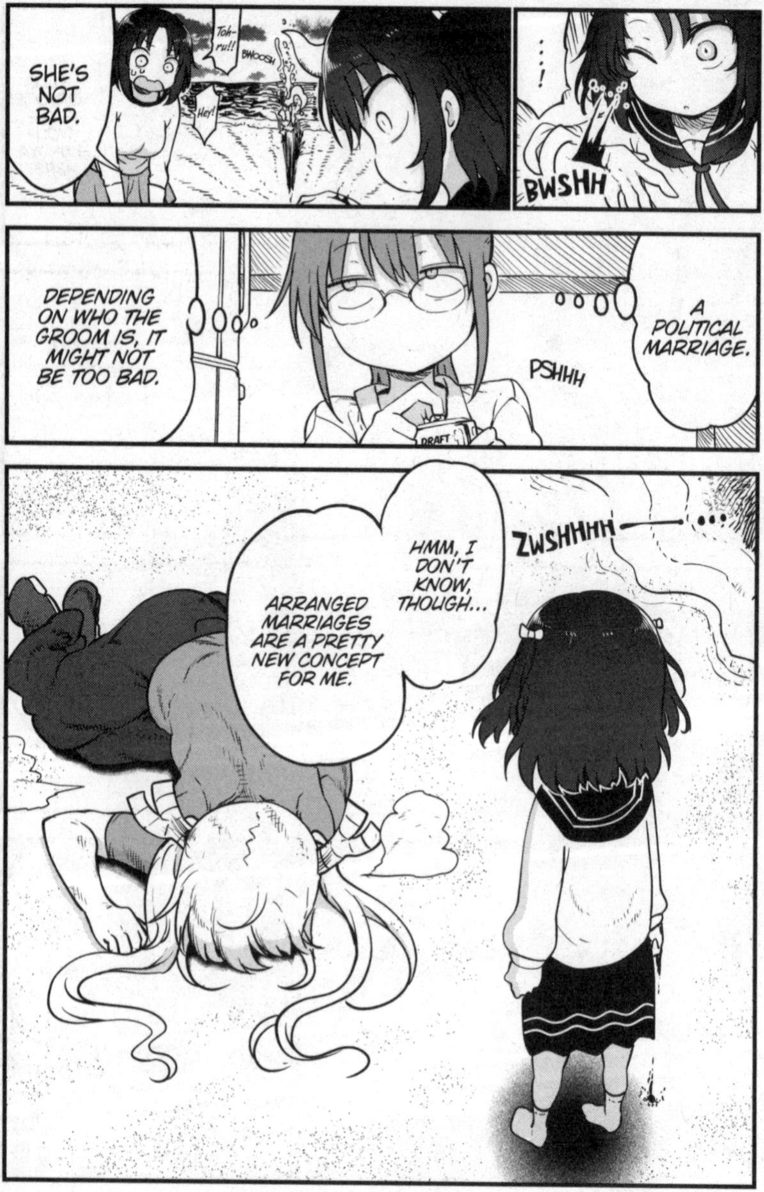
…!
BWSHH
Toh-ru!!
BWOOSH
Hey!
SHE'S NOT BAD.
A POLITICAL MARRIAGE.
PSHHH
DEPENDING ON WHO THE GROOM IS, IT MIGHT NOT BE TOO BAD.
DRAFT
…
ZWSHHHH
HMM, I DON'T KNOW, THOUGH…
ARRANGED MARRIAGES ARE A PRETTY NEW CONCEPT FOR ME.

CHAPTER 105/END

AFTERWORD

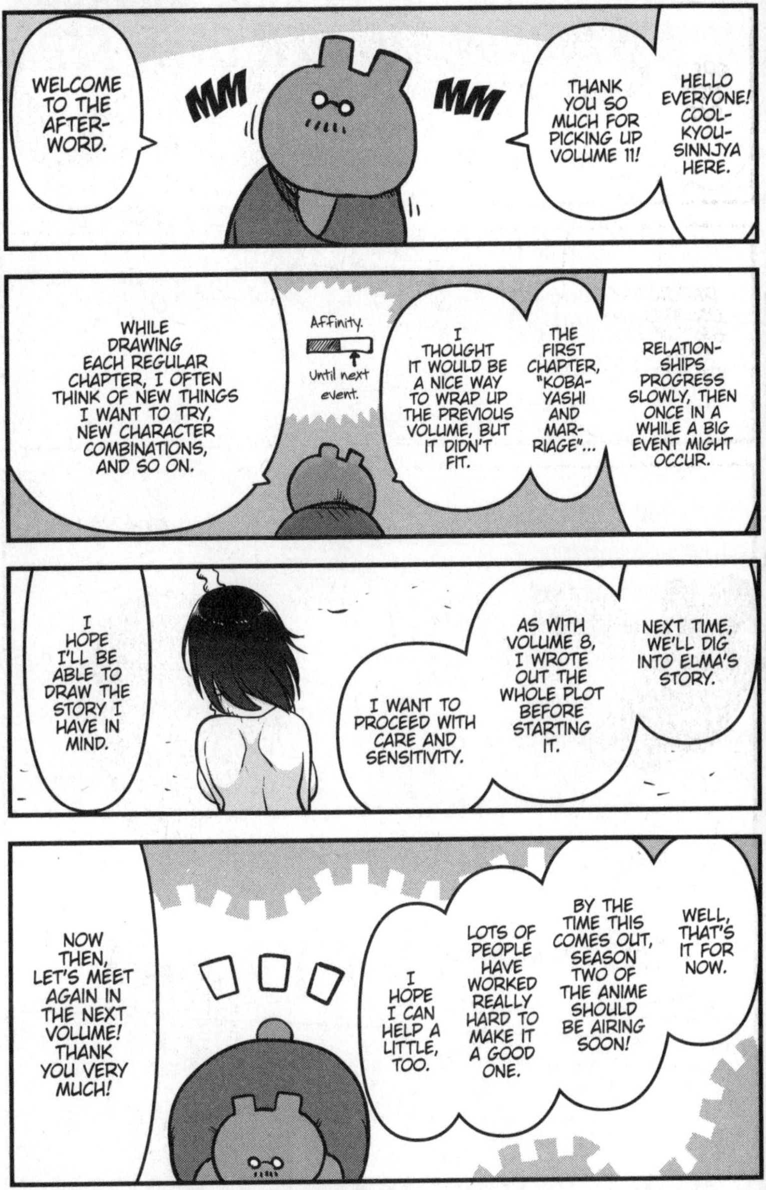
HELLO EVERYONE! COOL-KYOU-SINNJYA HERE.
THANK YOU SO MUCH FOR PICKING UP VOLUME 11!
MM
MM
WELCOME TO THE AFTER-WORD.
RELATION-SHIPS PROGRESS SLOWLY, THEN ONCE IN A WHILE A BIG EVENT MIGHT OCCUR.
THE FIRST CHAPTER, "KOBA-YASHI AND MAR-RIAGE"...
I THOUGHT IT WOULD BE A NICE WAY TO WRAP UP THE PREVIOUS VOLUME, BUT IT DIDN'T FIT.
Affinity.
Until next event.
WHILE DRAWING EACH REGULAR CHAPTER, I OFTEN THINK OF NEW THINGS I WANT TO TRY, NEW CHARACTER COMBINATIONS, AND SO ON.
NEXT TIME, WE'LL DIG INTO ELMA'S STORY.
AS WITH VOLUME 8, I WROTE OUT THE WHOLE PLOT BEFORE STARTING IT.
I WANT TO PROCEED WITH CARE AND SENSITIVITY.
I HOPE I'LL BE ABLE TO DRAW THE STORY I HAVE IN MIND.
WELL, THAT'S IT FOR NOW.
BY THE TIME THIS COMES OUT, SEASON TWO OF THE ANIME SHOULD BE AIRING SOON!
LOTS OF PEOPLE HAVE WORKED REALLY HARD TO MAKE IT A GOOD ONE.
I HOPE I CAN HELP A LITTLE, TOO.
NOW THEN, LET'S MEET AGAIN IN THE NEXT VOLUME! THANK YOU VERY MUCH!

Assistants: Namazenmai-sama, Giovanni Works-sama

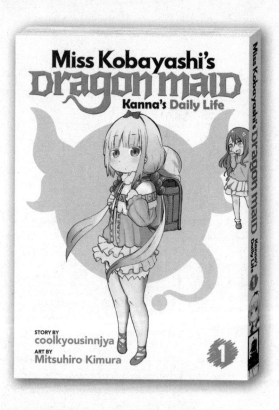

Miss Kobayashi's Dragon Maid S

COMING SOON TO ⓒ crunchyroll®

Miss Kobayashi's
DRAGON MAID

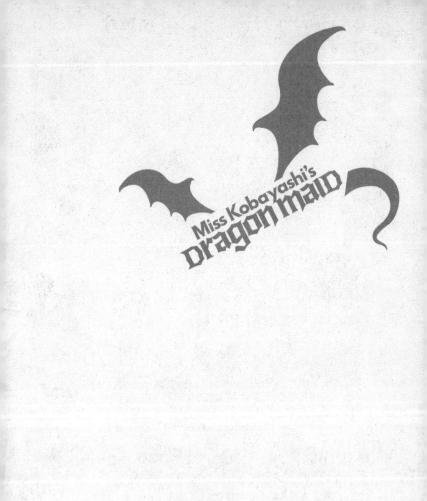

SEVEN SEAS ENTERTAINMENT PRESENTS

Miss Kobayashi's Dragon Maid VOL. 11

story and art by **coolkyousinnjya**

TRANSLATION
Jenny McKeon

ADAPTATION
Shanti Whitesides

LETTERING
Jennifer Skarupa

LOGO DESIGN
Hanase Qi

COVER DESIGN
Nicky Lim

PROOFREADING
Alyssa Honsowetz

PREPRESS TECHNICIAN
Rhiannon Rasmussen-Silverstein

PRODUCTION MANAGER
Lissa Pattillo

MANAGING EDITOR
Julie Davis

ASSOCIATE PUBLISHER
Adam Arnold

PUBLISHER
Jason DeAngelis

Seven Seas press and purchase enquiries can be sent to Marketing Manager Lianne Sentar at press@gomanga.com. Information regarding the distribution and purchase of digital editions is available from Digital Manager CK Russell at digital@gomanga.com.

ISBN: 978-1-64827-463-3

Printed in Canada

First Printing: December 2021

10 9 8 7 6 5 4 3 2 1

READING DIRECTIONS

This book reads from ***right to left***, Japanese style. If this is your first time reading manga, you start reading from the top right panel on each page and take it from there. If you get lost, just follow the numbered diagram here. It may seem backwards at first, but you'll get the hang of it! Have fun!!

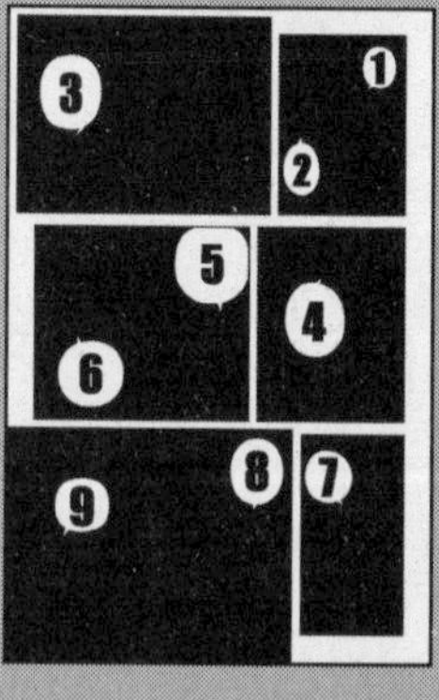
1
2
3
4
5
6
7
8
9